T3-BID-517

Miscellanies

OF

the Fuller Worthies' Library

IN FOUR VOLUMES

VOLUME 2

EDITED BY THE REV. ALEXANDER B. GROSART

AMS PRESS
NEW YORK

Original pagination has been maintained in this reprint.

Reprinted from a copy in the collections of the Harvard College Library
From the edition of 1870–1876, Blackburn
First AMS EDITION published 1970
Manufactured in the United States of America

International Standard Book Number:
Complete Set: 0-404-02670-2

Volume 2: 0-404-02672-9

Library of Congress Card Catalog Number: 70-129362

AMS PRESS, INC.
NEW YORK, N.Y. 10003

Miscellanies

OF

The Fuller Worthies' Library.

IN FOUR VOLUMES.

VOL. II.

CONTAINING

ANDREW'S 'ANATOMIE OF BASENESSE'—
LOK'S 'SONNETS OF CHRISTIAN PASSIONS,' &c.—
MARKHAM'S 'TEARES OF THE BELOUED' AND
'MARIE MAGDALEN'S TEARES'.

EDITED WITH

Memorial-Introduction and Notes:

BY THE

REV. ALEXANDER B. GROSART,

ST. GEORGE'S, BLACKBURN, LANCASHIRE.

PRINTED FOR PRIVATE CIRCULATION.
1871.

156 COPIES ONLY.

TO

WILLIAM HARRISON, Esq.,

F.S.A.,

Samlesbury Hall, Lancashire:

WORTHY SON OF WORTHY SIRE:

A 'COUNTRY GENTLEMAN'

WITH BOOKISH AND CULTURED LIKINGS:

This Volume of Miscellanies

IS INSCRIBED

BY HIS FRIEND,

THE EDITOR.

Preface.

I believe it will generally be admitted that the present Volume of the Miscellanies is of equal worth and interest with the former one. Its contents are all of the very rarest and costliest as books, and none having been re-printed for upwards of a couple of centuries, must be virgin to ninty-nine of a hundred readers.

As throughout, I have endeavoured in each case faithfully to reproduce the actual text of the Author, and to elucidate or illustrate in foot-notes where deemed necessary. The Memorial-Introductions, as before, supply what has long been wanting in our literary biography.

HENRY LOK'S "Sonnets on Christian Passions" &c. having stretched out beyond our estimate, from the separate pagination (not continuous) of the two divisions of the original volume (inadvertently over-looked), I have thought it well to re-distribute the announced Miscellanies and to present them in four instead of three volumes. Accordingly a cancel general title-page as in four volumes is issued with the present to take the place of that given in the first. Even thus arranged these volumes are proving much thicker than was intended.

With reference to HENRY LOK I have a somewhat important correction to make. Accepting somehow the impression that Zachary Lok was *son* of our Worthy while in fact he was his *cousin*, son of his uncle Michael, I have been led into error as to the age of our Henry Lok. By turning to pp. 9 &c. of the Memorial-Introduction, it will be seen that his father could not have been born until about 1530. He appears to have married in 1551, and as the Poet was the second son of the name, it is probable that his birth was about 1553, so that in 1608 when we last hear of him, his age could not have been more than 55. Our mistake therefore as to the extreme age of our Worthy in the several references (pp. 28, 29, &c). must thus be corrected. I am anxious to relieve Colonel Chester of all responsibility for the misapplication of Zachary Lok's letter. By favour of J. G. Nichols Esq. I have had an opportunity of consulting a large volume from America entitled "Book of the Lockes" &c. &c. (Boston 1853 8vo) It shews amazing research: but unluckily the English department of the family-history is confused and erroneous.

Through the kindness of Clements R. Markham, Esq. I am enabled to add a privately-engraved head of Gervase Markham (in large paper copies) before Marie Magdalen's Teares.

At close of Vol. IV. will appear a short series of supplementary Notes to the entire Miscellanies from materials obtained subsequently.

ALEXANDER. B. GROSART.

St. George's,
Blackburn, July 6th, 1871.

MISCELLANIES
OF
The Fuller Worthies' Library.

THE

ANATOMIE OF BASENESSE
(1615)

BY

JOHN ANDREWS:

Edited, with Introduction and Notes.

BY THE

REV. ALEXANDER B. GROSART,
ST. GEORGE'S, BLACKBURN, LANCASHIRE.

PRINTED FOR PRIVATE CIRCULATION.
1871.

156 COPIES ONLY.

Contents.

Memorial-Introduction.

THE "Anatomie of Basenesse" was published anonymously, that is to say only the initials I. A. in the Epistle-Dedicatory to Sir Robert Sydney guide to its authorship. Apologizing for his dedication, the Writer says among other things, that he prints not 'vaine-gloriously' or he would have 'subscribed' his 'name' and that he forbore to have his name published 'out of some respects'. We shall not err probably if we interpret the 'some respects' as having reference to his being a 'Preacher' of God's Word, as deeming his trenchant, vehement satire liable to misconstruction if known to come from a clergyman. Anthony a-Wood in his *Athenæ* and his erudite Editor Dr. Bliss, fill in the initials with "J[ohn] A[ndrews]" and thus write of him: "John Andrews, a Somersetshire man born, was entred a student in Trin. Coll.

1601, aged 18, took one degree in Arts,[1] left the University, became a painfull[2] preacher of God's Word and a publisher of these books following" —of which more anon—. Then, "When he died or where he was buried, I know not." DR. BLISS appends the following: "He seems to have been the same person with John Andrews, minister and preacher of the Word of God at Barrick Bassett in the county of Wilts., who was the author of "Christ's Cross: or the most comfortable doctrine of Christ crucified and joyful tidings of his Passion. Oxon. 1614 qu. in two parts. To this writer we may ascribe a very rare poetical work, entitled the 'Anatomie of Basenesse.' . . . . . . By 'Barrick Basset' is intended the small hamlet of 170 inhabitants, 'Berwick Bassett': but our enquiries there directly and in the county-History, have resulted in nothing. SIR RICHARD HOARE in his huge book on Wilts (1843) thinks it important to record that a "Master James Andrews, Mayor" . . . . . was fined for "selling strong ale" (p. 274): but has not a syllable for the "painfull Preacher". It does not appear that he was Incumbent: prob-

[1] *Viz.* Master of Arts: (*Fasti. s. n.*)

[2] = Painstaking. G.

ably he was a Curate or assistant, or what the Puritans supplied and named, Lecturer.

The identity of the "Preacher of God's Word" with the author of the "Anatomie", seems to be confirmed by an examination of the pious books euumerated by Wood, and others that must have escaped him. We glean what of Verse is found in those that we possess ourselves or have come upon.

Passing "Andrewe's Golden Chaine to linke the penitent sinner unto Almighty God" (1645) we have the "Converted Man's New Birth" (1629) and "Andrewe's Repentance, sounding alarum to returne from his sinnes unto Almighty God, declaring his repentance: published by John Andrewes, Minister of the Word of God, in the County of Wilts" (1623). These details of this quaint little volume will interest. On reverse of the title are these Lines:

> The Author did this little booke forestall,
> And from the presse he did it take,
> That none thereof might haue the sale,
> But he himselfe which did it make,
> Except it be his speciall friend,
> Which may it sell, and giue, and lend.

Then follows a prayer (2 pages). Then "To all Christian Sinners, (2 pages,) ending thus :

Prayer with practise,
Oft times on your knee,
Gets fauour with God,
As daily we see.
But prayer with lips
Where heart is away,
Returnes into sinne
Their soules to destroy.

Then follows " The Author to the Reader " (2 pages,) in which he says that " by the handy-work of God, in sending contrary windes, I have lost to the value of threescore pounds by the yeare, in spirituall livings within the realme of Ireland, to the vtter impouerishing of me, my wife and children for euer, except God in His mercy open the harts of welldisposed gentlemen and others, by their good liking of these my labors to relieue me in these my present wants, that thereby I may attaine unto some better estate againe."

Then comes "An humble Petition " &c. (12 pp).

Then this : (2 pages) " The Praise of Wisedome " Prouerbs, Chap 3.

Blest is the man that Wisdome finds,

And he that doth obtaine
True vnderstanding, and thereof
Doth know the precious gaine:
For better 'tis to get the same
Then siluer ready told,
And better profit it doth bring
Then merchandize of gold.
Wisedome doth precious stones exceed
And all things else that are,
There is nothing thou canst desire,
To be compared to her.
Vpon her right hand is long life,
Which neuer is bereft,
Riches and honor doe attend
And waite vpon the left.
Her wayes are passing pleasant wayes,
Her paths are full of rest,
She is a tree of life to those
Which her to seeke are prest.
Shee is I say a tree of life
To such as on her hold,
And such as alway keep her fast,
Are blessèd manifold.
My sonne let not these things depart,
Nor from thine eye to passe,
But keepe my lawes and counsels eke,
And thou shalt finde them grace.

Vnto thy mouth, and to thy soule
They shall be perfect life.
So shalt thou safely walke the way
Whereas there is no strife:
Thy foot from stumbling so thou maist
At all times surely keepe,
When thou lyest downe thou needst not care,
But rest and sweetly sleepe:
Thou shalt not need to be afraid
Of any sodaine feare,
For violent force of wicked men
Which chance, take thou no care.
For violent rushing in of such
As the vngodly are,
Of them thou needst not to account,
Nor let them not thee scare.
For why, the Lord with thee shall be
At hand, and keepe thy foot,
That by deceiuing sleights of foes
Thou neuer shalt be tooke.

Then follows (1 page)

The Author to his Booke.

Go thou my Booke with the zeale of my hart
To all that shal come view thee:

When thou hast past from the Presse, and art
print
Cry daily, Come peruse me :
If that thou canst giue to them all content,
Then is my labour ended,
Which is the thing that I haue desired
For my paines on thee spended.

Turning now to another, viz.

"A golden Trumpet sounding an Alarum to Judgement" &c, "By John Andrewes Minister and Preacher of God's Word". "The Nine and twentieth Impression, London. 1648". (22 pp small 8vo), on reverse of title are these Lines:

The Author to the Reader.

Sound to Judgement this Golden Trumpet,
Into the eares of every one ;
Early be ringing here thine owne knell,
O sound t' alarum, for time will be gone.
Weep for thy sins, and watch for the day
Here of the coming of Christ our Judge ;
Each day and houre slips quickly away ;
No time is set, therefore doe not grudge.

Make this Trumpet to sound in thine eare,
A day of Judgement is almost come :

Delay no time, we all must appeare,
Now still prepare for the day of doome.

On 3d page of text is the following:

To morrow, some wil say, I will a convert be;
O when tell me I pray, shall I this morrow see?
Let never wise man say, tomorrow mend I will;
Who is not fit to day, is lesse and lesse fit still.

Again, we have

" A Celestiall Looking-Glasse" &c., by John Andrewes, Preacher of God's word" London, sm. 8vo 1639. (pp 21.) On reverse of the title is the following

The Avthor to the Reader.

If Logick's arts could heavenly joyes define,
Or Geometry celestiall wayes but measure,
Here mortall men might shew these workes divine,
Now in the heavens where saints doe reigne with pleasure.

Arithmeticians ne're can number right,
Nor yet the tongues of rhetoricians rare,
Describe that blisse which saints have in God's sight,
Reioycing with Christ our Saviour there.

Esteeme you this *Celestiall Looking-glasse*,
Which I have penn'd Heaven's beauty to behold:
Each day and night pray God to bring to passe,
Such joyes unto our soules for to unfold.

Anagramma,

Nonne Deus eras via ?

Finally, there is,

"Andrewes Caveat, to Win Sinners" &c. "Newly published by John Andrewes, Preacher of God's Word"—London, 1655, small 8o. (22pp). On last page is the following

Sinne no more.

Christ's mercy is to such as doe repent,
But not to sinners that remaine in sinne,
Who were a sinner, if he have intent
To change his life, he may His mercies win;
For in the world He hath His mercy plast,
Whilst it endures, so will it ever last.

If sinners' conscience tremble for to thinke
Of their accounts upon the dreadfull day;
If that their terrors make their hearts to shrinke,
Then let their mind drive sinfull thoughts away,
And dare not doe their wicked actions here,
In which they durst not at that day appeare.

God's justice doth, as ever heretofore,
Call on, that sinners may receive their due,
But Christ's endeavours now, as evermore,
For man's repentance, and salvation sue.
At Jesus sute, God ever granteth grace,
And for repentance giveth sinners space.

Certainly the sentiment excells the poetry in these homely, Bunyan-like rhymes, and they lack the *elan*, the terseness, the quick touches, of the 'Anatomie of Basenesse.' Still they go to shew that the Verse-taste was in the Writer, and so, that Wood and Bliss's filling in of the initials I. A. may be accepted.[1]

Of the "Anatomie of Basenesse," only the solitary exemplar in the Bodleian is known. It must consequently be a surprize—a pleasant one surely—to most of our Readers. It is characterized by uncommon vigour and high-toned *morale*.

---

[1] In Trinity College Library, Cambridge, is the following book: "An Historical Narrative of the judgement of some learned and godly English Bishosp, holy martyrs, and others, &c. London, 1631. 4o. The Epistle to the Reader is signed J. A. of Ailward, which has been expanded in MS. to Jo. Andrewes of Ailward, *Doctor*. I have failed to discover where Ailward was, and so to identify Dr. Jo. Andrewes with our Worthy.

You can't help laying up in memory some of its lines that are condensed as any aphorism of a Master, *e. g.*

"You like the meate because the sauce is sweete"

and

"You quite forget neere honie lies a sting",

and

"Beheading him that honestly reproves you"

and

"Tel the sun he'es brighter than the moone"

and

"Still to be doing though you do amisse."

There is humour in this retort "To the ungrate-full":

I'st long of thy short memorie, that thou
yeeld'st not due thanks, where thou the same
do'st owe ?
Alas, good man, *why dost thou not forget*
to begge as well ?"

Sometimes there is a happy epithet, as in the Feast of the envious, Envie is "the *meager* cooke" and finer as deeper, and worthy to be put beside Mrs. Clive's grand "*insuperable* threshold" is this: "the hand of *reconciling* Death" as vain to arrest the cruel speech of Envy. The context is worth adducing:

"Nor can the hand of reconciling Death
Free men from this iniurious monster's sting
which through the bowels of the Earth doth pierce
and in the quiet vault appeares more fierce
Then Death—the graue's sterne tyrannizing king."—

This too is noticeable:

"An honest fame—like spice—the more 'tis bruis'd
sauors the sweeter, which when we are dead
Will be the sweetest seare-cloth can be vs'd
to wrap vs in; it will outlast the lead
Wherein that bodie lies, in which did liue
a spotted conscience, a detracting spirit;
Which to itselfe an earthly heauen did giue,
and of heauen's ioyes it selfe did disinherite."

And this:

Doe not you thinke that man deserues much blame
who findes his owne infirmitie, yet feedes

Daily on that which nourisheth the same,
  and dangerously the braine's corruption breeds?

Altogether, independent of its *unique* existence, the "Anatomie" is intrinsically worthy of wider preservation and study.

ALEXANDER B. GROSART.

Anatomie of Basenesse.

1615.

Note.

Below will be found the original title-page of the "Anatomie of Basenesse"—for the *unique* exemplar of which I am indebted as in other cases, to the world-renowned Bodleian. G.

THE

ANATOMIE

OF

BASENESSE.

OR

The foure quarters of a knave;

Flatterie,
Ingratitude,
Enuie,
Detraction.

He that hath these foure parts, neede no more haue
To be recorded for a complete *Knaue*.

Imprinted at *London* for *Richard Redmer*, and are to be sold | *at the West dore of* Paules *at the signe of the Starre.*

1615. |

[4to. 18 leaves.]

Epistle-Dedicatory.

To THE TRULY enobled both by vertue and birth,
Sir ROBERT SYDNEY, Knight of the BATH:[1]

I. A. wisheth the reward of his vertue, honour in this world, glorie in the next:

HONOURABLE SIR,

To immitate the common methode of Epistolizers in this kinde, were rather to write of you then to you; which course though I affect[2] not, I cannot altogether neglect, though I shall thereby either wrong you or myselfe; for in publishing—though sparingly—my knowledge of your worth to the world, such, to whom you are vnknowne will so much iniure mee, as to taxe me with—what I condemne in others—flatterie; whereas some—

---

[1] The illustrious brother of the still more illustrious Sir Philip Sidney. He was knighted for his bravery at fatal Zutphen. His name is imperishably linked with his brother's. It were superfluous to annotate more here. G.

[2] Choose. G.

to whom you are no stranger—will censure mee as much on the cōtrary to haue dealt with you rather, according to the pouertie of my abilitie, then to the fulnesse of your merite.

It will peraduenture seeme strange vnto you—if this poore worke chance to come to your view—what assurance of your good acceptance begat such presumption in me as to dedicate the same vnto you. I must first answere, I haue not done it mercenarily; for then I would haue presented it to your hand: nor vaine-gloriously ; for then I would either haue craued your allowance, or subscribed my name; but freely and honestly out of that respect which I owe to that innate goodnesse which I know to be in you. Though I forbeare—out of some respects—to haue my name published; yet I can acknowledge the booke to be mine without blushing. If it bee—by anie—ill digested, the fault must be in the taker not in the Author. It was written with a right hand, and I wish it may not be sinisterly intertained by any; but if som wil needs be so forward, the care is taken. In you I am made so confident by that—I might iustly vse honourable, noble, worthy, or some such high epithete : but I will rather say—honest—a poore phrase will some thinke—and vertuous disposition which accompanies you, that I must account it my happinesse that I liue to knowe a second, whose brest Goodnesse makes her habitation; yet pardon mee if I say, I enioy not this happinessse without some touch of griefe ;[1] I shall not need to implore your protection, though your pardon. I acknowledge I haue presumed, and know you can and will remit the errors of affection in him that is,

The wisher of your honour,
and honourer of your
VERTVES
J. A.

[1] The death of Sir Philip Sidney is in J. A's thought. G.

The Anatomy of Basenesse.

Of the Flatterer.

They that compare the fawning Parisite,
  vnto the spaniel, do the curre much wrong;
  for he will often heare his master's tongue,
When in the field he follows his delight:

Yet neuer quest;[1] but th' ecchoing Sicophant
  at euery word, by his weake fauourer spoken,
  cries 'good', ''tis true'; and this is held a
    token
Of much respect and loue; though from the haunt

Of worth and merit his base nature range
  as farre as falshood, from the strong built nest
  of Truth and Goodnesse, which in euery brest
Should like two twinnes be nourisht; but 'tis
    strange

---

[1] To give tongue, as usually the spaniel does on scenting game. G.

To see how this poore worthlesse humour liues,
euen in those bosomes where good bloud and parts,
haue their abiding, poisoning generous arts[1]
With that, to which no language spoken giues

An epithete too bad: and to those men
—if I may tearme them so—whose only words
such sweetnesse to the flattered eare affoords;
To yeeld a fitting title by my pen.

I am as much vnable, as vnapt
to imitate their basenesse; which indeede
had I not chanc't t'haue heard, into my creede
Could nere haue come; but it hath often hapt

To sownde within the compasse of my hearing;
whereby mine eares as to the pillory,
seem'd to be nailde in such grosse flattery;
Yet in their cheekes no signe of shame appearing.

It may seeme strange—yet I dare say 'tis true—
that I haue blusht to see their impudence,
while they—vn-man-like—seem'd to haue no sence
Of their own basenes: of this thriuing crue.

---

[1] Query, arts = hearts? G.

I haue observ'd both sexes to be free ;
too free in some respect, though in some kinde
more bound then slaves, for our best part—the minde—
Was chiefly given diuinest things to see.

And not to be by ought that shares with vs,
in the short course of our mortalitie
so fetter'd, least vnhappily it be,
Depriv'd of its best good in being thus.

Haue I not heard one tell the crowe, shee's white,
and Midas-like preferre the pipe of Pan
before Appollo's harpe ? wherein this man
—Who thus from Art and Nature teares their right—
Thus from the Phrygian differs : Midas weares
—as the reward and badge of ignorance—
th'eares of an asse ; but 'tis the other's chance
To thriue by clawing th'ignorant asse's eares.

Haue I not heard some tell the prodigall,
'tis for his honour to be bountifull :
and with applause commend the humourous gull[1]
In all his actions ? I haue seen them fall

---

[1] The 'gull' given to 'humours' or changes. Cf.

And kisse the feete of a great golden calfe ;
whose very best of his admirèd worth
was by a taylor to the world brought forth,
To whom his honour ought[1] his better halfe.

Let a man chafe—though no iust cause there be—
and then obsequious apes will fret as fast,
as had they seene a verier slaue t'haue past
By, then themselues : or be your humour free

And iouially dispos'd, they'le Janus-like
straite shew a cleerer face, where you may see
the true proportion of hypocrisie
Drawne to the life ;—which loues as others like—

Many yeeres since the famous CHAUCER[2] writ,
that these same men which bear a double visage,
are as meere monsters in good Nature's linage,—
And for good mens societie vnfit.

Like your chameleons these wil change their hew

Sir John Davies' Epigram on the 'Gull' : our edition pp 346 – 7 *et alibi* G.

[1] Owed. G.

[2] Is the allusion to Chaucer's account of *Fals Semblant* in the later part of the *Romaunt of the Rose ?* (that is a a summing up of the character.) In line 1070 is this of the lozenger " No good man loueth her companye ". G.

as you your colour, be it good or ill;
change nere so oft, yet you shall finde them still
—From what they were—transforme as fast as you

Seeme to be most vnlike your selfe, or speake
what you least thinke, they'le be, and speake
like you;
tell them they're knaues, they'le smile and say
so too;
Faine your selfe ill, they'le sweare they finde you
weake.

To the Flattered.

OND man, that suck'st the pleasing
poyson in
—which from the Syren's vnsuspected
tongue
Is kindly offer'd to thine eare—wherein
are all the drugges and dregges of vildnesse[1]
wrung:
Assure thy selfe, if in thy bosome liue
ought that deserues the name of worth, 'tis
knowne

[1] Vileness. G.

More then thy selfe, nor shalt thou neede to giue
Fame a reward to haue thy mercy blowne.
For 'tis her care, the more she findes thee slow,
or carelesse, whether thy desert shall be
Knowne vnto any, but thy selfe, or no;
to sound the louder:—so to honour thee—
Thorough her golden trumpet—good mens throats—
or if thine eare shall loue, and itch to heare
Thine own praise sung in smooth and pleasing notes,
—which makes true worth vnlike it selfe appeare—
She hath another trumpet blowne by those,
whose mercenary tongues shall sownd thy praise;
But with a breath which blasteth as it blowes,
and ruines that which it pretends to raise.
For do but note, you shall perceiue their plots,
are—being once assur'd of you as friends—
To thrust their blankes amongst your high priz'd lots,
so by your losse to compasse their owne ends.
But selfe-conceipt so much corrupts your sence,
that to your iudgement, onely that same man
Seemes wise and honest, and giues no offence
that by this art, can make a goose a swanne.
If by the breath of these, you striue to raise

your reputation, your ambition's weake ;
You must resolue of such to buy your praise ;
not for the trueth, but for reward they speake.
If on the former—who for Vertue's sake
honour that good is in you—you relie,
Their approbation shall have power to make
your glory liue to all posteritie.
Doe not you thinke that man deserues much blame
who findes his owne infirmitie, yet feedes
Daily on that which nourisheth the same,
And dangerously the braine's corruption breeds ?
Such is your case—weake men and women—for
you like the meate because the sauce is sweete ;
What bitter is—though wholsome—you abhorre,
disabling that which iudgement holdeth meete.
But iudgement is no iudgement, if it seeme
to contradict your humour ; but the longer
Y'are constant to this poorenesse,—which you deeme
worth in your selues—your weakness proues the strõger.
Though to the palat pills distastfull be
they to the health more beneficiall proue,
Then things more pleasing to the sence ; we see
cutting doth oft in curing much behoue :
But you like Herod thinke, that he most loues you
who cries, you speak more like a god then man ;

Beheading him that honestly reproues you,
  not caring though it be baptizing John :[1]
Let a man seeme but cheerefully to sing
  '*Placebo*' to your words and actions, then
You quite forget, neere honie lies a sting ;
  and that the diuell—clarke-like—sayth 'Amen'
Where flatterers—his chaplaines—reade the Masse
  whose superstition—making you their saint—
  you doe allow as currantly to passe,
For truth, as Gospell—which no tongue can,
    taint—

To the Flatterer.

THOU that canst grieue because another
    smiles.
  and giue to vndeseruing spirits, stiles
Which thou dost filch from gen'rous noble minds ;
  because thy poore obsequious humour findes
Cold intertainment there ; tell me, dost thinke
  that all are blinde that are content to winke ?
Or that thy shamelesse flattery beguiles
  euery man that at thy glozing smiles ?
Assure thy selfe thy thoughts deceiue thee much ;

[1] St. John the Baptist : cf. Acts of Apostles xii. 22 and St. Matthew xiv. 1—12 G.

for many smile to see thy basenesse such :
And such as thou think'st blind more truly see
thy heart, then they that hugge thy flatterie ;
And—scorning by thy pitch to be defil'd,
or by thy sweet tun'd lullabies beguil'd—
Doe loath to view thy vilde[1] deformitie,
which pleasing is to such as fauour thee.
That euery man be master of his owne
all men allow ; but it is lately growne
To such a custome,—first by thee brought in—
among th' ambitious of this world of sinne,
That to a man—if I professe to loue him—
I must giue titles some degrees aboue him :
Or else be tax'd with enuie or neglect,[2]
though my soule knowes, I giue more true respect
Then you that id'ly light a torch at noone,
and tell the sun hee's brighter then the moone ;
Which argues only that your humour is,
still to be doing though you do amisse
In guilding gold. This I obseruèd haue
in some, whose age did homage to the graue,

---

[1] Vile. G.

[2] Even so in this year 1871. Every Smith, Brown, Robinson and Jones must be dubbed 'Esquire', will be quite offended with plain 'Mr.'. G.

Whose words in prairs more fitly had been spent,
and with deuotion on embassage sent
To make their peace with heauen, then to obay
that which would guide them by the broader way.
If it be hatefnll euen in younger yeeres
to temporize and gloze, sure it appeares
Monstrous in Age, whose part it rather is
to grieue for what in youth it did amisse;
Then in the last act of a life mis-led,
To heape more blow es vpon a wounded head.
Could I instruct, or might I but aduise,
I'de teach, or wish you to become more wise:
But 'twill be thought preposterous in Youth
To tutor Age, though by the Word of Truth:[1]
Such proofes as it doth bring approouèd be:
Therefore I leave you to your humour free;
Wherin—no doubt—you'le one day finde this true,
You make your fav'rers fooles, they knaues of you.
Too mild a stile, for that's a tearme for men;
if so, too good for any flatterer then:
What, shall I call thee diuell, monster beast?
if not all these, thou'rt one of them at least

[1] Perhaps this may be taken as an intimation that the Poet was now in early youth. G.

Transform'd to th' shape of man; nor seemes it
strange
if thy grand Master—who himselfe can change
Into an angel's likenesse—make thee seeme,
A saint-like man in many men's esteeme;
Instructing thee vpon what vaine to worke,
And where thou maiest the most securely lurke,
With best assurance bids thee plie that minde;
where thou the weakest easiness shalt finde:
Such thou maiest puffe as butchers do their meate,
and with thy breath perswade them they're as
great
As thou dost make them; and aboue the rest,
be sure—my child—thou suff'rest not a iest,
Bee't nere so poore, to passe without a 'good,'
though by none else the same were vnderstood
How to deserue applause; and then thou hear'st
amongst that sect—where gracious thou appears't
—A tedious talker, sencelesly discourse
till he dull others, and himselfe grow hoarse—
Let thy attention—till his tongue ly'th still—
stare in his face, then let him finde thy skill.
These be the rules, and many worse then these
thou must obserue, if thou desir'st to please,
Thy tutor sayth, whose helpe will nere deceive
thee,
and to whose fauour wretched man, I leaue thee.

Of the Ingrateful.

OME haue compar'd—and not improperly—
him that is tainted with this worst of ills
vnto the swine, who—freely daily—fills
His hungrie mawe euen to sacietie.

Vpon such maste as from the fruitfull tree
falls to the ground, yet his deiected eye
is fixèd only where his food doth lie,
And neuer rais'd the Giuer's face to see.

Guilty of this vnpardonable crime,
were[1] diuers kinds of these inhumane men,
discoursed by th'industrious famous pen
Of heathen Tully, liuing in his time.

The first dissemblers were of fauours reap'd
proportioning the same—being more or lesse—
To the small measure of their thankfulnesse,
Though a full hand on them the same has heap'd.

The next acknowledg'd freely that occasion,
off'ring it selfe—ioyn'd with abilitie—
to make requitall—for each curtesie—
Seem'd deafe to Opportunitie's perswasion.

---

[1] Misprinted 'where'. G.

An other sort there was, whose shamelesse crauing
  would not admit deniall, but being made
  master of their desires, could soone perswade
Their tongues—too basely—to denie the hauing.

The fourth and last—and worst my Author
    writes—
  were such as, what they had receiu'd, forgot.
  Vnthankfull he then, that remembers not;
He that denies, dissembles not requites.

Let me adde one kinde more, which I conceiue
  worse then all these, who like the frozen snake,
  stings that same bosome, whence it warmth did
    take;
And would, what gaue it life, of life bereaue.

Such there hath been, my obseruation knowes,
  who—from a poore, deiected miser state—
  being rais'd—by great ones—prouèd so ingrate,
To bring their rayser's necke neere th' axe's blowes.

Should I demaund why such unnumbred were
  among the former, some man might reply;
  —as vnto him who ask't the reason why,
Among so many lawes, so strict, seuere,

Made by the Romans, none was knowne to touch

the childe, whose hand should guide the fatall
knife,
to cut his throat who gaue his being life :—
Because that Tully thought there liv'd none such

But since the time perfidious Judas dyed
—who at his end—I feare—bequeath'd his
curse,
to some that do in these daies beare the purse—
Such there haue been, such haue been deifide.

If your prosperity strike sayle, be sure
These kites, that stoop to you while you can
feede them,
come to an other's fist; and if you need them
They soare aloofe, checke at your empty lure.

Much like their embleme, which—for the full
payles—
followe the maide that beares them : if she
fall
and spill the meate, to that they run, and all
Respect of her that vs'd to feede them, failes.

Or cuckoe-like, they to your Summer's sunne
sing merrily — though sucke your egges
withall —

but when they finde your Summer faile, and
Fal[1]
Draw neere, they're gone, and their harsh musicke
done.

To the bovntifvll.

F on the waters you shall cast your bread
it is not lost,[2] but if your pearles you
throw
Vnto the swine, be sure the same they'l tread
vnder their feete ;[3] good seed['s] in good ground
sowen.
Fauours ill plac'd, are numbred with ill deeds ;[4]
for if that hand which liberally bestowes,
—Though it—in giuing—other mens exceedes—
not the true vse of Bountie rightly knowes,
'Twere better be more sparing ; for to giue
is proper to all creatures in their kinde :

---

[1] Fall = Autumn, from the '*fall*ing of the leaf' as Spring from the '*spring*ing' See our edn. of HENRY VAUGHAN : Index of words under "Fall". G.

[2] Ecclesiastes xi. 1. G. [3] St. Matthew vii. 6. G.

[4] Beneficia male locata malefacta sunt. A.

The meanest thing which we can say doth liue,
in some respect we beneficiall finde,
But vnto man is only giuen the powre
to limit bounty, know when, how, on whom,
Best to bestowe; not like a heedlesse showre
to let faire flowers die in their mother's wombe
For lack of moisture, whil'st vpon wild weedes
it—in aboundance—poures refreshing droppes;
This kinde of giuing naturally proceedes
from partiall hands, which in the course soone stoppes.
Nor should your bountie—like the sunne—runne round
and shine on all alike, though—like the beames—
The same should seldome in the eclipse be found;
truest bountie liues betweene extreames.
Your hand should neuer be so lockt from all,
as to deserue a couetous report :[1]
Nor still in action like your Prodigall,
who makes expence his most delightfull sport:
Long since were none then[2] goodmen held more fit
to taste your bountie—then t'was rightly vs'd;—

---

[1] Non ita claudenda est res familiaris vt eam benignitas aperire non possit, nec ita reseranda vt pateat omnibus. A.

[2] = than. G.

But in those daies, such men must naked sit:
thus is true liberality abus'd.
He that can now most temporize, best thriues,
and great men, more then good men, bounty taste;
Honie is brought vnto the fullest hiues,
small riuers giue vnto the sea—in waste—
Many—againe—like husband-men doe lay
Their seede in th' bosome of the fattest ground;
Whose richnesse will with much aduantage paie,
where for each graine there shall an eare be found:
And some of you, to gaine a knaue's good word;
or by a iester to be highly prais'd
Will giue with both handes, place them at your boord;
when good-men are not ore your threshold rais'd.
Bountie's pure current in this muddie time,
Is by the fogges of Prodigalitie
So steinch't, with stinking ayres, so re-spread with slime,
that—as it were not—no such thing we see.
Wee finde the streame as contrary to runne,
vnto that course which it should rightly hold,
As is the West to th' rising of the sunne,
or Southerne heate vnto the Northerne cold.

Nay more, this vertue suffers wrong,
as to be made a subiect, nay a slaue.

The Anatomie.

EUEN vnto such whose base malitious tongue
the giuer's reputation dare depraue :[1]
Yet haue they still gift after gift receiu'd,
Euen to the full of their desires : shall I
Say this was bounty ? I might seeme bereav'd
—in saying so—of sence and honesty.
If a curst dogge—fed at your table—bites you,
you'le kick him—if not hang him—at the least :
And in a man—which doggedly requites[2] you—
reward you that, you punish in a beast ?
I know not to tearme this kinde of giuing :
nor will I make my braine a minte for phrase ;
But wish that men—whil'st their faire fame is liuing,
would manifest it comes of Vertue's race ;

---

[1] Defame, depreciate G.
[2] Misprinted 'requires' G.

Whose true-borne children should releive her
friends;
but Vertue starues, they go degenerate
In sucking base ones, for their priuate ends,
whil'st she and her's—though prais'd—are
desolate.
Alas! poor Vertue,—onely poor to such,
as do not know thy worth, who liue and die
Without all sence of goodnes, or a touch,
of ought but beast-like sensualitie:—[1]
Or rather let me pittie them then thee.
for though the strange deformèd brats of Vice
Be richly clad now, thine in pouertie;
they valued high, but thine at meanest price;
The time may come when Bountie shall appeare
pure, like it selfe, and like faire Vertue's freind,
When Ostentation shall not dare come neere,
nor Prodigalitie perswade her spend,
But vpon such as merite more then craue;
then shall no bauling foole, no wit-bare iester,
No fawning base insinuating slaue
presume, the place where Bountie liues, to pester
And you that now it thus abuse, shall then

---

[1] Talis benignitas vanitati est coniunctior, quam liberalitati. Cic[ero]. G.

[2] Virtus laudatur et alget. G.

curse your much-giuing and mis-giuing hand,
When you shall see the deeds of other men,
grauen in brasse, your's written in the sand.
Such mettle are men's hearts, the thankfull part
cannot forget the good it doth receiue,
But—as in brasse—record it in his heart,
of which no time can ere the same bereaue.
Th' ingrateful nature—sand-like—doth retaine
th' impression of your hand, and more perceiues,
An aptnesse in it selfe to take againe,
then to make shew it anything receiues.

To the Ingratefvll.

IS'T long of thy short memorie, that thou
yeeld'st not due thanks, where thou
the same do'st owe?
Alas, good man, why do'st thou not forget
to begge as well? or do'st thou thinke it fit
For men to craue thy thankes because to thee
vnask't their fauours came not? can there be
Excuse allow'd for such a fault? O no
But contrarie, no tyrants lawe can show
A torture too seuere for such an ill:
Looke how an ore-charg'd peece breaking doth
kill

The gazers on, and yet the gunner stand
not hurt at all, though from his fatall hand
Death tooke his flight ; so doth thy want of art
rightly to vse a friend, make many smart
And suffer too vniustly : for, thy fault
makes honest hearts—with no such basenesse fraught—
Suspected ; which approues the proverbe true
men scalt with hot, cold water do eschewe.
The guiltlesse seruants of that Carmelite[1]
inurbane[2] foole, who did with ill requite
Fauours receiu'd—had been to death pursuade
—but for his wife—for his ingratitude.
Art[3] thou reliev'd in want, and canst forget
—vnworthy wretch—what gracious hand did set
Thy mis'ry free ? doost thinke ther's nothing more
to be perform'd when of thy leaprous sore
Of pouerty thou'rt cur'd ; no thankes, no praise,
rendred to Him which chang'd thy painfull daies
To times of ease ? more grieuous is thy sore

---

[1] Naball. [See 1 Samuel c xxv. G.]

[2] = uncivil. G. [3] Misprinted 'Arr.' G.

—through thy neglect—by much then 'twas before.
Thine out ward sence then only felt the smart;
but now it sticks so close to thy false heart,
—And vl'cring ly'th in thy corrupted bloud—
That not from thence proceedes a thought that's good.
If by sinister meanes thou hast obtain'd
What thou inioyst, thou canst not say 'tis gain'd.
By wealth that's purchast with the losse of fame,
men do growe rich in nothing else but shame:
In whom desert, no thankfulnesse doth moue,
they do noe lesse then cheate men of their loue.
Thou with a hollow heart, false, stopp'd within,
on thy best friends wilt play, so thou mais't win:
Gaine sauours well to thy misiudging sence,[1]
whose facultie can easily dispence
With any stocke, with any ground, or dung
—bee't ne're so base, or vild[2] for any tongue
But thine to touch—from whence it doth proceede,
though in thy bosome with the same doth breed
Hatefull Ingratitude; whose brasen brow
—bold impe of Impudence—will not allow

---

[1] Dulcis odor lucri. A. [2] Vile, as before. G.

A blush to touch it. I confesse my fault
from misconstruction came, in that I thought
Thou had'st been man, as well in deed, as name,
which title di'd to thee, when thou to shame.

Of the Envious.

OE we not hold him mad, that in his hand
Dare gripe an adder, though he crush it dead?
or seemes it strange, if he by whom is fedde
A lyon's whelpe, or hath of beares command,

Shall haue his bloud by them vntimely shed?
What shall we thinke him then that entertaines
a viper next his heart, which from his vaines
Sucks his best bloud, and leaueth in the stead

A fretting poyson? whose effect is this,
it makes him grieue and rage at others good,
to stabbe himselfe to spill an other's bloud,
And thinke himselfe curs'd in an other's blisse.

Let him be gorg'd euen to the very throate;
yet will he vexe to heare an other call

---

[1] Dulcis odor lucri. A.

for a poore crust of bread ; it frets his gall
To see a sayle belongs not to his boate.

If with the price of one of his owne eyes
he can buy both an other man's, hee'l doo't :
'Tis to be fear'd too, for a soule to boote
Hee'l giue his owne to hell a sacrifice.

This is the man which from his mother's wombe
hath been peruerse and froward, whose vild life
is nourisht only by the breath of strife ;
Which birth and breathing cannot want a roome

At last in hell ; for he that trauell's[1] heere
—this monster-like—with mischiefe, cannot finde
a place more suting to his diu'lish mind,
Then where his friends and father may be neere,

To be deliuerd of his hell-bred seede :
for there some damn'd infernall hagge or other
may be the midwife fit for such a mother
From whom—at best—some Fury must proceede.

This is the man[2] who sits, and laughs to spie

---

[1] Travails. G.

[2] Vix sunt homines, hoc nomine digni quamque lupi senæ plus feritatis habent, perfudere manus fraterno sanguine fratre. A.

where men do—wolfe-like—by throate, each
other
teare: how the inhumane brother kills the
brother,
And by the hand of children, parents die.

When he perceives an other's downe-fall nigh,
he thirsts to see their ruine, more then they
whose high-flowne falcons—watchfull for
their prey—
Threatning to bring destruction from the skie,

Long to behold the fearefull game strooke dead.
'Tis ENUIE's life, soule, *summum bonum*, all
which we tearm deere, to see an other fall,
Though't be the man that giues his hunger bread.

To see his neighbour fast is his best foode,
it makes him leane to see another fat;
he pines to nought, when he finds nought
whereat
He may repine. To haue him vnderstood,

And to the full describ'd, thus in a word,
it grieves his staru'ling spirit more to see

---

[1] Inuidus non minus discruciatur aliena felicitate, quam suo infortunio. A.

an other's good, then his owne miserie:
Though it cut deeper then Affliction's sword.

To the Envied.

S it not strange, that such can liue, whose foode
Is dres'd by ENUIE, and with poyson mixt,
Whose heart's the kitchen, and whose canker'd bloud
the meager cooke carowseth; while betwixt,
His master and the diuell are begotten
prodigious monsters, which appeare as barren
Of honestie as Hell, their ioints as rotten
through want of marrow, as a peece of carrion?
By these th' art malic'd; but be not dismaide
nor grieue thou at them, rather for them grieue
If so thou canst thy charitie perswade,
—which as thou'rt flesh and bloud, I scarce belieue.—
When a fierce dogge comes running at thee, stay,
and thou shalt finde hee'l rather back retire
Then offer to assault thee: if away
from him thou fly'st thou further'st his desire:

So these—farre worse then dogges—will fiercely bite,
when they perceiue their venome makes thee stirre :
For nothing giues such fulnesse of delight
to th' snarling spleen of a malitious curre,
As to behold the mischiefe that he doth.
But where well-temper'd patience doth preserue
—As a safe antidote th' rankling tooth
of Enuie's whelpes — they pine awaie, and starue :
This to thy farewell ; if thy vertues make thee
hatefull to th' bad, their enuie is thy glorie :
If loue to vice make good men's loue forsake thee,
resolue thyselfe they enuy not, they're sorrie.[1]

To the Enuious.

UT that I know thy face, I must confesse
I should haue trembled ; for an obiect lesse
Fearefull, were able without physick's art
To make a costiue man play a loose part.
I cannot thinke the worst of Pharoe's kine

---

[1] Inuidia virtute parta gloria, non inuidia putanda est. A

Look't halfe so bare, as this poore trunke of thine ;
Which like Sir Cranion,[1] or a starv'ling capon
Staukes here and there, proportionately shapen
To thy leane spirit, whose repining hate
Hath brought thy carcasse to this pining state.
I see there are more ways to th' wood then one ;
Not age, or wedlocke, bring'th a man alone
Vnto a night-cap; for a wretched minde
Gaue thine to thee ; O had it been so kinde
T'haue put a nose-gaie too into thy hand ;
And in thy ruffe's roome plac'd a falling band,
Many had lookt to haue seene you turne, and
Hope,
Would haue presum'd that next had come a roape:
Whereto thy hanging ominous lookes presage
Thou must do homage; in th' meane time, ingage
That little hope thy wretched soule enioyes
Of heauen, to him who thy best good destroyes,
In feeding thy insatiable spleene;
Which—had not helpe from Hell transported
been—
Could not haue been so diuelish as't hath proou'd,
But it in thee, infernall powers haue mou'd:

---

[1] Query = Sir Crane. G.

To the Enuious.

CARCE Hell itself could conster[1] that for ill,
Which—damnèd—thou—to satisfie thy will—
Hast vr'gd—I know— as an extreame offence,
Against vnguiltie, harmlesse Innocence.
Which hath[2] by some,—too credulous weake men—
—Out of their wisdomes—been found faulty; when
Had they been masters but of so much sight,
As to distinguish betweene day and night,
They had beene lesse iniurious, or more iust;
But to such iudges must the guilty trust,
Whil'st Innocence must suffer; yet not so
But it may liue to see their ouerthrow
Who moale-like heaue vnseene, till at the last
Their working be discouer'd and they cast
Out of their hollow trenches, and withall
Trod on by them, whom they desir'd might fall;
Then shall your sable cacodæmon be
Hang'd with a twigge vpon some willow tree;
To all which enuious vndermining slaues
I wish no fairer ends, no better graues.

---

[1] = construe. G. [2] Misprinted 'hiath'. G.

Of the Detracter.

THIS comes in last, because he comes behinde
those whom he wrongs, though in his doing so
the diuell cannot him in skill foregoe
Vnto the last but this; this last I finde

To be as neere alli'd in basenesse, as
a brother can be to a brother twinne,
in feature, though—as oft—Nature within
Proportion them so like, that each doth passe

For other. Onely this one difference I note,
this last allow'th more freedome to his tongue
then ENUIE doth, and other men are stung
By him more then himselfe; he makes his throate

An open graue, where his contagious breath,
labours to blast the spotlesse fame of such,
whose reputation it shall chance to touch.
Nor can the hand of reconciling Death

Free men from the iniurious monster's sting,
which through the bowels of the Earth doth pierce,

and in the quiet vault appeares more fierce
Then Death—the graue's stern tyrannizing king—

Were a man here as free from actual ill,
as when he first mou'd in his mother's wombe;
or as the man that calls the Heauen his home
Guiltlesse of sinne; yet would this trie his skill

If in a bul-rush he can finde a knot;
or from pure hony—which the harmlesse bee
suck'd from those flowers which like it selfe
was free—
Straine poison'd iuyce; when if he finde one iot

Which he can iudge doth relish of a weede
—from which the toylsome bee cheerfully flies,
home to the hiue with hony laden thighs—
He straite concludes no good can thence proceed.

So strange is the distraction of this Tom
of Bedlam, that all places, times, and men
without distinction seeme alike: for when
The furious rayling fit comes on him, from

His stinking stomacke, hee'le belch forth such
geere,
such filth; and with such violence, as though
he meant to cast his rotten garbage: so
He ioyes to make his loathsomnesse appeare.

This—what shall I tearme him—will deuoure
your bread,
call you his master, crouch with cap in hand,
professe he falls, if you shall faile to stand;
Yet curse you liuing, ioy when you are dead.

He'le be the herald of your infamy,
and scandalize your worth, though you haue
bred
him to the shape of man euen from a shred:
This is a *black-one*,[1] full of trechery!

To the Detracted

THOUGH wolues against the siluer moon
do bark,
they blemish not her brightnes; nor
the spight
Of bauling curres—which she disdains to mark—
can any whit eclipse her of her light.
So mai'st thou slight the railing of ill tongues,
if a cleere shining conscience be thy guard;
Which to defend thee from the world of wrongs
will, as a wall of brasse, be found as hard.
Men are by nature apt to blame, and hate

---

[1] Hic niger est, &c. A.

such as distaste what they approue as good:
If thou dislike to heare a parrat prate,
and tell a tedious tale of Robin-hood:
He'le shoot Detraction's boult against thy braine,
terming it shallow, barren, poore, and dull;
Because not vented by a windy vaine
empt'ing it selfe to make thy mouth shew full.
But wiser men then he assures them no;
They are most fooles—say they—that vse most words: [1]
That silence argues folly, 'tis not so;
for Vertue's branches no such fruite affords.
Admit a Turke should call thee Infidell;
wouldst be offended? or imagine, that
One dubbe thee knaue, in whose owne heart doth dwell
basenesse enough, to make him wondred at
By all that know him; shall the first perswade thee,
that thy religion knowes more gods then one:
Or to denie the sacred power that made thee,
or t'giue His honour to a caruèd stone?
Or can the second force thee to confesse.
through his report, thou art so base as he?

---

[1] Loquacita certissimis fatuitatis argumentum. Eras[mus.]

If none of these thou wilt, their power's the lesse,
thy worth the more by their detracting thee.
An honest fame—like spice—the more 'tis bruis'd
sauours the sweeter, which when we are dead
Will be the sweetest seare-cloath can be vs'd
to wrap vs in; it will out-last the lead
Wherein that bodie lies, in which did liue
a spotted conscience, a detracting spirit;
Which to it selfe an earthly heauen did giue,
and of heauen's ioyes it selfe did disinherite.

To the Detracter.

THINK'ST thou it makes thy reputation faire,
if by thy muddy tongue thou can'st impaire
An other man's? looke how a murtherer can
—whose fatall hand shall kill an other man—
Adde to his owne by shortning others daies;
so by detracting others grows thy praise.
Perchance thou feed'st thy selfe with a conceipt,
that euery man that heares thee raile, doth straite
Belieue that all thou sayst is true, for that
they contradict thee not; I'le tell thee what,

In my opinion thou shouldst rather feare,
it makes them tremble and amaz'd to heare,
How diu'lishly thou second'st what thou sayst
with oaths, and curses; admit thou maist
Light vpon some who—knowing not thy vse—
may be perswaded, that from some abuse
Offer'd to thee, proceeds thy railing fit:
Yet all the glory thou enioy'st by it
Is, that they'le note thee euer after, for
a creature which all good men should abhorre.
Or say, thou shalt some man to some depraue
who know him honest; think'st thou for a knaue
They can do lesse then iudge thee? and beware
thou ray'lst to no one that iuditious are:
For they'le soone finde that thou dishonest art,
and therefore know thou tak'st no good man's part:
Whose prayse they iudge is equally the same,
Where iust men doe applaud, or thou defame.
I might haue spar'd my breath in wishing thee
to men of iudgement not to be too free;
For thou art chiefly carefull in this point
to plie his eare whose iudgement's out of ioynt:
By whom as yet was neuer vnderstood
how any cause could, but the first, be good;
Whose ignorance—I thinke—might argue rather

Th' vicar of fooles will prooue their ghostly
father.
And as for thee, thou dost resolue I know
thou must die mad, thy braine's distemperd so.
Which will be for thy credit when thou'rt dead:
for some will lay the fault vpon thy head,
And say thy braine inforc'd thy tongue to raue:
Better be thought a mad-man then a knaue.

Finis.

Qui ducis voltus, et non legis ista libenter,
Omnibus inuideas liuide, nemo tibi. Mart[ial
Ep. 20. I. xli. Paley's edition (1868) pp 12, 13.
Freely rendered we may take the couplet thus:
Who readest my Anatomie,
with envious spleen:
May he still envy all, and envied
be ne'er seen. G.]

MISCELLANIES

OF

The Fuller Worthies' Library.

POEMS

BY

HENRY LOK, GENTLEMAN:

(1593-1597)

Edited, with Memorial-Introduction and Notes,

BY THE

REV. ALEXANDER B. GROSART,

ST. GEORGE'S, BLACKBURN, LANCASHIRE.

PRINTED FOR PRIVATE CIRCULATION.

1871.

156 COPIES ONLY.

Contents.

Memorial-Introduction.

OF HENRY LOK, the Worthy to whom it is now our privilege to introduce the Reader, little or nothing has hitherto been known beyond the bibliographic-accounts of his extremely rare volume of 1597. RITSON and similar authorities, give us the merest morsel. Mr. J. PAYNE COLLIER was the first to disinter two letters of his from the State-Paper Office: and to shew that the ascription of "Orpheus and Euyridice" to him because of the initials H. L., was a mistake,—these representing the Publisher not the Author.

It is our pleasant task greatly to encrease the number of Letters of LOK from the treasures of the "Record Office"—including a correct text of the two somewhat blunderingly printed by Mr. Collier, as will be seen on comparison—and through one of the Sonnets as a first-guide, to trace his ancestry and connections. If still the light is dim and troublous, it will nevertheless be allowed that as in other cases our additions to the stock of literary biography herein, are considerable—all the more that incidentally the great name of JOHN LOCKE emerges.[1]

In the HERALD'S COLLEGE, in a volume, known there as VINCENT'S MIDDLESEX, there is a Pedigree of the family of LOK or LOCK or LOCKE[2]—such is the arbitrarily various orthography. It is meagre in its details : but an examination shews it to be accurate as to names and relationships. Taking this Pedigree as a basis, we shall add many particulars obtained from Wills, Parish Registers, and other authentic manuscripts.

The first person named in VINCENT (as *supra*) is WILLIAM LOCK, who had two sons THOMAS and JOHN. The latter has heretofore been identified

---

[1] I have had on former occasions to acknowledge the full and ever-ready stores of my Anglo-American friend, Colonel Chester, *the* Biographer of England's proto-martyr JOHN ROGERS. To him I owe nearly the entire *data* of this Introduction and of the Notes to the additional Sonnets. It is a pleasure to receive the most onerous favours from one who is so genial in rendering help to fellow-workers.

[2] At page 309 : I have to thank Mr. Adams of the Herald's College for his invariable interest and attention.

with one of the name who was Sheriff of London in 1461: but as *he* did not die till 1519, it may be doubted if they were identical. Further: in several of the Biographies of JOHN LOCKE the Philosopher, his descent has been deduced from him: but erroneously, as according to his Will he had no children. The error originated in assuming that THOMAS above named was his son, while he was certainly his brother.[1] This THOMAS LOCK (or as sometimes Lok and Loke) was a Mercer of London. He died in 1507 and was buried in Mercer's Chapel. His wife was JOANNA, daughter of...... Wilcocks of Rotherham, co. York: and she too was buried in the same Chapel in 1512. They appear to have had one son only, viz WILLIAM LOK, who was born according to the Pedigree in 1480. He also became a Mercer of London, and one of the aldermen of the city. In 1548 he was Sheriff of London, and was knighted at Westminster in that year. He was Mercer to King Henry VIIIth. with whom he was an especial favorite, so much so that it is said he held a key to the king's private chamber—a fact which

---

[1] See particularly in Gentleman's Magazine 1792: Vol. 62. Part 2. pp 798 *et seqq*.

had been an equivocal compliment before Froude wrote. One of his daughters, Rose, who by marriage became ancestress of the Hickmans of Gainsborough, and of the Earls of Plymouth, left an account of his sufferings during Queen Mary's reign, which is printed, at length, in Stark's Gainsborough. It may serve to lighten up dry genealogies to quote from its commencement, briefly, as follows: " Of my father, in Holinshed's Chronicle, I find this story. In the 25th yere of the reign of King Henry 8. being the yeere of O^{r} Lord 1534, at the sute of the ladye Katherine, dowager, a curse was sent from the Pope, which cursed both the king and the realme. This curse was set up in the town of Dunkirk in Flanders: for the bringer thereof, durst no neerer approach, where it was taken down by Mr. Lock of London, Mercer. Now I, his daughter, Rose Throckmorton, widow, late wife of Simon Throckmorton Esq, and first y^{e} wife of Anthony Hickman, a merch$_{t}$ of London, reading this of my father, have thought good to leave to my children this addition to it, y^{t} for y^{t} act y^{e} king gave him £100 a yeere, and made him a gent of his privy chamber, and he was the king's Mercer, and his Majest^{y} vouchsafed to dine at his house. Moreover he was knighted, although he was never Maior, but only sherief of London, and so was never any Londoner before him". All honour to the stout heart of Master William Lok in pulling down the 'Bull'! Evidently the fair Rose's eyes—she must have been fair—kindled over Holinshed.

SIR WILLIAM LOK was buried in Mercer's Chapel 27th August 1550. His Will dated 15th March, was proved 11th September in that year. He had four wives : (*a*) ALICE, daughter of..... SPENCER, of London, Fishmonger, who died in 1522 and was buried in Mercer's Chapel : (*b*) CATHERINE, daughter of WILLIAM COOKE of SALISBURY, who died in childbed 14th Octr. 1537 and was buried at Martin Abbey in Surrey : (*c*) ELINOR (widow of WALTER MARSH) who died in 1546 : (*d*) ELIZABETH (widow successively of..... Hutton and of ROBERT MEREDITH) who was buried in Mercer's Chapel 5th Decr. 1551. By his last two wives there were no issue. By his first wife he had 9 children, viz. 8 sons and 1 daughter. From the latter descended the EARLS of ROMNEY. Six of the sons died in their father's life-time and without issue. By his second wife CATHERINE COOKE, Sir William Lok had 5 sons and 6 daughters of whom JOHN, FRANCIS, ALICE and THOMAZINE died young, or without issue. DOROTHY, the eldest daughter, married first OTTIWELL HILL, a mercer of London, and secondly JOHN COSWORTH—of whom more anon. CATHERINE, the second daughter, married first THOMAS STACEY, mercer of London and secondly WILLIAM MATTHEW, of Braddon, co. Northampton. ROSE, third daughter married, as already brought out in her own Narrative, first ANTHONY HICKMAN, secondly SIMON THROCKMORTON. Elizabeth, the youngest daughter and 19th child (*not* 20th as is sometimes stated—as the mother died of her son John, second of that name) married first RICHARD HILL, and secondly NICHOLAS BULLINGHAM, Bishop of Worcester: (her daughter MARY HILL, married SIR THOMAS MOUNDEFORD M.D., and their daughter BRIGHT, became the wife of SIR JOHN BRAMSTON, Chief Justice of the King's Bench.)

MICHAEL LOCK, who appears to have been the 18th child of Sir William, and the 9th by his second wife, became an eminent Merchant in London, and has the renown of having been patron of FROBISHER's first Expedition. His name often occurs in the Histories of the period: but he evidently met with great reverses of fortune in his later life. He was living as late as 29th of August, 1611, when he administered the estate of one of his sons: but no subsequent trace of him has been discovered. He is sometimes called SIR

MICHAEL, but he certainly never was knighted. It is from him, through sometimes a son MATTHEW, and sometimes a son CHRISTOPHER, that JOHN LOCKE is made to descend. But he had no son MATTHEW or CHRISTOPHER, unless, which is most improbable, they were ignored by his wife and several of his sons, whose Wills are extant. His children were Zachary (who was M.P. for Southwark in 1600, and several of whose letters are preserved in the Public Record Office), ELEAZAR, GERSHON—a Puritan trait of the family as fetched from the Bible-story of the "sons of Levi" (Genesis xlvi. 11 *et alibi*)—BENJAMIN, WILLIAM, ANNE, JOANE, and ELIZABETH.

The remaining son of Sir William Lock by his second wife Catharine Cooke, was HENRY LOK or Loke or Locke. He was the 17th child of the Knight, and the 8th by his second wife. He is mentioned in VINCENT'S Pedigree as a Merchant of London. In his Will, dated 28th January and proved 31st October, 1571, he described himself as a Mercer. He mentioned no children, but leaves all his estate to his wife, who proved the Will as ANNE LOCK. In the Pedigree she is called ANNE VAUGHAN. She remained a widow: for in the Register of Burials of St. Giles, Cripplegate (London) is this entry "Buried 1573, June 12th,

Ann Locke, widow."[1] In the Visitation of Cornwall of 1620, this Henry LOCK is described as of Acton, Middlesex: but a careful search there shews no trace of them in the Parish-Registers. He must have died comparatively young, as his birth—according to the dates exhibited in the preceding details,—must have occurred after 1530.

The Pedigree at Herald's College assigns him four children, thus:

HENRY LOCK of London, Merchant = ANNE VAUGHAN

Henry s.p. | Michael s.p. | HENRY LOCK = Anne.... Moyle of Cornwall.

HENRY. | CHARLES.

The second HENRY above named we have no difficulty in identifying as our Worthy. The clue is furnished by one of his own sonnets, which is dedicated to his brother-in-law ROBERT MOYLE, of BOKE, county Cornwall. Thus our HENRY was son of HENRY LOK, *not* of MICHAEL, as Mr. COLLIER too facilely surmised,—with girds at the HAKLUYT editor which we must be pardoned regarding as

[1] See our Memorial-Introduction to Henry Vaughan: Vol. Ist. p. xxvii, for a little hereon.

sufficiently uncalled for in the face of three errors for one, of his own, on the very page he gives way to such girds.[1] Thus the author of the "Sundrie Sonets of Christian Passions" proves to have been of good descent: for then to be a Merchant was to be indeed a 'prince' in the deepest sense: his father HENRY LOK: his mother, ANNE VAUGHAN. His own birth-date and birth-place we have not been able to find. The first glimpse we get of him is as Author of a Sonnet to King JAMES prefixed to that monarch's "Essayes of a Prentise" (1591)—which we have added to the extra-Sonnets. Our next, in the following entry from the Baptismal-Register of St. Giles, Cripplegate: "1592, April 21, Henry son of Henry Lock, Gent., from widow Hall's in Fore-street." Our next, in another entry, from the Stationers' Registers, of the subject-matter of the earliest form

[1] Mr. Collier says, "We feel the more interest about Henry Lok and his Ecclesiastes, because we take him to have been the son of Michael Lok, *civis Londinensis*, who dedicated to Sir Philip Sidney one of the two maps in Hakluyt's "Divers voyages touching the discovery of America," &c., 1582: and then follow severe remarks on a few (relatively) trivial errors of the Hakluyt Society editor. (Bibl. Account: Vol. I. pp. 480-1).

of a portion of our reprint as follows: "The first parte of christian passions, conteyninge a hundred Sonnets of meditation, humiliation and prayer." [London, by *Richard Field*, 1593] "authorised under the hande of the Lord Bisshop of London."[1] More of this in the sequel. Our further chancing on his name introduces him as intermixed with home and foreign Service for the State, through all which there runs a plaint, if we ought not to say a cry of hardship, wrong, ingratitude—a sorrowful revelation altogether. The Record Office contains a series of Letters from and concerning him: and we proceed to unfold their contents for the first time. It were wearying and superfluous to give all *in extenso*: but we shall present some wholly and cull whatever of interest is found in the remainder. We begin with the two Letters of Mr. Collier's "Bibliographical Account", which, in order to correct his copies, we reprint in full. These shew that in 1596 and in 1598—before and after the publication of his Poems—he was a solicitor to Sir Robert Cecil for a small public appointment.

---

[1] Hazlitt's Hand-Book: *s. n.*

"R$^{t.}$ Ho$^{bl.}$

By your countenans had my trauels their first grace, and my hopes thair comfortes w^{ch} (with your h^{rs} present fartherans) I dowpt not shal sort to sum present stay of my nedy state: For I am by the La^{y} of Warwick incoraged to make vse of hir hig^{s} gratius inclination towards me, wch to farther she offereth her ho$^{.}$ assistans. Wherto (I having had latly so ample testimony of your h^{rs} most effectuall indeuors) I am the more incoraged to bend my self, and dowpt not (God now moving your ho^{l} heart to the fartherans therof) but it may prove to the competent stay of me & my poore family herafter, whos passed deserts, if they have not bin according to the proporsion of my many resaived fauors, yet God may in future time bles to the testification of my dutiful memory thereof. May it then pleas your h^{r} to vowtsaf me the direction of my coors herin, & to procure me your h. father's allowans therof, w^{ch} (sins Monopolis ar scandalus, Reuersions of offices vncertain, Consealments, litigius, and Forfetyrs but rarely recouered) I must be forsed to attempt by crauing of porsion of hir m^{ts} lands by leas or feefarm; or sum Pension til an office or forfeture may fall to my relefe. Wherin I beseech your h$_{r}$ to excuse my boldnes, sins my sute is not for to consume on vanities, but on the mere necessitis of life & dischardg of honest dutis. Wherin the fauour which I shal by your ho[l] travel resaiue, I hope God shal bowntifully reqwit to you & your posterity To whos gratius protection I, in all sinserity of hart, commit your h[r], & my servis to your h[s] perpetual command. This 16 of Janu. 1597. Your h[r] in all duty.

HENRY LOK."

The second letter, printed by Mr. COLLIER, is as follows:

"Rt. Ho[ll]

Vnderstanding that by the death of Mr. Ralph Bows diuers things retorn to hir M[st] disposition of thaim, I thowght good to craue your h[l] fauer in renuing to her hig[s] memory, hir late promis to releve my estate (w[ch] to be performed was referred to your ho[r] retorn) & the dayly occasions pressing me to solisit the same, ar to my grefe and your troble to much known vnto yourself. What is fit for me, or that I am fit for, is in hir M[ts] pleasure to censure, & by your h[rs] woonted fauor most likly to be bettered; w[ch] whatever it proue, (so it protect me from beggery & reproche) shal be as much as I desire, who wold rather haue my deserts, then woords, pleade for me ; if God had in any caling inabeled me to serue hir M[ty], and to apere thankful to your h[r], by whom only I as yet brethe in the hope of a good issue of my long sute. It is better to be a Beareherd, then to be bayted dayly with great exclamations for smal depts. But I dowpt I shal speak to late for things now ; when menn are deade so many are redy even to justel with the liuing for preferment in this adge. I knowe my lot shal fall where God hath asigned, & trust your h[r] shal be the happy Doue to giue token of rest to my floting fortune. To whose servis (even in al most particular dutis and imploianses) withowt any respect of trauils or perils I protest I shal most reidely, whilst I liue, dedicate al my powres, so far as shal be commanded. And thus crauing pardon of this my forsed importunasy, grownded on the occasion thus offerd, I commend my petition to your h[rs] best oportunity, and your h[r] to the protection of the Almighty. Your h[rs] in al duty.

HENRY LOK."

The date of the latter communiction is ascertained from the endorsement, viz., 8 June 1598 : the endorsement of the first is 1596 instead of

1597, the Secretary and Lok commencing the year at different periods, as was then not unusual.

Whatever resulted from LOK's candidature for the office of Keeper of the Queen's Bears and Mastiffs, which had been held by RALPH BOWES until his decease, he was taken into government service of an extremely confidential kind, not without peril, as emerges in the correspondence. Previous to his application for BOWES' post he had applied for the 'collectorship of Devon', but (under date 31st of March, 1598) writes to Secretary Cecil that he "no longer opposes the petition of one Mr. Hals" for it, conditioning merely for his charges "in riding down about the same"[1] Then comes an exceedingly familiar petition to Cecil on certain private affairs touching on Papists and the scare of them at the period, as thus—dated 12th July 1598 :—

He has, according to Cecil's advise, examined the estate of his (Lok's) aunt, and finds that by an inquisition taken in August last, it appeared to be £68 pr. an. for her life, which being a competent portion for a lone woman, he craves may be allotted to him to keep her with, "wch I rather crave

[1] Cal. Dom. Eliz. Vol. 266. No. 97.

may be elswhere rather then in prison, becaws papists doe com̄only repair together there, as at this time of hir imprisonment doe & did, when she was drawn to this peril of life: howbeit the prest to daye diing hath chardged his sowl wth clering hir & Barns, for euer knowing him a prest, hering him say Mas, or so much as praing wth thaim, for wch thay were indited. By w^{ch} (her Maj^{y} being in mersy likly to be moued to saue Barnse's life also, as she hath by his repriual giuen hope of) if it wold also pleas hir M^{ty} to bestowe for ful recompens of any seruis, and inabeling me for farther imploians, to bestowe on me the benefit of Barnse's liuing (wch with his deth is lost) I shold I trust apere thankful for your h^{ll} mediation, & hensforth les troblesom: his estate whilst he liveth is held woorth £140 a yere, wch might both releue him somwhat & satisfie my p'sent wants, & preuent I trust the future. If my merit seme not fit to carye it all, your h^{r} may dispose of sutch porsion in me as shal seme fit."[1]

On 16th July, 1598, he writes from "Coort, Grinwich" — simply recommending some person not named, to his lordship's confidence and good services.[2]

---

[1] Dom. Eliz. Vol. 268. No. 3. [2] *Ibid*, No. 6.

Again on 26th July, 1598, he communicates news concerning various matters before referred to "And for that it apereth ther is soom credit giuen by hir M^ty^ to Mr. Toplif's reports, I here send yowr h^r^ Barnes'es own certificat of his state and Mr. Osborn's of my awnts, then wch if yet any better might growe (as I trust) hir M^ty^ wold not much dislike. Yet I protest I wil be true to yowr h therin, & refer myself & it to be disposed of, whom I most humbly beseach (if this satisfye not hir M^ty^) that I may haue warant to Commissioners for farther trial, only I humbly craue that I may not be cownterpesed [*sic*] in this sute by sutch a riual's intrusion, thre daies after by the parti's owne mosion, I had labored your H^or^ fauor herin. Espesially he being one by his place abeler to liue then myself & hauing obtained £1000, more by his seruis (then I am like) alredy."[1]

We have next a Letter from ZACHARY LOK to Secretary Cecil, dated 9 Dec. 1598. He was our Worthy's son, and it is sorrowful to find both so pathetically if persistently pleading. This Letter is of deep biographic interest, opening up as it does the Past: "I humblie besseeche yow not to

---

[1] *Ibid*, No. 10.

think that naturall affection in my father's cause doth transport me. He was drawne (for that Companie's busynes) out of his Contrie almost 6 yeares past, being then above 64 yeares of age. In Turkey he passed muche hardnesse allmost to ye Hazarde of his life, by ye unfitting usage of ye Companie's servants ther. It were too long to troble yr Hrs. eares wth repeticon of yt. I doe assure yor Hr yt hath and will cost him above £500 more then ever he shall receue of ye Companie if he be concluded wthin this Awarde: whereas if he had continewed out his lymited tyme of 4 yeares resydence at Alepo, his estate had byn bettered by a thowsand marks and his credyt preserued. All wch doth not greeve me soe much as this letter of Sr Jo: Spencer's man to him, wch yt may please yor H: to reade & judge of accordinglie. And therfore I humblie desyre that either somme exemplarie punishment may be should upon him or that my father (notwithstanding this ende betweene ye Companie and him) maye be lefte to his remedie against this George Dorington for his manyfowld abuses towards him, wch I trust in yor honorable wisdomes shall be thought fitt "[1] We pass now to 1599 and Henry

---

[1] *Ibid*, Vol. 269, No. 7.

Lok himself addressing again Secretary Cecil (dated 31st March 1599) he thanks his lordship for a gelding rec^d this morning. Delays his departure until to morrow—hopes he will not have to use a certain letter of his lordship's—suggests the use of a cipher, &c.[1] He is now abroad, and in a short Letter dated at Bayonne, 30th May 1599, communicates sundry naval intelligence in that neighbourhood, and then this personal bit: "Of Mr. Le Grands time of going in I here not, but hope yor Hr wil farther my sute."[2] Next month "10 June 1599, at St. John de Luis" he intimates that he is engaged in a troublesome and somewhat perilous service, and craves some safe and perpetuall employment[3]—evidently on some special or secret service. Again in England at "London 25 Decr. 1599," he encloses certain letters received from France, and mentions his late services at Bayonne and elsewhere. Then "towching the particulars of my sute in my late Lrs commended to yowr hr. I attend yowr more leisure to be directed, as one whom no wants shold incoradg to be importun or offensive to yowr hr" &c.[4] Further, from "Strand, 26 Apl. 1600," "being

[1] *Ibid*, Vol. 270, No. 67. [2] *Ibid*, 121.

[3] *Ibid*, Vol. 271, No. 6. [4] *Ibid*, Vol. 273, No. 54.

nuely arrived out of the West Country" he encloses a letter from the coast of Spain which he finds awaiting him "touching the succes of my jorny with T. Killigrew, this his letter will testify it to be litel to my present relefe and holy depending on your hl favour to make it hopeful or not." The enclosure is a letter from Bayonne, containing general news, addressed thus:
"To the Worshipfull and his verry good frend Mr. Henry Locke, Esquire, in London, at on Mr. Thomas a talyor, in the Strand p. the Diana of Portchmouth whom God preserve." [1]

The Secretary has somehow taken offence: for in a Letter indorsed 1600 on the back, but without date in the body of the document we read as follows:

"The hope wch I have that your ouer just reprofes tend rather to my reformation then utter relinquishment of me, is the only brething life of my languishing hart, whilst that your natiue bownty cannot lightly abandon the distressed, but (imitating the divine goodnes) then showe itself most powrful when (not in faith thowgh in frailty, the suppliant hath falne". "A more hevy acsident on earth (I protest) cannot befall my

[1] *Ibid*, Vol. 274, No. 112.

declining years and setled thowghts then to be iustly abandoned from your grace." He earnestly desires restoration to favour, and offers to take any service, however perilous or expensive to himself, inclosing sundry suggestions as to how he could be serviceable in foreign parts, evidently as a secret emissary of the government, when his better services might cancel his former errors, and he be relieved from his creditors, &c., &c.[1] Our next are two letters from THOS. NICHOLSON to HENRY LOK "at Mr. Harwood's, Strand, opposite the old Lord Treasurers", dated at Calais 10/20 Sep., 1601,[2] and from Mr. Tresham to Henry Lok, "the Strand, London." dated, Paris, 5 Nov. 1601,[3]—neither of further interest. The 'great Queen' is gone and JAMES ignobly fills her splendid throne. Our Worthy is still in correspondence with the State-Officers. Under date 8th Novr 1615, he writes to the Earl of Salisbury (Lord High Treasurer) "Finding the importunity of times unfit to troble your Lp by speach, I herin send a memorial of what I can gather from the Keper of Cambridg Castel. If it be held fit to be farther proseded in, I rest to be directed by your

---

[1] *Ibid*, Vol. 276, No. 32. [2] *Ibid*, Vol. 281, No. 80.
[3] *Ibid*, Vol. 282, No. 45.

Hr. And if your Lp. pleas to dispose of a Burgeship [i. e. seat in Parliament] in Cornwall, I haue a kinsman her, a Justise of peas of that contry, caled *Cosworth* who wold comend it to your hs nomination of one, wch els I wold acsept of,"[1] &c., &c.

With reference to the 'kinsman Cosworth' of the last Letter, in the Visitation of London of 1598, a John Cosworth, Mercer of London—descended from the Cosworths of Cornwall—married it will be remembered Dorothy, daughter, of Sir William Lok.

Difficulties and sorrows have multiplied around the now aged Suitor and Letter-Writer. He is in "Gate-Hows"—a prison chiefly for debtors in Westminster,—and from thence addresses the Earl of Salisbury, dated 31st March 1606:

"By yor hr fauour being licensed by my Ld Chamberlin to part wth my place and by his hrs order having this day agreed wth my creditor Mr. Grig, for £24, to be paid the next terme, or securing for it then, to pay it & the use at Christmas (wch I hope very shortly by my place to dischardg honestly) I rest now only in form of law to be quit herof & to pay his & my own

[1] Dom. Jac. Vol. 16, No. 27.

chardges, both wch exsede not 6 or £7, wherein if your h^r shal be plesed (as a blessed seale of al your fauors) to geue me so relefe, I may in the morning be dispatched & attend my former sute for a packet, wherin (as in any thing during life) If I may apere grateful God so bles me as my sowl (of al erthly things) desireth it, who shal in al fortunes & in the bitterest exile continually (wth my poore orphants) pray to God for his increas of happines & ho^r vppon your Lp: & hopeful posterity."

Onward on 18th May, 1608, the same debt-troubles are crushing him. He writes once more to LORD SALISBURY, from the "Clink in Southwark"—another prison—

"Whilst I have bin long a haples sutor to his M^ty & now lately seking to trye a titel of lands & to recover nere £1000 wch Sr Thomas Harris the elder Seriant oweth me for land (w_ch I sold him nere to years sins to pay my debts and so folow my sutes) I am (through his breach wth me) fallen in to the hands of an old creditor, for surtiship past 20 years sins of a dept then but 13, now grown to £120, for wch I lye & haue this senight, prisoner in the Clink, to the utter disabeling me to folow my sutes in the Tearms, & in peril of more actions, if I be not by God and your h^{e} fauour releved in this my humble sute, wch is that your Lp wold be presently pleased to lay yor h$_{rs}$ commandement uppon me here, wherby no more actions can cum nor be entered. And if farther your Lp. wold vowsafe to undertake my true imprisonment wth Mr. Davison Bayly of the Clink (he wold be content to make my servant my keper, and I shal be able to goe abroode to folow my sutes, and be in hope, if I recouer my lands or Sarient Harises dept, to pay my creditors, and live poorly, who els must pine. If therfore your H^{r} shal pleas to take my oth (on my faith to God, aleageans to prins and duty unto your Lps) for true performans therof, & in trust therof to vowtsafe this your warant to him for my commitment & licens by a keper to folow my sutes, it may be a relefe of the hole fortune of me and mine.

Thus leuing the lamentable state to your h$_{o}^{r}$ compassion, I humbly beseach your Lp. to think that I haue rather in hast euer desired to seru your Lp then to be thus dayly vnsauery vnto yow in this kinde (whereunto God knoweth extreme peryl & wants compel me) to whos holy protection

I commend your Lps incres in a perfect & perpetual $h^{r.}$ & happines, resting whilst I live

Your Lps

faithful beadsman

HENRY LOK."[1]

There follows—dated 22 Oct. 1608—another appeal for his lordship's consideration. As his lordship had not favourably answered his late petition to recommend his causes to the Ld Chf. Justices, he is now put off from trial until Midsummer term &c.[2] Finally—dated 26 Oct. 1608—he renews his petition for employment, or leave to withdraw out of danger.[3]

There is no after-trace of Henry Lok in the Calendars of the Record Office. Upwards of 64 as we have seen in 1592, he was by the close of 1608 well on to, if not beyond, the "four score years" vouchsafed "by reason of strength." It is to be hoped that he went away Higher to know there no more "labour and sorrow." When or where he died is unknown to us. The Fire swept away many Registers and Monuments: and his name has not been discovered in those that survive, nor in the old Chronicles of the dead.

---

[1] *Ibid*, Vol. 32, No. 53. [2] *Ibid*, Vol. 37, No. 26.
[3] *Ibid* No. 31.

It is plain that earlier with the 'Companie' at Aleppo and later in secret-missions on the Continent, our Worthy was frequently engaged in hard and onerous service: and somehow was suffered to blanch into hoariness in neglect and poverty. Other Letters in the Record Office—which may be summarized in a foot-note[1]—go to shew

---

[1] Dom. Eliz. Vol. 266. No. 24: Letter from Secretary Cecil to Lord Burghley, dated 17 Feb., 1597/8. Has received a letter from Colville, &c. "There are some ciphers which Lok can decipher, for he and Colville are sworn brothers."

Ibid, Vol. 271., No. 91: date 14 July, 1599: Account by Thomas Honyman of money disbursed for intelligence from Spain during the year 1599, to Fras. Lambert, [*Hen.*] *Lok* and Thos. Bradshaw. Total £278 13s. 4d.

Ibid, No. 125: Thos. Honyman to Secretary Cecil: dated 27 July, 1599.

"From Bayonne I understand that Mr. *Lok* had like to have been in trouble for showing his discontent at a vessel's bringing of corn out of England; the people questioned what he was and what he had to do there, and talked of banishing him the town. He said he was an English traveller that would pass into Spain with the French Ambassador. He is not acquainted with Spain, yet I told him it was the most dangerous country in Christendom, and that a man might be touched there in causes when the king might not speak for him. If he pass, I know not how he can escape. For Bayonne I told him it was a town

that he risked limb and life for the State. Pity that like all too many of the bravè hearts of the period, risk and loss fell so heavily on him and his "poor orphants"—the tender words accidentally informing us that his wife predeceased him.

Such is all we have to tell of this old Life-story in its outward facts. Whether living LOCKES in our own country and in America descend from the line of HENRY LOK, I know not. They might do worse than give us their family-history.

Turning to the one surviving book of our Worthy—for Mr. Collier has certainly disproved the alleged authorship of "Love's Complaint or

---

where he would quickly be noted, so he determined to travel thereabouts, and to come thither once a month till he passed. Contrary to this he took a chamber there, which was presently noted, for as it is a garrison town, none can be there without giving good reason. I told him if they once found he lay there upon intelligence only, the people would malice him. * * * The danger I conceive of Mr. Lok, if he pass, causes me to trouble you so far."

Ibid, Vol. 273. No. 13 : Thomas Honyman to Secretary Cecil, dated 20 October, 1599 :

I send a letter of old date from Mr. Lok. I have written him 6 in 3 months, but contrary winds have kept back his answers."

Ibid, Vol. 275, No. 133 : a letter dated 6 Dec., 1600, mentions having delivered certain letters to *Lok*, &c.

Legend of Orpheus and Euridice"—its title-page bears in the face of it that a portion of it at least had been previously in print. The entry from the Stationers' Registers given by Mr. Hazlitt confirms this. Still no copy of this prior impression is known to Bibliographers. Of the edition of 1597 our own exemplar is one of at the utmost *four* complete copies recorded. That in the British Museum is imperfect. The title-page also shews that the Poet gives prominence to his versification of the book of ECCLESIASTES. Its extent alone justifies this. We have found it as a whole a dilution of the robust and passionate thought of the original, without any of those felicities of wording, even occasional, that sometimes atone for pious common-place. We have had no hesitation in dismissing therefore, the idea of reprinting ECCLESIASTES: but as an Appendix there will be found such few things as seemed noticeable in it. We have prefixed also the Epistle-dedicatory and other preliminary matter, including the versification of certain of the Psalms. Of the Sonnets—as well those of the "Christian Passions" as of the extremely-rare additions brought together by the Printer, from (apparently) various scattered sources—we have formed a very much higher yet we believe equally accurate, estimate. In the former there seem to us pulsations and thrills of a true and deep experience of the truest and deepest things, while ever and anon there are bird-like snatches of real singing, and hidden away in unlooked for places, epithetic bits of colour, now gleaming as jewels, now coming and going as a dove's or peacock's neck, as were not usual at the period. I do not claim for HENRY LOK the supreme *aflatus*, the grandeur of thoughts "that voluntary move, harmonious numbers". Nevertheless I assert for him a place—whence he has been too long excluded—among the Christian Singers of England—all the more that there are in the Sonnets of the "Christian Passions" real passion, sprung of compassion, tremblings, penitence, sobs, shouts of joy, weeping, autobiographic confidences of unquestionable realness, and so of unquestionable worth pyschologically. His extra-Sonnets have the further interest of preserving many historic names of whom too little is known. There are in them, beneath their most exaggerate flatteries, traits that tell of personal knowledge.[1]

---

[1] See introductory Note to the extra-Sonnets, where Singer's misannotation of Bishop Hall's Satires, is corrected.

Our text, as usual, is a faithful reproduction of the Author's own. Our Notes elucidate or illustrate wherever called for.

ALEXANDER B. GROSART.

Sundrie Sonnets

OF

Christian Passions.

Note.

The following is the title-page of the Volume whence our reprint of Lok is taken:

ECCLESIASTES,

OTHERVVISE CALLED

THE PREACHER.

Containing Salomons Sermons or Commentaries (as it may probably be collected) vpon the 49. Psalme of Dauid his father.

Compendiously abridged, and also paraphrastically dilated in English poesie, according to the analogie of Scripture, and consent of the most approued writer thereof.

Composed by H. L. Gentleman.

Whereunto are annexed sundrie Sonets of CHRISTIAN PAS | SIONS heretofore printed, and now corrected and augmen | ted, with other affectionate Sonets of a feeling con | science of the same Authors.

PSAL. 144,

3 Lord what is man, that thou regardest him : or the sonne of man, that thou thinkest vpon him ?

4 Man is like to vanitie, his days like a shadow that vanisheth.

LONDON.

Printed by Richard Field, dwelling in the Blacke-friers near Ludgate.

1597. [4to.]

Though for reasons assigned in our Memorial-Introduction we have contented ourselves with a few short specimens of "Ecclesiastes" as an Appendix, we have prefixed these (*a*) Epistle-dedicatory to Elizabeth : (*b*) To the Christian Reader: (*c*) Certaine poems to the Author of the Work: (*d*) Sonnet to Elizabeth: (*e*) Adue to World's vaine delight: (*f*) Sundry Psalmes of David. The several parts of the Sonnets have also their Epistles, &c., complete. G.

Epistle-Dedicatory.

TO THE RIGHT EXCELLENT AND NOBLE PRINCESSE, LADIE OF RAREST VERTVES, Queene Elizabeth, our most gracious Soueraigne : her Hhighnes faithfull subject Henrie Lok, wisheth perfect and perpetuall felicitie.

THE purest liquor drawne out of the heauenly fountaine of Salomon's inspired wisdom, I here—with all zeale of your Highnesse seruice—in most hūble dutie, offer to your thrise sacred Maiestie, vnder whose most glorious Empire, hauing first receiued the breath of this life : and by whose shining beames of most gracious gouernement, that life hauiug tasted part of the common comfort of your many happie subiects, and peculiar fauor of your most princely countenance : I cannot but as I acknowledge all my powers of right to pertain to your Highnesse disposition : so to force my weake indeuors, to testifie the sinceritie of the same. This my present, which —in a rustic[1] caske, in steed of a golden cup—I have ventured to purchase for your Highnesse, is —I confesse—farre vnworthie of your Maiestie's tasting of—though in the benignitie of Dauid's spirit, I doubt not your Highnes will accept the same,—which, as it is borrowed from the labours of so mightie and worthie a King as was Salomon, the true Author thereof, it seems most fit the dedication to your Maiestie, who in Empire being a peere vnto him, in election a partner, in happinesse a riuall, and in wisedome a Sabian obseruer of his soundest doctrines, can perfectliest judge, and will kindliest—I assure my selfe—welcome this his child for his father's sake, which must be —and so I desire—his onely grace. For with me it is true that in the composition hereof, it fared as with more worthie Nehemias, when he attempted the repaire of the holy citie: who being oftentimes disturbed therein by the practise and malice of Sanballet, Tobia and Geshem, was sometimes forced to desist from his attempt, and in the end to effect it with sword in one hand and mattock in the other:[2] so whilst common cares and domestick duties—the direct enemies to all ingen-

[1] Misprinted 'rustie.' G. [2] Nehemiah iv. 18. G.

ous actions, and proper poyson of pure inuention —did many times confound my iudgement, disturbe my leisure, and in a maner vtterly disable my disposition for so waighty an affaire,—remouing so often my hand from my mind, and my mind almost from the affection of my heart—I—with half my weak selfe—haue bene driuen thus to peece together, this often broken off, and now vnworkmanly perfected taske. Which yet—as a well fauored person, euen in meane attires, seemes yet euer comely—will I doubt not shew some excellencie of the cōposer's spirit, though it be not artificially[1] clothed with borowed bewties frō my barren braine. And your Highnesse, whose course of life so wel conformeth with this his discourse—teaching vs your subiects, by holy practise, what he by deuine precepts instructed his—may as iustly chalenge—me seemeth—the publication of the like discourse: as we without defrauding God of His honor, and your Highnesse of your due, may not conceale the perfect resemblance your Highnes hath of him in name, disposition, and fortune: and we with his subiects in honor, prosperitie and peace: which albeit, we your inferior subiects—as the weake-sighted eyes

[1] Skilfully or with art. G

which cannot behold perfectly the face of the sunne, but looking downe in the water: nor see his first appearing in the East, but by looking for the shadow in the VVest—knowing our disabilities iudicially to observe the cleare brightnes of your shining vertues: referring to bordering Princes and attendant Peeres, the more fit recording of the same: we take palpable assurāces of the blessed Spirit of God working in you, by the like frute of peace, prosperitie and plenty, deriued by your Maiestie's most excellent gouernement and wisdome, vnto vs: whose first worke of building vp the Church of Christ, prouiding for learning, restoring the decayd strēgth and munitions of the realme, enriching the treasurie of the Land by refined coin, retaining with most princely magnanimity, the ancient ample bounds of your Empire, the establishment of so many profitable factories for vnfrequented trafficke, the chargeable discoueries of so many vnknown parts, the honorable repulsiō of so many foes, the bounteous purchase of so many neighbor friēds, the charitable relief of so many Christians oppressed, the equal distribution of iustice vnto all,—all tending to the glory of God, and prosperitie of your raigne—do sensibly, without any disparagement of the greatnesse of that mightie Prince, draw on a certaine liuely comparison of both your prosperities and blessings: which therefore might excuse me of flatterie, if in a few words I should point thereat. But I wil leaue the ampler relitaō hereof to future posterities, and herein hūbly crauing pardon of your Maiestie, for this my presumption—which indeed hath bene founded on your Highnesse gracious acceptance of my former Passionate present[1]—and recommending them anew to your Maiestie's fauor herewithall, augmented and reformed; I will with all feruencie of prayer, cōmend your Highnes to the protection of the Almightie: Who as He hath confirmed your throne these—now nigh fortie—yeares amongst vs, to the vniuersall peace and comfort of His Israel, the Church of Europe: so may He redouble and continue euen to the end—if so His Highnesse please—your Maiestie's most happie raigne ouer vs for euer.

Your Maiestie's most dutifull and
loyall subiect,
HENRY LOK.

[1] See Memorial-Introduction, *ante*. G.

To the Christian Reader.

IT is the most fit subject for the nobility of man's spirit to meditate of felicitie: and a true saying of ARISTOTLE, that *Omnia appetunt bonum.* Yea the common practise of our high-minded Age is to striue for the same in the superlatiue degree. But so foolish and new-fangled are our desires, that wishing we wot not what, and seeking it we know not how nor where: we come all farre short of the same, and some runne headlong to the despised contrary—looking for it on Earth—and therby groping for it to their graues, they are there cut off of their hopes, and die discontented with their haps. Wheras if they acknowledged it to be the tree of life, planted in the heauenly paradise, they wold lesse labor their bodies for attaining these transitorie shadowes of pleasure, and more exercise the faculties of the soule for atchiuing the same, so much the more despising these instable and imperfect happinesses of this life, as they found their foolish affections of the flesh—doting on thē—to worke neglect of the nutriment of their soule: and slacknes in the constant trauell in religion and vertue—which is requisit for the long iorney we haue to passe through life and death thereunto—. But this hauing bin the sickness of all ages, and specially of the Iews in Salomon's time,—which induced him, as it should appeare, to take so great paines in removing thē from that error,—I the lesse maruell, that our age florishing in the pride of like long peace and plentie, vnder her Maiestie's most happie raigne, be also sotted with the world, as they were dreaming of that pefection and perpetuity here, which God by nature hath denied vnto vs, and but by her Highnes raigne we could hope for. And since it is the dutie of euery part and member of the body, to ioyne in the assistance and cure of the whole, if any particular of it should suffer: I haue in a dutiful compassiō of this cōmon calamity endeuored to seeke forth some mithridate[1] for this poyson: by which so many perish; and haue here brought thee a doses[2] of the wisest

[1] (Medical) antidote, so named after its (supposed) discoverer, MITHRIDATES. See Index of Words in our Vaughan. G.

[2] See Index of Words in our Vaughan, *s. v.* G,

Physition's cōposition, that euer had practise of that cure: who did not—for th' experimēt of his potion's qualitie, first kill many patients in triall thereof—but applying it to his own wound first, dares confidently write *probatnm est*, and by the seale of the Holy Spirit and consent of the Church, doth warrant thee to tast of the same. It is a receipt so oldly composed perhaps, that thou respectest it the lesse, or of so small price, that thou shamest to take it, or perhaps knowing the bitternesse of the tast, thou hadst as liue continue sicke, as to trie it. But deceiue not thy selfe, it is of the nature of the perfectest drogs, which with age increase in strength: of the kind of Sibillae's works, which refused, grow higher prized:[1] and of the herbe called woodroofe, which onely handled hath an euill smell, but more forcibly rubbed, yeeldeth a sweet sauour. Receiue it therefore as confidently as he assureth it, and as kindly as I intend it: who in respect that the obscuritie of many places, the contrarietie—as at first would appeare—of some points, and strange dependancie of the whole together: haue done my carefull and studious indeuor—by consideration and imitation of the best interpreters hereof — to

[1] The well-known classical Sibyls' book. G.

explane the true sense, accord the different places: to ioine by probable cōnexion the whole discourse together: which—aswel to distinguish the seuerall arguments, as to varie the verse, and pawse the reader—I haue not altogether vnfitly distributed into three Sermons, each one containing foure Chapters a peece. The first especially shewing the vaine opinion of felicitie, which is not in Earth to be found. The second pointing more directly—by the lawfull vse of this life—the true way vnto her. The last, teaching her residence to be in heauen, and perswading the speedy pursute of her fauor. And that you might truly consider of the cariage of the matter, according to the scope of the Text, I haue caused the same to be quoted in the margent, reducing for memorie sake into the abstract lines of verse set in the top of euery leafe, the substance of euery page's content, which afterwards as thou seest, is paraphrastically dilated page by page, in the plainest form I can deuise.[1]

Whom respect of the grauitie of the argument did restraine my pen frō the helpes of much profane learning, and in consideration of the antiquity of the worke, and maiestie of the author, could

[1] See examples of above, in Appendix. G.

not—without great indecencie—haue vsed the authorities of men, or of so late times—as since the learnings florished, whence we now receiue our common light.—Like naked truth therefore I pray thee receiue it, for it[s] owne, if not for my sake: and if in anything I seeme to swarue from thy conceit of many points, I pray thee confer farther therin, with D. GREGORIUS, NEOCERASIENSIS EPIS. OLIMPIODERUS, D. SALONIUS EPIS. VIENNENSIS, THEOD. BEZA, JOH. SERRANUS, ANTH. CORRANUS, TREMELIUS, all interpreters and paraphrasers in prose vpon this worke, and J. LECTIUS, RO. LEMMANNUS, J. VIUIANUS, reducers thereof into Latin poesie, or any thou likest better of, so shal my errors be couered or excused, whilst their different formes, distributiōs of method, and interpretatiōs wil leaue thee—I am perswaded—in some points as litle satisfied as this my labor shall do: who in some things was forced to digresse from them all, when either too much in one place or too litle in another, they followed the forme of a Paraphrasis, which they vndertooke: into which error also it is not vnlike but I haue sometimes fallen my selfe, and I doubt not but many things more might haue bin said, and perhaps to more purpose then I haue done, but *non omnia possumus omnes.* According to my sufficiencie I haue discharged my self faithfully vnto thee, and therefore I trust—in these days when some pernitious, many vnciuil, and a swarme of superfluous and vnprofitable books passe from the presse—it shall not be needfull for me to vse great insinuation for thy fauour: since it lyeth not in the bounds of a Preface, to prepare a peruerse mind, or in the nature of such a worke, to go a begging for a grace. I will therefore cut off that labor, and only signifie vnto thee the excellency of this worke, compiled by the wisest man, and mightiest king of Israell, euen Salomon the king of peace: *Ydida*: the beloued of God: *Ecclesiastes* the preacher: who in his Prouerbs instructeth thee as a child, to a ciuill and honest life: in this worke, instituteth thy manly thoughts to the inquisition of the highest good. To the end, that by his last song of heauenly loue, thy ripened thoughts might be inflamed with that glorious bride Christ Jesus: to Whose holy direction I hartily cōmend thee.

H. L.

Sundry Sonnets of Christian Passions.

CERTAINE POEMS TO THE AUTHOUR OF THE WORKE.

Terra ferax vatum est Brittannia, non tamen omnes,
Aut vno, aut sacro flamine Phœbus agit
Hic canit obscuri certaminis arma virosve,
Alter laciui ludicra amoris alit.
Hos genio vt superas, sic carmine et argumento
Æquum et Reginæ est cedere Regis opus.

A. H. S.

AD SERENISSIMAM REGINAM ELIZABETHAM.

Regia Virgineæ soboles dicata parenti,
Virgo animæ, patriæ mater, Regina quid quid optas?
Chara domi, metuenda foris, Regina quid optas?

Pulchra, pia es, princeps, fœlix, Regina quid
optas?
Cœlum est? Certo at sero sit Regina quod optas.
Joh. Lily.[1]

AD LOCKUM EIUSDEM.

Ingenio et genio locuples, die Locke quid addam?
Addo, quod ingenium quondam preciosius auro.

AD AUTHOREM.

Non vane vanos sapiens per stringit abusus:
Nec vano enarras regalem carmine mentem.
Nec qui suasit opus, fuerat vanusve malusve.
Nec vanum diuæ sacrum dicare laborem.
Cuius quid vani? quid non memorabile dictu?
Non vanum est sceptro, populum rexisse potentem.
Non iusto regem bello, superasse superbum,
Non Antichristi vires fregisse furentis,
Non armis miseros, vicinaque regna fouere,
Si vanus repeto, ignosce O regia virgo
Vano. Perge tamen. Sola hæc et vera putato.
L. P.

TO THE WORKE.

The Prince's pen, now present to a Prince,
And poeme to a princely sprited Muse:

[1] The Euphuist: born 1553, died 1601. G.

Ye full sound Ethicks of the sweet essence
  Of heauenly truth, which all ought to peruse,
  View all, reape good, leaue ill without excuse.

H. A.

TO THE AUTHOUR.

For me to praise this worke, it were no praise,
  Whil'st thou doest publish it: it prayseth thee;
Thing—once called perfect—further prayse denayes,
Because all other words inferior bee.

With happie sight thy Muse appeares to see,
That could select a subiect of such choyce,
Which hath enforcèd many more then mee,
With silence—for thy blist attempt—reioyce.

Thy former vaine,[1] no vaine conceipt bewrayes
By Passions—patternes of a Christian sight—
But for this worke, yet highest honor stayes,
And therefore henceforth feare no other's flight,
  Thy zeale, thy theame, thy gift, thy fame to staine,
  Which imitate they may, but not attaine.

M. C.

[1] Vein. G.

TO THE QUEENE'S MOST EXCELLENT MAIESTIE.

To you thrise sacred Princesse of this Ile:
By God, by countrie, by true wisdome's praise,
Elect, annointed soueraigne, is the stile,
Religous empresse, Beautie of our dayes!
His Church you cherish, that your state did raise,
Our peace you purchase, where your throne is plast,
Eternall glorie on your actions stayes;
Rare, crownèd Vertue: holy, humble, chast,
Whom all heauen's high perfections fully grac't,
Whom all Earth honors, should, do, will adorne:
Whom all the Muses haue with loue embrac't:
Who doth pale Enuie, and blind Fortune scorne
To you wise king's discourse of blisse I bring,
Renownèd Queene, true type of happiest king.

ADUE TO WORLD'S VAINE DELIGHT.

Ye world's delights—blind guides to blisse—adue,
Weake helpes, which fit a carnall vaine desire:
My soule can find but comfort small in you,
Though—as true blisse—profane sort you admire.
My soule doth will my thoughts from ye retire,

In faith to place my hope of firmer stay;
To gaine true blisse, lesse hope it doth require,
Then world's vaine pleasure doth, by farre away.
Your false and fickle grounds do well bewray,
Your liking, base effect of fond desire:
The Earth—your seat—doth perfectnesse denay.
My soule's true hope—inspir'd with heauenly fire—
There seeks to liue, where blisse is firme and true,
And by reformèd life, would heauen pursue.

SUNDRY PSALMES OF DAUID TRANSLATED INTO VERSE, AS BRIEFLY AND SIGNIFICANTLY AS THE SCOPE OF THE TEXT WILL SUFFER; BY THE SAME AUTHOR.

PSALME 27.

1 The Lord He is my sauing light, whom should I therefore feare?
2 He makes my foes to fall, whose teeth would me in sunder teare.
3 Though hosts of men besiege my soule, my heart shall neuer dread,

4 So that within His court and sight, my life
shall still be lead.
5 For in His Church from trouble free, He shall
me keepe in hold:
6 In spight of foes, His wondrous prayse, my
song shall still vnfold.
7 Have mercie — Lord — therefore on me, and
heare me when I cry;
8 Thou badst me looke with hope on Thee, for
help to Thee I fly.
9 In wrath therefore hide not Thy face, but be
Thou still my aide;
10 Though parents fayle, Thou wilt assist, Thy
promise so hath said.
11 Teach me Thy truth, and Thy right path, least
that the enemy
12 Preuaile against my life, whose tongues intrap
me trecherously.
13 My heart would faint for feare, vnlesse my
faith did build on Thee,
14 My hope, my God, and comfort's strength, Who
will deliuer mee.

PSALME 71.

1 In Thee—O Lord—I trust, therefore from
shame deliuer mee;

2 Performe Thy promise, saue Thou me, who call for helpe to Thee.

3 Be Thou my rocke of strength and shield, Whose powre is great and might.

4 Deliuer me from wicked men, and put my foes to flight.

5 For in Thee onely from my youth, haue I my trust reposd;

6 Thou hast had care of me, whilst yet in wombe I was inclosd.

7 Thee will I praise, Who art my helpe, when men at me do scorne;

8 My mouth Thy mercies still records, Who helpst the mind forlorne.

9 In time of age forsake me not, or when my strength doth faile,

10 Least that the counsels of my foes, against my soule preuaile.

11 Who say, my God hath me forgot; they therefore me pursue:

12 But be thou Lord at hand to me, who canst my strength renue.

13 Shame and reproch let be their share, which my destruction seeke;

14 But on Thee alwayes will I waite, with humble hart and meeke.

15 My mouth Thy mercies shall rehearse, Whose measure doth excell:

16 And in Thy trust my steps shall walke, and tongue Thy truth shall tell.

17 Euen from my youth Thou hast me taught, Thy wonders well I know:

18 And while I liue,—if Thou assist—I will Thy iudgements show.

19 Thy iustice Lord, I will exalt: Whose workes are like to Thine?

20 Who threw'st me downe, and raisd me vp, who else in dust had leine.

21 Thou canst man's honor soone increase, and shew Thy chearefull face:

22 Vpon the vyall will I sing Thy prayse, O God, of grace.

23 My lips shall ioy to talke of Thee, Who hast my safety wrought:

24 My freed soule, shall still confesse, Who hath my safety bought.

PSALME 119.

1 Blessèd are those whose wayes are right, and in Gods lawes do walke,

2 Whose heart obeyeth to His will, and lips thereof do talke,

3 Such do not worke iniquitie, but so their wayes direct,

4 That in their life, by straying steps, Thy lawes they not neglect.

5 O would to God, my deedes therefore, so straightly I might frame,

6 That with regard of Thy precepts, I might be free from blame ;

7 Then shold I prayse, with vpright hart, Thy righteous iudgemēts known,

8 Which whilst I study to obserue, Lord let my helpe be showne.

PART. 2.

9 By looking to Thy lawes, most soone a man may perfect grow :

10 Since then my heart hath sought the same, astray let me not go.

11 Thy promises in mind I beare, which me from sinne withdraw :

12 Thou gracious God and blessed guide, teach me Thy perfect law,

13 My tongue hath testifi'd Thy prayse, and iustice thou doest vse :

14 To follow freely Thy beheast, I'le worldly wealth refuse.

15 For of Thee will I meditate, and studie whilst I liue;

16 And to obey Thy iust precepts, my mind will wholly giue.

PART. 3.

17 Be gracious to Thy servant Lord, giue life and powre to mee;

18 Open my eyes, that of Thy lawes, I may the wonders see.

19 I am a stranger upon Earth, hide not from me Thy will:

20 My heart doth swell with hot desire to know Thy iudgements still.

21 Thou hast destroyd the proud, and curst are they which go astray:

22 Shame and contempt yet take from me, who keepe Thy lawes alway.

23 Though princes hate me for Thy truth, yet will I Thee obay:

24 Thy lawes shall be my studie still, and comfort night and day.

PART. 4.

25 My soule with sorrow is opprest, giue me Thy promist aide:

26 Thou knowst my sinnes I do confesse, Thy
wrath makes me affraid.

27 But teach Thou me Thy truth, that I Thy
wonders may admire :

28 For shame of sinne so daunts my hope, it dares
not helpe desire.

29 If thou redresse my blinded steps, and teach to
me Thy will,

30 Thy ordinances will I keepe, and looke vpon
them still.

31 Thou art the portion I do chuse, O Lord confound me not ;

32 But guide my steps to run that race, the which
Thy lawes alot.

PART 5.

33 Teach Thou Thy statutes vnto me, that I may
keep them all ;

34 Give Thou the knowledge of Thy will, and turne
my hart withall.

35 Direct me in Thy path, O Lord, therein is my
delight :

36 Incline my mind vnto Thy word, and sinne
put Thou to flight.

37 Turne Thou my eyes from vanities, and do
Thou quicken mee :

38 Performe Thy promise made to me, whose hope depends on Thee.
39 Preuent the shame I feare, because Thy iudgements all are iust:
40 Behold I would performe Thy will, Thy grace relieue me must.

Part 6.

41 Then let Thy promise kindly made—O Lord—fulfillèd be:
42 So shall I 'scuse my iust rebuke, and giue the praise to Thee.
43 Take not away from me Thy truth, for on Thee I attend;
44 But let my lips speake of Thy praise, vntill my life doe end.
45 My feete shall freely follow Thee, vntill the truth I find.
46 I will not shame, to kings Thy truth to preach, with constant mind;
47 Yea all my solace shall be still, my loue of Thee t'expresse:
48 My lifted handes vnto the heauens, Thy glory shall confesse.

PART 7.

49 Remember then Thy promise made, wherein
Thy seruant trusts;
50 In trouble it doth comfort me, my soule thereafter lusts.[1]
51 The wicked haue derided me, Thy lawes yet
haue I kept:
52 I cald to minde Thy iudgements past, whereby
in peace I slept.
53 Sorrow and feare afflicted me, to see how
wicked men
54 Thy lawes transgresse, in pilgrim's life yet
sing I to Thee then:
55 In darknesse and by night, Thy name and
lawes I keepe and feare;
56 Which blessing Thou bestowest on me, Thy
will in mind to beare.

PART 8.

57 O Lord Thou art my portion, I Thy law will
still obserue;

---

[1] See our Lord Brooke, Vol. I. 158: II. 88, for like use of lust as = (simply) desire, not necessarily evil. G.

58 My hearty prayers made to Thee, and promise Thine preserue.

59 I haue reform'd my wayes, and will to Thy behests obay :

60 With speed I will my life amend, and make no more delay.

61 The wicked haue intic̀ed me, but I will turne againe :

62 At midnight will I rise to pray, till iustice I attaine.

63 My company shall such be still, as do Thy precepts know ;

64 Thy mercie fils the Earth, O Lord, to me Thy pleasure show.

Part 9.

65 According to Thy Word—O Lord—Thou graciously hast dealt ;

66 Teach wisedome to Thy seruant Lord, who in Thy law hath dwelt ;

67 Before I felt Thy scourge, as them my feete did go astray ;

68 But gracious God direct me now, that keepe Thy lawes I may.

69 The proud against me worke deceipt, yet will I follow Thee :

70 Their hart on folly feedes, Thy lawes yet shall
my comfort bee.
71 This fruit affliction brought to me, which made
me learne Thy law,
72 A greater treasure to my mind then hertofore
I saw.

Part 10.

73 Thy hand hath fashioned me, therefore teach
me Thy holy will :
74 So shall Thy seruants all reioyce, and I obey
Thee still.
75 Thy iudgements Lord—I graunt—are iust, I
did Thy wrath deserue ;
66 Have mercie yet and pardon me, Thy promise
cannot swarue.
77 Lord let me liue I Thee beseech, Thy law is my
delight :
78 Bring Thou to shame my foes, and driue the
wicked out of sight ;
79 And let Thy seruants all behold, Thy mercies
showed to me,
80 Who walking in Thy statutes iust, shall not
ashamèd be.

PART 11.

81 My soule is almost faint for feare, yet on Thy word I trust :

82 My eyes are dim with looking sore ; send me Thy comfort iust.

83 My bones are withered with despaire, till Thou Thy promise pay.

84 My life is short, Thy iustice on the wicked Lord bewray.

85 By fraud they seeke to take my life, contrary vnto right ;

86 But Thou art iust, vniust are they, therefore put them to flight.

87 They had almost consumèd me, my faith yet did not faint :

88 Reuiue Thou me, and with Thy truth, my mouth I will acquaint.

PART 12.

89 O Lord, Thy word immutable in heauen doth still indure :

90 Thy truth from euer was, Thou laid'st the Earth's foundation sure.

91 All things continue as a stay, and do Thy people serue :

92 Vnlesse Thy word did comfort me, my faith with griefe would sterue.

93 I neuer therefore will forget, Thy lawes which
quicken me ;
94 I am Thy seruant, saue Thou me, who vnto
Thee do flye.
95 The wicked seeke me to destroy, but in Thee
will I trust,
96 Thy truth endures for aye, but else all things
returne to dust.

PART 13.

97 So much I loue Thy law O Lord, I studie on
it still :
98 Thy grace beyond my enemies doth me with
true knowledge fill.
99 I better vnderstand Thy will, then they which
do me teach ;
100 I better know Thy lawes to keepe, then they
which should them preach.
101 That I Thy word might keepe, my feete
refraine each euill way :
102 My iudgement 'grees vnto Thy law, which
taught me what to say.
103 Then hony combe vnto my tast, Thy word is
far more sweet,
104 Thereby Thy will I learne, and falshood shun
as most vnmeet.

PART 14.

105 Thy word is light vnto my feete, and guides
me in my way :
106 My hart hath sworne, I will performe, Thy
statutes night and day.
107 My soule is sore opprest O Lord, do Thou me
ioy now send ;
108 Teach me Thy will, to my request a gratefull
hearing lend.
109 Though I in daunger daily be, Thy lawes I
not forget,
113 But keepe them still, while me to snare, the
prowd a bayt haue set.
111 They are the portion I haue chose, they are
my hart's delight ;
112 My hart is vowd Thy lawes to keepe, with
all my power and might.

PART 15.

113 Thy word I loue, but do detest the vanities
of minde :
114 My shield Thou art, my refuge safe, in Whom
I trust do finde.
115 Away from me ye wicked men, my God alone
I serue ;

116 He will performe my hope, His word from truth doth neuer swerue.
117 Support Thou me, then am I safe, in Thee is all my trust ;
118 Thou hast supprest the proud, and such as follow worldly lust.
119 I loue Thee Lord, because Thou doest from Earth the vaine remoue ;
120 Yet do I feare Thy iudgements Lord, which shall my sinnes reproue.

PART 16.

121 Let me not then oppressèd be, I iustice do obserue :
122 Plead Thou my cause gainst wicked men, which frō Thy will do swerue.
123 My eyes are dim with longing Lord, to see Thy promist ayde ;
124 Teach me my God, and let Thy seruant be with mercy payd.
125 I wait on Thee, let me therefore of wisedome Thine haue part :
126 Helpe Lord in time, for all the world do from Thy lawes depart.
127 Yet do I Thy precepts esteeme, more then the richest gold :

128 Most iust are they; but such I hate, as vnto sinne are sold.

Part. 17.

129 Thy testimonies I admire, on them my soule doth muse:
130 The wayes thereto do shine so bright, the simple it may chuse.
131 The zeale I bare vnto Thy law, did make my hart to moue;
132 Looke on me then in mercy Lord, because thy law I loue.
133 Direct my deedes, so that no sinne may beare in me a sway:
134 I keepe Thy will, to wicked men let me not be a pray.
135 Thy shining face vnto me turne, Thy statutes teach Thou mee:
136 With teares my eyes do daily flow, because they trespasse Thee.

Part 18.

137 Thou righteous God, most iust indeed Thy iudgements all are found;
138 To truth and equitie alone, Thy lawes Thy seruants bound.

139 My zeale doth burne, because my foes Thy lawes haue cleane forgot,

140 Thy word we finde most pure, and I haue chose it to my lot.

141 Though I be poore and in contempt, I do remember well,

142 Thy righteous precepts, which for aye, in glorious truth excell.

143 Anguish and cares vpon me come, Thy law yet do I loue :

144 Teach me Thy truth, that I may liue eternally aboue.

PART 19.

145 Heare me O Lord, to Thee I cry, Thy statutes I wil keepe :

146 Saue me, and graunt that in Thy house, I may in safetie sleepe.

147 Before the twylight vnto Thee I call, and wait Thy will :

148 By night I watch, to meditate and studie of Thee still.

149 Heare me O gracious God, in time, and quicken Thou my spright ;

150 They are at hand that hate Thy law, and me pursue with spight.

151 Thy promises assure me Lord, that Thou art nigh at hand :

152 I knew long since Thy high decree, should firme for euer stand.

PART 20.

153 Behold my sorrowes then and helpe : Thy pleasure I obay ;

154 Plead Thou my cause, deliuer me, vpon Thy word I stay.

155 The wicked they are farre from helpe, which do not Thee regard :

156 But for Thy seruants we do know, Thy mercy is prepard :

157 Many they are that me pursue, yet will I follow Thee :

158 I see the wicked scorne Thy word, and much it grieueth mee.

159 Consider Lord my loue to Thee ; so quicken Thou my minde :

160 For, from for aye, Thy word of truth, and righteousnesse I finde.

PART 21.

161 Princes of might do me pursue, yet onely Thee I feare :

162 Thy word delights my hart, as if my richesse great it weare.

163 Thy law I loue, but do abhorre all falshood and deceit,

164 Seauen times a day I praise Thy name, and on Thee alwayes wait.

165 The keepers of thy law, shall stand from danger alwayes free ;

166 I keepe Thy heasts,[1] because I hope Thy sauing health to see,

167 Yea for the loue I beare to them, I will them not transgresse.

168 Thou seest—O Lord—in all my wayes, Thy name I do confesse.

PART 22.

169 Let then my plaint before Thee come, and be Thou still my guide :

170 Giue eare vnto my sute, and let Thy promise firm abide.

171 When Thou hast me Thy statutes taught, my lips shall speake Thy praise ;

172 My tongue shall tell Thy word of truth, and walke thy righteous wayes.

---

[1] Hests or commandments. G.

173 Helpe with Thy hand, for I entend, Thy precepts to pursue:

164 Thy sauing helpe and law I seeke, Lord do my faith renue.

175 Let liue my soule, to praise Thy name, Thy mercie me vphold.

176 I feare Thy law, then clense my sinnes, and bring me to Thy fold.

PSALME 121.

1 Vnto the hils I lift my eyes, from whence my helpe shall grow;

2 Euē to the Lord which fram'd the heauens, and made the deeps below.

3 He will not let my feete to slip, my watchman neither sleepes,

4 Behold the Lord of Israell still His flocke in safety keepes.

5 The Lord is my defence, He doth about me shadow cast;

6 By day nor night, the sunne nor moone, my limbs shall burne or blast.

7 He shall preserue me from all ill, and me from sinne protect;

8 My going in and comming forth, He euer shall direct.

PSALME 130.

1 From pit of deepe perplexities to Thee for helpe
I cry,
2 O Lord giue eare vnto my plaint, and aide me
speedily.
3 If strictly Thou my sinnes behold, O Lord what
flesh is iust ?
4 But mercy proper is to Thee, and thereto do we
trust.
5 Vpon Thy promise I attend, Thy word is alwayes true,
6 With morning and with euening watch, I will
my sute renue.
7 Thy seruant must depend on Thee, in Thee is
mercie found,
8 Thou wilt redeeme their soules from death, Thy
grace doth so abound.

LORD'S PRAYER.

Our Father which in heauen art, Lord halowed
be Thy name;
Thy kingdome come : Thy will be done, in Heauen
and Earth the same :
Giue vs this day our daily bread: our trespasses
forgiue,

As we for other men's offence, do freely pardon
giue :
Into temptation leade vs not, but 'liuer vs from
ill ;
For Thine all kingdome, glory, powre, is now and
euer will.

Christian Passions

AND

Extra-Sonnets:

1597.

SUNDRY CHRISTIAN
PASSIONS, CONTAINED

in two hundred Sonnets.
Diuided into two equall parts:

The first consisting chiefly of Meditations, Humiliations and Prayers.

The second of Comfor, Joy, and Thankesgiuing.

By H. L.

Call vpon me in the day of trouble, so will I deliuer thee,—
and thou shalt glorifie me.

LONDON,
Printed by Richard Field. 1597.

To the rIght renoVVneD VertVoVs VIrgin ELIzabeth, VVorthy QVeene of happIe EngLanD, her hIghnesse faIthfVL subIeCT, HENRY LOK, VVIsheth Long Lyfe, VVith eternaL bLisse. IVne VII.

My worthlesse pen Presumeth to deuise,
To eternize Your peerles vertuous fame :
In holy flame Of zeale my heart doth rise,
VVhich doth dispise A theame of vulgar frame
Thee sacred dame The graces haue select,
That should protect The holy Muses hill ;
VVhose phœnix quil The heauenly crowne affect,
And those hath dect VVhich Romane trophies fill :
Heauens do distill Their happie iufluence,
As come from thence, You there your portion haue;
Ioue long you saue, VVhose scepters you dispence,
For whose defence, True English hearts He gaue :
Venus would craue, And Dain[1] doth that due,
VVhich Pallas wils Mee yeeld alone to you.

---

[1] = Diana. G.

THE OBSERUATIONS OF THE SQUARE FOLLOWING.

1. A Saint George's crosse of two collumbs, in discription of her Maiestie, beginning at A, and B, in the middle to be read downward, and crossing at C and D to be read either single or double.

2. A S[aint] Andrew's crosse, beginning at E and read thwartwaies, and ending with F, containing the description of our happie age, by her highnesse.

3. Two Pillers in the right and left side of the square, in verse, reaching from E and F perpenddicularly, containing the sum of the whole, the latter columbe hauing the words placed counterchangeably to rime to the whole square.

4. The first and last two verses, or the third and fourth, with seuenth and eighth, are sense in them selues, containing also sense of the whole.

5. The whole square of 100, containing in it self fiue squares, the angles of each of them are sense particularly, and vnited depend each on other, beginning at the center.

6. The out-angles are to be read 8 seuerall waies in sense and verse.

7. The eight words placed also in the ends of the S. George's crosse, are sense and verse, alluding to the whole crosse.

8. The two third words in the bend dexeter of

the S. Andrew's crosse, being the middle from the angles to the center, haue in their first letters T. and A. for the Author, and H. L. in their second, for his name, which to be true, the words of the angles in that square confirme.

9. The direction to her Maiestie in prose aboue, containeth onely of numerall letters, the yeare and day of the composition, as thus, DD. C. LL. LL. LL. LL. VV. VV. VV. VV. VV. VV. VV. VV. IIIIIIIIIII. For, 1593. June V:

In — Hoc

E			Hæc.	A	B				F
God 5	hath	pourd	forth	Rare	Grace	On	this	Isle-	And
Makes	cround 4	your	rule	Queene	In	the	same	so 4	still
Kings	lawd	THis 3	saint	Faire	that	with	truth 3	doth	stand
Rule	so	long	time 2	milde	Prince	ioy 2	land	it	will
For	proofe	you	showes	1 wise	1 of	earths	race	whome	There
Heaues	haue	vp	held	Iust 1	choice 1	whome	God	thus	sheilds
Your	stocke	of	Kings 2	worlds	rich	of 2	spring	and	feare
States	fame	Known 3	farre	Praise	Isle	which	ALl 3	blisse	yeilds
Hold	God 4	there	fore	sure	stay	of	all	the 4	Best
Blest 5	is	your	raigne	Here	Builds	sweet	Peace	true	Rest 5

Forma C — Quadrata

Vinces — Signo

Firma

THE SQUARE PLAINELY SET DOWNE.

God hath powr'd forth rare grace on this Ile, and
Makes crown'd your rule, Queene in the same so still;
Kings laud this saint faire, that with truth doth stand;
Rule so long time mild Prince, Ioy laud it will.
For proofe you showes, wise of Earth's race whom there
Heauens haue vpheld. Iust choyce whom God thus shields.
Your stocke, of kings—world's rich offspring and feare,
State's fame knowne farre—praise Ile which all blisse yeelds.
Hold God therefore sure stay, and port the best;
Blest is your raigne, here builds sweet peace, true rest.

TO THE CHRISTIAN READER.

WHO so shall duly consider the whole progresse of man's estate from life to death, shall find it — gentle Reader — to be nothing else but a very pilgrimage through this Earth to another world; for whether we obserue the common course of all flesh, which from the mother's wombe to the graue, is still trauelling with change of bodily constitution, from youth to age, from health to sicknesse, and so from one estate to another. Or if we behold the particular incounters which each man findeth in himselfe, in the variable change of hopes and crossing of his purposes: in both it shall by a generall experiēce of all men's calamities be assuredly confirmed to be too true. But how much more may we find in the direction of our soules to the proper hauen of their habitation—euen to heauen—a multitude of aduersaries lying in the way to hinder our trauell to that Promised Land; how many affections of the minde, frailties of the flesh bayts of the world, and snares of Satan, are bent against vs, to slacken—if not clean to diuert—our due course thitherwardes, in such sort as if God of His infinite mercie and prouidence did not oftentimes preuent and stop our willes and powers, and bridle the malice of these aduersaries, we should all assuredly perish by the way. But now—such is His fatherly care and loue to vs in Christ—that He hath left vs a direction and ready way of safetie in the midst of all assaults or afflictions how perillous soeuer, euen praier; which being formed according to the rules prescribed vnto vs by His

Sonne, and with feruencie of faith offered vp vnto Him, are of power to penetrate the heauens, purchase our safetie, pay our debts, and procure vs peace of heart in the midst of all earthly perils: yea—knowing our coldnesse herein, and feare of our owne guilt, deterring vs from His presence—He doth not only licence vs to this boldnesse, but allureth vs by many sensible blessings felt in our owne consciences; and calleth vs by a supernaturall courage, sometimes with confidence to come vnto Him, and euen to hope against hope in our most desperate necessities. He doth direct our tongues oftentimes herein before our mindes, and our mindes before our hearts; being Himselfe readier to giue then we to aske, and giuing with more regard of our good, then we can craue or conceiue: for all which He expecteth nothing else at our own hands, but continually to flie vnto Him, and to yeeld Him due praise: to relie on Him onely in the day of tryall, and to encourage others thereto; for in this sort alone He will be honoured of vs. This our earthly pilgrimage being then so daungerous to all flesh, and so readie a way prescribed vnto vs for our safer passage therein, he were very vnwise that would not furnish himselfe with such prouision—which costs so litle as our wils to haue it—and more vncharitable, that would not do his best to assist his cōpanion in his iourney, with both coūsell and cōfort of the same. For this cause—gentle Readers—I hauing—through God's great goodnes—felt in the direction and protection of my vnstable youth, a plentifull portion of the wonderfull care He hath ouer vs, and of the vnspeakable force of praier and thanksgiuing in all extremities: the more to stir vp my selfe to a memorie thereof, haue thought good to set downe these abrupt passions of my passed afflictions, as witnesses of the impediments most stopping me in my Christian pilgrimage, and testimonies of the meanes of my euasion hitherto, which may serue for presidents for my selfe in the like future occasions: and not be altogether vnprofitable for others to imitate. In which—as in a glasse—may be seene, the state of a regenerate soule, sicke with sinne, sometimes—ague-like—shiuering with cold despaire, straight waies inflamed with feruencie of faith and hope. One while yielding vnder the burden of sinne to eternall death, and presently incouraged to runne chearefully forward the appointed course of this his pilgrimage; and like a practised traueller, vsed to the change of company, dyet, heat, cold, paine, pleasure, plentie, aud want, not to amaze himselfe long with any change; but by a consideration of pleasures passed, or rest expected, patiently to passe, ouer this world, full of incombrances; from a sence and feeling whereof in some measure, no true child of God is any long time—as I suppose—exempt. Now, although I doubt not but euen these reasons will carry the iudgement of the godly Christian Reader to a fauourable interpretation of my purpose herein, and to some delight in the taste thereof, to whom no person or occasion, style or phrase, will seeme vnseasonable, being imployed to the glorifying of God, and profit of the Church, or proceeding from a zeale of that effect: yet the consideration that the greater number to whose handes this treatise may happen to come, are either not so well affected, or so discreet and temperate as were to be wished, maketh me thinke it needfull to say something in declaration of my purpose herein: not in excuse of my exercising my selfe in such theames, which in deede ought to be the common action in some measure of all men, as oft as necessary affaires of this life will permit them, neither in that I make common with others this my exercise, which seemeth in secret only to be practised by my selfe: for that I take it not to be alwaies a token of pride or vaine-glory, to make knowne for a common good to others, that which may breed a suspect of ambition in the Author, among the prophane or cauelling multitude; though how herein I am caried my selfe, I leaue to God the searcher of hearts to iudge: only I would satisfie them first in the cause of my writing them in verse, then of the confused placing of them without speciall titles. To the first I was induced, for that I find many oftentimes —speciallie such as had most neede to praie and meditate—to reade bookes rather for the affection of words than liking of matter, and perhaps more to controll the compiling, then to commend the contents. Such yet—so as they read—shal giue me al that I craue, and find I hope, that good they loked not for, if not in all, yet in some among many of these Sonnets. As for the apt nature of Poetrie to delight, to contriue significatiuely in fewe words much matter, to pearce and penetrate affections of men, with the aptnesse thereof, for helpe of memorie, I will not saie much: but for my deducing these passiōs and affections into Sonnets, it answereth best for the shortnesse, to the nature, and common humor of men, who are either not long touched with so good motions, or by their worldly affaires not permitted to continue much reading. To the cause of my so preposterous placing of them, and deuision onely into three sorts, I confesse indeed I am perswaded their disorder doth best fit the nature of mankind, who commonly is delighted with contraries, and exercised with extreames; and also as they were by God ministred vnto my mind to set downe by sundrie accidents: so I suppose my prouidence could not—by a formall placing of them—so soon hit the affection of euery reader, as God's direction—by that which mē call chance—might often do. As they are therefore, I recommend them to thy courtesie in reading, and thee to God's Holy Spirit in the perusing of them. If they may haue the same working in thee, that I praise God some of them had in me, they shall not be vtterly vnprofitable. If in matter they iumpe not to thy passions in all points, thinke that in the great arsenall of Satan's armor he hath choice of weapons for sundrie assaults, and disposeth of them diuersly, according to the strength or weaknesse of the partie he besiegeth: which—being as difficult in particular persons as God's gifts are to them—thou shalt doe well—to thy abilitie—to reforme or supply my defect therein. If in manner of the verse or stile, they be—as I doubt not but they are—to be amended much, I do not greatly seeke the praise of a curious architector, neither—without neglect of more necessary duties—could I attaine to the required obseruances that way. And therefore craue that thy discretion may excuse my intention and abilitie. And thus I hartily recommend thee to the Almightie.

The first Part of Christian Passions:

CONTAINING A HUNDRETH SONETS OF MEDITATION, HUMILIATION, AND PRAYER.

PREFACE.

IT is not Lord the sound of mnay words,
The bowed knee or abstinence of man,
The filèd phrase, that eloquence affords,
Or poet's pen, that heauens do pearce, or can:
By heauie cheere, of colour pale and wan,
By pinèd bodie of the Pharisay,
A mortall eye repentance oft doth scan,
When iudgement doth on outward shadows stay,
But Thou—O God—doest heart's intent bewray
For from Thy sight Lord nothing is conceald;
Thou formdst the frame fro out the verie clay,
To Thee the thoughts of hearts are all reueald,
To Thee therefore with hart and minde prostrate,
With teares I thus deplore my sinfull state.

SONET I.

How should my soule Lord, clad in earthly mold,
—The prison where it readie is to pine,
Where vile affections captiue it do hold,
And threaten naught but ruine in the fine[1]—
Vnto one thought or hope or helpe incline,
Or raise my eyes vnto the heauens bright?
How may it Lord take hold on mercies Thine,
Or presse it selfe in presence of Thy sight?
Or how canst Thou therein at all delight,
If Mercy be not spokesman in this case,
If merit of Thy Sonne should not acquite
The common guilt of Adam's sinfull rase?
Which since by faith alone man may attaine,
Grant me first grace not faithlesse to remaine.

SON. II.

Fro out the darknesse of this sea of feare,
Where I in whale remaine,[2] deuourd of sin,
With true remorse of former sin I reare
My heart to heauen, in hope some helpe to win.
I do confesse my fault, who did begin
To flie from Thee, O Lord! and leaue vndone

---

[1] = *finis*, end. G. [2] Jonah i. 17 G.

Thy seruice, which of right should first haue bin
Performed, by which so many should be wonne
To praise Thy name: but feare alas! begunne,
To represent to me my iourny long,
The dangers of the world my life should runne;
Which made me to my soule to offer wrong.
But since by show of death Thou caldst me backe,
Thy gracious helpe at need let me not lacke.

SON. III.

WITHIN this arke where in my soule doth dwell,
My bodie floting on worlde's troubled waue;
Which winds of fierce affections cause to swell,
And hardly can my power from sinking saue,
I crie to Thee O Lord, and comfort craue:
Close vp this fountaine of stil flowing sin,
Let me by faith againe once footing haue
On frutefull Earth, and holie life begin;
Lighten the burden so vncleane within,
Of brutish vices raging in my minde,
Let cleane affects[1] the greater partie win,
And so increase, that plentie I may finde
Of sacrifices pleasing in Thy sight,

[1] = Affections. G.

Of faith and loue, which are Thy soule's delight.

SON. IIII.

In humble wise as fitteth best my state,
An abiect wretch deuoyd of all desert,
I here approch before Thy mercy gate,
O Lord of life, with broke and contrite hart:
I neede not to reueale to Thee my smart;
A lump of sin and shame I am I know,
Wounded so deepe with deadly poysned dart
Of serpent's sting, which did from parents grow,
That now my humors so do ouerflow
With foule affections of my feeble minde,
As presseth downe my eyes on Earth so low,
As dares not search the heauens, true helpe to finde.
Yet since Thou hast made known to me my griefe,
Guide me by grace to fountaine of reliefe.

SONET V.

Unto Thy princely wedding Lord are bed,[1]
Of euery sort some guests to feast with Thee;

---

[1] Bid. G.

One that a spouse but late before had wed,
One oxen bought, one taken land to fee:
They from the banket therefore absent bee,
Regarding not Thy messengers of grace.[1]
In number of the like, Lord, hold not mee,
But let me haue I craue, the offred place:
Yet ere that I appeare before Thy face,
A wedding garment first I must put on,
My owne vnrighteous cloathing is too base,
And marchandise of merits now are gone;
Then since Thou cal'st, with faith do Thou me cloth,
A lame blind beggar Lord, do thou not loth.[2]

SON. VI.

In pride of youth when as vnbridled lust
Did force me forth, my follies to bewray,
I challengèd as patrimony iust,
Each vaine affection, leading to decay:
And trusting to that treasure, post away
I wandred in the world's alluring sight:
Not reason, vertue, shame, or feare could stay,
My appetite from tasting each delite,
Till want and wearinesse began me bite,

---

[1] St. Matthew xxii. 1-14. G. [2] = loath G.

And so perforce to father I retire,
To Whom I prostrate kneele—vnworthie wight—
To name of sonne not daring to aspire;
Receiue me yet, sweet Sauiour, of Thy grace
Poore penitent, into a seruant's place.[1]

SON. VII.

Lame of my limmes, and sencelesse of my state,
Neere fortie yeares Lord haue I groueling line,[2]
Before Bethesda poole,[3] yet still too late,
To wash me in the fountaine I encline,
Whence health wold come, when angel giues the sine,[4]
If any one to aide me readie were;
But helplesse thus, I readie am to pine,
My selfe vnable duly vp to reare:
Vouchsafe Thou then me to this bath to beare,
By the assistance of Thy heauenly grace.
Let not the force of foule affects me feare,
To prease forth first when Christ appeares in place,
Who is the fountaine, angell, and the man,
That bath, that blisse, that cure my senses can.

---

[1] St. Luke xv. 11-32. G. [2] = lain. G.
[3] St. John v. 2. G. [4] Sign. G.

SON. VIII.

Thy thundring voice and angell, Lord of long,
Hath cald my soule from slumber where it lay,
The harmony of heauenly musicke's song,
Hath made my wandring feete at last to stay:
Direct Thou me also the readie way
Vnto Thy church, that in Thy holy place,
Thy word and law I may in heart obay,
And worship Thee before Thy people's face.
Grant me I say, such measure of Thy grace,
That greedily by faith I swallow vp
Thy booke of truth, and so Thy word imbrace,
That frutefully I taste saluation's cup.
Thou who doest rule the Earth, the sea and land,
In my defence, with power and glory stand.

SON. IX.

Among Thy sheepe, O Lord, I seemd to feed,
By sacraments receiu'd into Thy flocke:
By preachèd word I watred was indeed,
And works with fleece did seeme inrich my stocke:
But at my doore true faith did neuer knocke,
—Which should be shepheard of my soule's defence—

But—thiefe-like—fond affections reason mocke,
And by the window of my wilfull scence
Do enter to my heart, and steale from thence
Each motion of amendment which doth rise,
And shepheardlesse of grace, transported hence
By Sathan—rau'ning woolfe—in fearefull wise,
I call to Thee—sweet Sauiour—shepheard true,
Teach me to know Thy voice and Thee insue.[1]

SONET. X.

Behold, O Lord, the citie Thou hast built,
Jerusalem, this fleshly frame of mine,
By sin—Assyrian's sword—is almost spilt,
And like to yeeld to Rabsake in fine,[2]
Yet lo—alas !—my soule doth much repine,
To see proud Satan so blaspheme Thy name,
To threaten ruine to this temple Thine,
Since Thou art praysd and honord in the same :
Thou able art the rage of lust to tame,
The force of pride and furie to subdue ;
Against Senecharib Thy angell came,
And all his host in one night ouerthrew :

---

[1] = follow : transition-word for 'pursue'. G.
[2] Isaiah xxxvi. G.

So let Thy Holie Spirit me defend,
And to my plaints and praiers comfort send.

SON. XI.

SINCE with Goliah[1] I am now to fight,
And lacke the slight[2] of holie Dauid's sling,
Arme Thou me Lord with heauenly armor bright,
Which power of flesh and world to foile may bring:
Thy righteous brest-plate gird on me with truth,
Prepare my feet with Gospel of Thy peace,
The shield of faith—which firie dartes beare forth,
Of wicked Satan, whose assaults not sease—[3]
The helmet of saluation, and the sword
Of Spirit, which is founded on Thy law;[4]
All these my praiers are, that Thou afford,
To make me stedfast, spight of lyon's claw,
Who roaring, daily seekes as wishèd pray,[5]
My silly soule from Thee to take away.

SON. XII.

Now that Thou hast prepard me to confesse,

---

[1] 1 Samuel. xvii. 23. *et seqq*. G. [2] Sleight or skill. G.
[3] = cease. G. [4] Ephesians vi. 14-18. G. [5] Prey. G.

Thy seruice Lord, the which I vndertake,
I Thee beseech, my purpose so to blesse,
That I a good account to Thee may make:
A Nazarit I am, who do forsake
The delicacies of the world's delight,
Whose thirst Thy purest fountaine still shall slake,
With faith and truth, the which with sin shall fight:
I will not tast the wine of Satan's slight,
Which doth confound all reason and all sence,
My vow shall be to serue Thee day and night,
And trust in Thee shall be my true defence,
Till death dissolue this promise made to Thee,
Whose strength herein Thy heauenly graces bee.

SON. XIII.

I seeke O Lord to shew Thy powrefull hand,
Which hath conuerted this my sinfull hart,
Into a rod of strength, which still might stand,
Strong in Thy truth, Who powrefull onely art:
But Jannes pride, and Jambres lustfull hart,[1]
By slight imposture of slie Satan's mitgh

[1] 2 Timothy iii., 8. G.

Two serpents frame, which will not thence
depart,
But seeke against Thy powreful hand to fight.
But let my faith their fury put to flight,
And Vertue Thine, deuour these imps of sin;
Let not these fleshly frutes appeare in sight
Of truth, which only can the conquest win.
Let faith shew forth the finger of Thy hand,
And cleane consume ech power doth it with-
stand.

SON. XIIII.

Behold O Lord a tree by high way side,
Unfrutefull yet of any good for Thee;
In high way side as yet I do abide,
Where passers to Jerusalem I see:
Thow Sommer grow, I cannot frutefull be,
Vnplanted by Thy grace in garden Thine:
I do confesse I am a wild fig tree,
For want of moisture which am like to pine;
Vnto my praiers Lord do Thou incline,
Remoue me home into Thy garden faire,
Let me behold the face of Thy sunne shine,
Which may my withered leaues with life re-
paire:

So maist Thou tast a frute of wholesome kinde,
And leaue a marke of mercy great behinde.[1]

SON. XV.

WITHIN Thy garden Lord I planted was,
And watred well with Thy most carefull hand,
But yet vnfrutefull I remaind—alas!—
And these Thy blessings did not vnderstand.
In vaine I did employ possessèd land,
Ten times three yeares Thy seruants did replant
My stocke, and sought to bend my crooked wand,
And did supply ech aide I seem'd to want.
At length my frutes which daily grew more scant,
Wil'd Thee resolue to haue me weeded out.
My foule affections were with folly brant,[2]
My roote of faith was shakt with feare and doubt,
And lo I pine; sweet Sauiour water me,
Paul and Apollos' worke else lost will be[3]

SON. XVI.

A wicked Pharisie I long haue bene,
Whom sight of mercies Thine, alluro to Thee,

[1] St. Luke xiii. 6 *et seqq.* G. [2] Branded. G.
[3] 1 Corinthians iii. 6. G.

Ashamèd Lord of my faire-clothèd sinne,
In secret night I seeke Thy face to see:[1]
That Thou art God, Thy workes reueale to me,
That Thou art mine, Thy Sonne doth me assure,
Vouchsafe, that I regenerate may be;
And that my praiers pardon may procure.
Purge by Thy Sprite and faith, faire fountaine pure,
The senses dull that cannot vnderstand
The heauenly birth, which shall in blisse endure,
Not subiect vnto Satan's sinfull band.
And with Thy Sonne let world's affections die,
My soule from hell, with Him ascend on hie.

SON. XVII.

Fiue foolish virgins[2] in my senses dwell,
And seeke to make me slumber ouer long,
They dreame, that all my deeds do fall out well,
Whereas indeed I headlong run to wrong:
To vanities their humours do belong,
And Sin, who doth their fancie chiefly feed:
They cheinèd are to linkes of lust so strong,

---

[1] St. John iii. 1. *et seqq.* G.

[2] St. Matthew xxv. 1. *et seqq.* G.

That their best soile, brings forth but bitter
weed;
They lacke the oyle which should be vsed indeed,
To lead them to the euerlasting light:
It growes not Lord in frute of humane seed:
Man sleeps all day and gropes his way at night:
Vnlesse Thou lend Thy hand and fill our
lampes,
Our light goes forth with smothering sinful
dāps.

SON. XVIII.

Ovt of the fountaine of eternall life,
I poore Samaritan here readie stand,
—To sinfull lust an old betrothèd wife—
With pitcher readie in my trembling hand,
To wraw[1] a draught of liquor most diuine,
To quench the thirst of my inflamèd hart
With heauenly deaw: ere that my soule do
pine,
And qualifie the rigor of my smart.
A Prophet true Thou art I vnderstand,
Or rather Father of all truth Thou art,
A stranger I from faire Judaca land,

[1] = draw. G.

With these Thy blessings craue for to impart :[1]
Then guide my hand, and teach my soule to tast.
True faith, the fountaine where all blisse is
plast.

SON. XIX.

A WICKED soule sold to all fleshly sin,
Lord here I prostrate at Thy feete do lie,
To gather crummes of grace, soule's health to
win,
Which Lord to giue me do Thou not denie :
The precious oyle of innocence will I,
Powre forth with teares, fro out my melting
eyes,
To bath Thy feete, and after will I drie,
Them with my haires,—which balms no trea-
sure bies[2]—
Though worldly loue—when he my fact espies—
Repine to see my soule so well inclind :
To my defence O Lord vouchsafe to rise,
And fructifie this first-frute of my minde ;
Vouchsafe to sup with humble seruant Thine,
And that of seruice, better choyse be mine.

---

[1] St. John iv. 7. *et seqq.* G. [2] = buys. G.

SON. XX.

A poore Arabian whom base Agar[1] bare,
First borne of flesh, but last of promist grace,
Of bastard kinde, bred vp with honest care,
In wildernesse of world, for a long space:
And famishing before my parent's face,
Whose workes vnable were to lende me aide,
A bond man vnto sin as fleshly race,
To whom heauen's heritage Thy lawes denaide:
Amidst my wandring course by Thee am staide,
And haue a promise, not to die but liue;
Thy couenant Lord abundantly is paide,
If grace—to feed by faith—Thou doest me giue:
My bondage thus release, make Thou me free,
My barren branch shall so bring fruit for Thee.

SON. XXI.

A Marchant, I full long abroad haue straide,
By sea and land true happinesse to gaine;
The riches of the Earth my eyes haue waide,
And see their profit to be light and vaine:
Such trifling trash my soule doth now disdaine,
And iewels of more value I espye;
Among the rest, one doth all other staine.

---

[1] Ishmael and Hagar. G.

Which with my wealth I wish that I might
buye:
But this rare pearle is of a price so hie,
As all the Earth cannot esteeme the same
Much lesse to purchase it, can it come nie,
Yet doth the loue thereof, my heat enflame;
Be Thou the pledge—sweet Sauiour—then
for me,
That heauenly blisse shall so my riches be.[1]

SON. XXII.

Among the prease[2] of many that draw neare,
Vnto the feast of grace in temple Thine,
I silly widow also doe appeare,
With humble heart, O Lord, who here encline,
And vnto Thee a mite for offering mine, [3]
Present as precious, to my poore estate;
For heards or flocks, for sto re of corne and wine
Without obedience Lord Thou aye didst hate,
But broken hearts, and soules which lye prostrate
Before Thy throne of grace, and mercy craue,
Do mercie finde, though it be nere so late;
Thy promise hereof vs assurance gaue,

---

[1] St. Matthew xii. 45. G. [2] Press or pressure. G,
[3] St. Mark 12. 42. G.

In trust wherof, obaying Thy behest,
My praiers to Thy praise, O Lord, are prest.

SON. XXIII.

Into Thy vineyard Lord—vnworthy—I
Desire to come, to trauell out the day:
Thou calledst me thereto, and didst espie,
Me loytring idle, by the world's high way:
At first to come my follies did me stay,
Whom cold and hunger now to worke compell:
Though halfe my daies be spent, say me not nay,
The other halfe to trie, employed well.
I doe not hope my paines so deare to sell,
As they that beare the brunt and heat of day,
They merit most whose trauels most excell:
My slender seruice craues but single pay:
But—if Thy bountie giue,—behold me prest,
With thanks Thy grace to taste, amongst the rest.

SON. XXIIII.

As Thou art pure and iust in all Thy waies,
—O Lord—so should Thy offrings also bee:
The tongue vncleane, cannot set forth Thy praise,
The wanton eye may not Thy secrets see:

The lame of faith, the blind of skill, not hee,
That Thou alotst Thy sacrifice to slay;
The heart that is found cleane in each degree,
Is fittest for Thy church, wherein to stay:
Such is no flesh, O Lord, the truth to say:
But as Thou pleasest them to purifie,
By faith and by repentance euerie day,
Who then with Christ, may boldly Thee come nie:
Behold me then, thus Thy adopted chyld,
Let me not from Thy temple be exyled.

SON. XXV.

I FOLLOW Thee, O Lord, but far behinde,
As Peter did, when he did see Thee led[1]
To prison, where the traitors Thee did binde:
Amazèd much with worldly feare and dred,
When as I saw the world all ouerspread
With hatred and disdaine vnto the iust,
My courage it was quayld, and quickly fled,
And had no liking to Thy helpe to trust,
But Lord I know perforce I forward must:
If I intend to gaine the crowne I craue,
I must abandon flesh and fleshly lust,

---

[1] St. Luke xxii. 54 G.

And in Thy promise all my hope must haue.
Grant Thou me boldnesse then, and constant will,
To perseuere in Thy obedience still.

SON. XXVI.

Of parents first two brothers borne that were,
The bodie and the soule did represent;
The elder Cain, who Henock's wals did reare,
The yonger Abell dwelt in silly tent:
First man with plough the virgin soile he rent,
The other seru'd, and shoare the silly sheep:
To worldly lustes of flesh the one was bent,
Thy heauenly lawes the other sought to keepe.
A deadly discord 'twixt them so did creepe.
The elder did the guiltlesse yonger slay;
That ancient hatred grounded is so deepe,
It striues in me —alas!—vnto this day.
Accept my sacrifice, Lord me defend,
My powres vnto Thy holie pleasure bend.

SON. XXVII.

Like pinèd chyld O Lord, from nurse's brest,
Whom churlish stepdame ouer soone doth waine,[1]

[1] Wean. G.

By wicked will alas! I am opprest,
And crie to cruell flesh, behold, in vaine:
Who lets me languishing in sin remaine,
And sends no comfort to support my need:
My faults I know, I do confesse them plaine,
That folly doth my weake affections feed.
I see my ruine neare at hand indeed,
And cannot call for aide whose tong is dum;
My feete so feeble cannot helpe at neede,
Although I see at hand Thy vengeance come;
Vnlesse Thou giue me grace to see and feare,
To pray in faith, and Thou Thy hand forbeare.

SON. XXVIII.

POLLUTED with the carelesse leprosie,
Of sin, which is hereditarie now,
So lothsome growne, that I dare not come nie
Thy holy temple, where my heart doth bow:
I craue, O Lord, it please Thee to allow,
The High Priest Christ Thy Sonne to view my sore,
Whose holy hand may guide and teach me how
To cure this griefe, it may returne no more.
I know, O Lord, Thou hast of mercy store,
And onely Thou dost pittie man's estate,

Which though my stubburne heart refusde
before,
Repentance yet and faith comes not too late,
Whose sparrowes of repentance I present:
An offering here through worldly desert sent.

SON. XXIX.

A VIRGINE pure, O Lord, by birth I was,
The daughter of Thy Church, adopt by grace:
But lothsome Lust—foule fiend!—did me alas!
Pursue, and sought with me his dwelling place.
As many vertues as did seeke my grace,
By wedding's band to me to be vnight,
So many did this fiend, first night deface,
So oft was I depriu'd of my delight.
Seuen times a widow I with shame and spight
Am left, and liue now hopelesse of redresse:
Till Thou with Raphaell[1] send that medicine
bright,
Of God to giue me grace, to sinne suppresse.
Thy Sonne thus made, my spouse shall soone
restore
Tobias sight, wealth, comfort, lost before.

---

[1] Tobit iii. 17. G.

SON. XXX.

Of sinfull race, of man's licentious seed,
Whilst heauenly ofspring with faire humane
kinde,
Do ioyne affects,[4] where wicked lusts do breed,
And so pollute the frutes of vertuous minde,
A bastard brood my selfe alas ! I find,
Whose nature doth in tryannie consist:
Of grace and reason growne so dull and blinde,
That I in wrong with stubburnesse persist :
Who seeing father Nature ere he wist,
Asleepe with sottish wine of worldly loue,
To hide his shame by wisdome had no list,
Which iustly curse of God on me did moue.
A slaue to sin, therefore I did pursue,
—Like Nymrod—grace of God, which now
I rue.

SON. XXXI.

As oft as Thou by grace would drawe me backe
From sin, whereto I am by Nature thrall,
So oft alas ! I finde my will to lacke,
And power to follow Thee when Thou doest call;
From sin to sin, I headlong thus do fall,

[1] Affections. G.

And quench repentance by a peruerse will;
I see my fall, but haue no feare at all,
And to my vomit, dog-like turne I still.
My frailtie doth Thy wrathfull cup fulfill,
With flowing measure of reuenge and wo:
When I returne a little backe from ill,
To wallow in the myre againe I go.
No powre is in me Lord my life to mend,
Vnlesse Thy hand from heau'n me comfort send.

SON. XXXII.

Faine would I fence this feeble flesh of mine,
From Satan's furie, who me thus assailes,
Which doth besiege my soule, and meanes to pine
My conscience, which my sin so sore bewailes;
His busie braine to win me neuer failes,
And leaues no stratagem at all vntride:
My fainting hope I know not what it ailes,
But it doth feare the battery to abide.
The safest way must be—what ere betide—
To set a watch to looke vnto my waies:
Lest pride, or lust, or wrath do let him slide
Into my hart, which yet vnyeelded staies

But like a theefe he stealeth me vpon ;
Watch Thou me—Lord—ech houre : else I
am gon.

SON XXXIII.

My sinnes behold—O Lord !—are manifold,
Which do incamp my soule each houre about,
Still me intrenchèd with distrust they hold,
So that no frutes of faith can issue out :
Their fleshly champion is a soldier stout,
Who is assist by world and Satan's aide,
And foule affections readie are in rout,
To further force to lust, but hardly staide.
The earthly treasures haue with pleasure paide,
The hatefull army which doth hast to hell :
My natiue powre their passage not denaide,
Which makes their pride and peruerse wil to
swel.
I see no way to helpe to shun decaie,
But on Thy grace's rescue Lord to staie.

SON. XXXIIII.

The gredinesse of this my corrupt minde,
Which tasteth not but of the earthly gaine,

And in Thy glorie can no profit finde,
But seekes with symonie my soule to staine:
Makes me—alas!—for carnal treasor vaine,
Like Elizeus'[1] seruant, to desire
A present of worlde's pleasure mixt with paine,
As recompence of heauenly comforts hire.
I sorcerer like do also oft require,
—Like merchandise—Thy graces oft to buye,
Supposing morall vertues may aspire,
To saue my soule, and sin to mortifie.
But lo! I see soule's leprosie herein,
And craue that praiers may my pardon win.

SON. XXXV.

Voyd of true life, and buried in the graue
Of wicked flesh—alas!—I long have bin,
No earthly comfort can my conscience haue,
Which was corrupted with all lothsome sin.
My sister vertues to despaire begin,
Of euer seeing once my life's restore,[2]
Ne is there any other way to win
True life indeed, which shall decay no more.
But prostrate Lord, Thy helpe for to implore,

---

[1] = Elijah, as in St. Luke iv. 27. G.

[2] Restoration. G

And craue Thy gracious presence at the last,
To aide the soule Thy Sonne hath lou'd before;
For time of grace with Thee is neuer past.
Roll backe hard stone from heart, bid him arise,
Who slaue to sin, in earthly coffin lies.

SON. XXXVI.

My bodie—Lord!—the house which hath bene long
Possest with spirits,[1] to ruine of the same,
Which forst me forward vnto open wrong
Of conscience, by defacing of Thy name,
Hath found some comfort, since Thy message came,
Vnto my soule, which in Thy word was sent;
Whose powerfull truth hath bound, and seeks to tame
The furious lust which to my ruine bent.
Grant Lord from heart I may indeed repent,
And therewith chase these fiends fro out of me,
Sweep cleane my house, fro out of which they went,
And garnishèd with graces let it be:

[1] St. Luke iv. 33. and xi. 25. G.

Let puissant Faith henceforth possesse the
place,
Let sin returne[1] with legions of disgrace.

SON. XXXVII.

AMIDST this famine of Sarepta soile,
Where I a widow dwell,[2] poore and abiect,
Compeld by sin, with sweat of browes to toile,
To gather stickes, from cold, me to protect:
Behold me Lord, a catiue thus neglect,
Whom sin hath banishèd Thy blessed land:
Who yet in heart Thy prophers do affect,
And with Thy Church to life and death wold
stand.
I offer all my treasures here in hand;
That litle sparke of grace yet left behinde,
Increase it Lord, vnto a great fire-brand
Of faith, which may a frutefull haruest finde.
My meale and oyle, O Lord! do Thou in-
crease;
My selfe and sonne, shall praise Thee so in
peace.

---

[1] = go away or retire. G.
[2] St. Luke. iv. 26. G.

SON. XXXVIII.

BORNE blinde I was, through sinfull Adam's fall,
And neuer since could see with carnall eyes :
Ne know I where or how for helpe to call,
From out of sin to holie life to rise.
It pleasèd Thee, —O Lord !— that in this wise,
Thy powre and glorie might to man appeare,
Who gracelesse groueling in Earth's darknesse lies,
And wants the eyes of faith his soule to cheare :
But since Thou sentst Thy Sonne, my Sauiour deare,
To shine in light to those in darknesse weare :[1]
To dym the worldly wisdome, seeming cleare,
And sinfull soules frō hell to heauen to reare.
Touch thou my eyes with faith, wash me with grace,
In Sylo poole[2]—Thy word—which I embrace.

SON. XXXIX.

How drunken are my humors all, alasse !
With wine of vanitie, and sensuall lust,
Which from one sin do to another passe,
And after euill daily more do thrust.

[1] = were. G. [2] = Siloa. St. John ix. 7, 11. G.

Of force my faults—for shame—confesse I must;
My lauish vsage of Thy graces sent;
My soule's consent to action so vniust,
As death of prophets, teaching to repent:
Like Herod I about the matter went,
To please the follies of my flesh delight:
Incest'ous I, to sin so much was bent,
That offred mercie, pleasèd not my sight:
But Lord! prepare my heart to see my sin,
That sorrow may, a way to mends bigin.

SON. XL.

Though with Thy saints, O Lord, I choise haue made,
To spend my daies in praising of Thy name,
And in the studie of Thy word to wade,
To feed my faith with portion of the same;
Yet can I not my choice so rightly frame,
Amidst the spacious fields where truth doth grow,
But whilst to gather healthfull herbe I came,
A bitter bud I found of fearefull show,
Which threatneth me with death and ouerthrow,
Vnto my soule, which feedeth greedely
On sin, the weed which Satan did bestow:
By poisoned tast thereof I pinèd lie;

But Christ, Thy Sonne, by faith me helth
shall bring,
Discharge the Law, and bruise this deadly
sting.

SON. XLI.

According to the promise of Thy word,
To giue the victorie,—O Lord!—to those
That fight thy battels with a faithfull sword,
Against the world, flesh, diuell and Thy foes:
I seeke, O Lord! proud Iericho t'inclose.
Incouragde by Thy graces from aboue;
My shooes of foule affects I pray Thee lose,
Before on holy earth my path I moue;[1]
Thy powerfull hand by prayers let me proue,
Which daily seu'n times[2] I to Thee direct;
Shake Thou the walls of sin for my behoue,
And in this skirmish do Thou me protect:
The frutes of flesh, pride, lust, and error all
So shall be wract, and sin not raise a wall.

SON. XLII.

Amidst the graues of death this many a yeare,

[1] Exodus iii. 5. G. [2] Psalm cxix, 64. G.

My soule—possessèd with all sorts of sin—
Hath liu'd, and held that frutefull place so deare,
That from the same no counsell could me win:
To beate my selfe my follies neuer lin,[1]
No reason can with chaines binde so my will,
But to vnlose my lust I do begin,
With helpe of furious fiend, who aides me still:
But since Thy Sonne appeareth me vntill
I craue I may no more tormented bee,
Lest that my soule eternally he kill,
But from the force of Satan make me free;
These brutish sinnes in swine more fit to dwell,
Drowne in repentant seas of teares which swell.

SON. XLIII.

In deadly sleepe, O Lord! sin hath me cast,
Wherein secure I lie, and so remaine:
Raise me, O Lord! out of this dreame at last,
And let me sight and light of heauen attaine:
The heauie humours which my iudgment staine,
And dazell so the reason of my minde,

[1] = cease. G.

Grant that they may their proper vse attaine,
And comfort in Thy grace and promise finde.
All fleshly wisedome of it selfe is blinde;
Till Thou by knowledge cleare their wandring sight,
Out of the snare of sin flesh cannot winde,
Vnlesse by faith they see Thy Sonne so bright;
Him let me still, both see and eke admire,
And Thee in Him, O Lord! I Thee desire.

SON XLIIII.

My wicked flesh, O Lord! with sin full fraight,
Whose eye doth lust for euerie earthly thing,
By couetise allurde, hath bit the baight,
That me to Satan's seruitude will bring.
By violence I vertue's right would wring,
Out of possession of the soule so weake;
Like vineyard which the wicked Achab king,
Possest by tyrant's power, which lawes do breake:
Let prophets Thine—Lord—to my soule so speake,
That in repentant sackcloth I may mone,
The murther of Thy grace, which I did wreake,
Whilst to my natiue strength I trust alone;

And let my Sauiour so prolong my daies,
That henceforth I may turne from sinfull
waies.

SON. XLV.

If Thou vouchsafdst Lord of Thy goodnesse rare,
To sanctifie with holie presence Thine,
The Cana marriage, where Thou didst not spare,
First miracle of water turnd to wine;[1]
Then be Thou present at this wedding mine,
Which twixt Thy Church and me by faith is
ment:
To see the want in me Thy eyes encline.
—Whose wine of grace by wanton youth is
spent—
But—being toucht with view thereof—repent,
And craue that water of Earthe's healthles well,
May issue forth from heart with sorrow rent,
And turnd to wine, may so with grace excell,
That all that see and tast this change in me,
May grant this worke, of Thee alone to be.

SON. XLVI.

Since it hath pleasèd Thee,—O Lord!—to fend,

[1] St. John. ii. 1. *et seqq.* G.

Now in my barren age of hope and grace,
Repentant childe, from ruine to defend,
My name and soule to liue before Thy face,
Thy blessings I do thankfully embrace,
And in Thy feare will frame his tender yeare;
The world's regard in me shall haue no place,
If once Thy word and will my heart do heare.
And when Thou calst, we both will then appeare,
Before Thy aulter in Moriath land,
To offer vp Thy gift, my sonne so deare:
Obedient childe to faithfull father's hand:
Which sacrifice—not worthie gift for Thee,—
With Christ my Sauior's suffrings quit let bee.

SON. XLVII.

Of euerie creature vncleane to fore,
Whereof Thy holy people might not tast,
Thou didst present, O Lord! to Peter store,
Which were from heauen in sheet before him plast.
Which he at first refusde with minde most chast,
Not touching things polluted or defilde:
But afterward Thy counsell he embrast,
And saw himselfe had bene before beguilde,
To think all sinners were for aye exilde,

From presence of Thy mercies, which abound;
Whom oft Thou dost receiue as Father milde,
If faith in Christ Thy Sonne in them be found.
By praier's faith, by faith, Thy grace doth grow,
Cornelius blessing—Lord—on me bestow.[1]

SON. XLVIII.

How hard it is—O Lord—for man to frame
His minde—corrupt—to be preparde for Thee:
With tongue vncleane to praise Thy holie name,
With fleshly eies Thy glorie for to see:
Homeward I bring Thy blessings vnto me,
And make my soule their dwelling-place to rest:
But so forgetfull of Thy lawes we be,
That this my action Lord! I see not blest;
Pride and contempt the waies haue so opprest,
That danger is the carriage ouerthrow:
Grant that Thy grace, to staie it may be prest,
That so my soule Thy sauing health may know,
For to my flesh vnsanctified to trust,
Were aie to hasten death by iudgement iust.

---

[1] Acts of the A ostles, x. 22. G.

SON. XLIX.

My traiterous heart which long time hath rebeld,
Against Thy Spirit, which should feed me still,
A secret counsell in it selfe hath held,
To contrarie Thy knowne reuealèd will:
Whose mutinie my sences so do fill
With deeds repining to Thy holie law,
That raging pride and lust lead me to ill,
Forgetting tokens of Thy wrath they saw;
As Dathan and Abyram had no awe
Of Moyses and of Aron, Thine elect,
But sought a way Thy people how to drawe,
And prophets Thine by pride for to reiect:[1]
So doth my soule alas! Thy grace resist,
And in the follies of the flesh persist.

SON. L.

A tenant most vntrue, O Lord! to Thee,
In vineyard of my bodie haue I bin:
To craue Thy rent Thy seruants came to me,
But nothing but intreatie[2] bad, they win: [3]
My trauell therein was to nourish sin,
And wast the wine of Thy abounding plant;

[1] Numbers xvi. G. [2] = treatment. G
[3] St. Mark xii. 2, 3. G.

The more to call me backe Thou didst begin,
The more to Thee my gratitude did want.
Ne would my lacke of grace let me recant,
When Thou Thy onely Sonne to me didst send,
For sin and Satan did me so supplant,
That to His ruine I did also bend :
But Lord me lend in time repentant hart ;
That from this vineyard I may not depart.

SON. LI.

Whilst in the garden of this earthly soile,
My selfe to solace and to bath I bend,
And faine wold quench sin's heat, which seems to boile
Amidst my secret thoughts, which shadow lend :
My sence and reason which should me defend,
As iudges chosen to the common weale,
Allur'd by lust, my ruine do pretend ;[1]
By force of sin, which shamelesse they reueale.
They secretly on my affections steale,
When modestie—my maides—I sent away,
To whom for helpe I thought might appeale ;
But grace yet strengthens me to say them nay :
Yet they accuse me Lord ! and die I shall,
If Christ my Daniell, be not iudge of all.

---

[1] = portend. G.

SON. LII.

I JUSTLY am accusde, and now am brought
By law and gilt of conscience—I confesse—
Before Thy throne, conuict by deed and thought,
Of sinfull lust which did me so possesse,
That quickning graces Thine I did suppresse:
By fading loue of world procliue[1] to ill,
Whose dome[2] eternall death, and nothing lesse,
My soule doth see, to threaten to me still.
But since that frailtie so the world doth fill,
That no one fleshly wight thereof is free,
For mercy Lord to Thee repaire I will,
Who seest the hart, and canst best comfort me:
Quit me from death, grant I may fall no more,
But remnant of my daies Thy grace implore.

SON. LIII.

A HUSBANDMAN within Thy Church by grace,
I am O Lord! and labour at the plough;
My hand holds fast, ne will I turne my face
From following Thee, although the soile be rough:[3]

[1] = prone or having proclivity. G.
[2] = doom. G.
[3] St Luke ix. 62. G.

The loue of world doth make it seeme more tough,
And burning lust doth scorch in heat of day :
Till fainting faith would seeke delightfull bough,
To shade my soule from danger of decay.
But yet—in hope of grace from Thee—I stay,
And do not yeeld, although my courage quaile ;
To rescue me be prest, I do Thee pray,
If sinfull death do seeke me to assaile.
Let me runne forth my race vnto the end,
Which—by Thy helpe O Lord !—I do intend.

SON. LIIII.

A BASE-BORNE sonne to sin by kinde I am,
From natiue soile by want of grace exilde,
Of idle fancies captaine I became :
Whilst I in Tob,[1] my resting place did bilde,
With worldly vanities I was defilde,
Till home Thou caldst me by Thy heauenly word :
Who—trusting to my selfe—was soone beguilde,
When I sought workes to be a conquering sword,
Whose vowes did seeme a present to afford,
Of frute of victorie at my returne :
Which rashnesse hath a mischiefe great incurd,

[1] Judges xi. 3, 5. G.

Compelling me my owne deserts to burne,
And now I mourne, and better frute do craue;
The blessing of Thy Sonne Lord let me haue.

SON LV.

When Thou vouchsafedst—Lord!—to raise my state,
From base degree of common humane kinde,
And gau'st me knowledge, and a will to hate
Each wickednesse contrarie to Thy minde,
By promise Thou didst me most strictly binde,
To slaye each wicked seed which doth possesse,
My sinfull flesh—Amalekite most blinde!—
Which vertue and Thy grace seekes to suppresse,
But wretched I alas! I do confesse,
Haue kept a part of that accursed spoile
Vndaunted, which Thou seest nere the lesse,
And therefore wilt accurse my sinfull soile,
And take from me the kingdome Thou didst giue,
Except Thy mercy do my soule relieue.

SON. LVI.

The onelie daughter Lord of my delight,

—Dina[1] the vertue of my iudgement best!—
Is rauishèd alas! by Satan's might,
Whil'st I secure in Hiuit's[2] countrie rest;
In worldlie vanities a wandring guest,
Amongst the wicked I remainde a while,
Where—sillie—she, by foolish will addrest,
Gazde on those godlesse youths which her beguile:
For lustfull Sichem,[3] sonne to sin most vile,
Did lay a traine of loue, which led to shame:
Whose flattering speech did modestie exile,
And left a spot of guilt and foule defame.
But faith and zeale—the first-frutes of my strength—
By grace shall 'venge my honour iust at length.

SON. LVII.

The silly babes—the motions of the minde,—
Which natiue vertue seeketh forth to bring,
Concupiscence—the midwife most vnkinde—
To deadly sin, and Satan straight doth fling:
The mother's power suffiseth not to wring,
Out of this tyrant's hands her dying childe;

[1] Dinah: Genesis, xxx. 21 *et alibi*. G.
[2] Hivites. G. [3] Schechem. G.

Her mone to see, it is a piteous thing,
When Reason's lawes so lewdly are defilde.
But in Thy fauour Lord be reconcilde,
By loue vnto Thy Sonne, by Him to mee:
Then though my hope of grace be neare exilde,
Yet Thou a childe of faith wilt let me see.
A coffin[1] Lord of comfort, for me make,
Where safe I may swim in the wor[l]d's wilde lake.

SON. LVIII.

Where shall I build O Lord! a quiet rest,
To bring forth birds of turtle—pigeons kinde?
My wearied wings do wander without rest,
And cannot gain a harbour to my minde.
The swallow Lord! a setling place doth finde,
Within Thy temple, free from eagle's claw,
Not mouèd with tempestuous stormes of winde,
Or dangers, which their kind doth stand in awe:
A place as fit for me, my faith once saw,
Whereas my soule might safely be inclosd:
Thy Church inuisible, to which I draw,
My life retirde, therein to be reposd.

[1] A noticeable use of the word 'coffin,' now limited to the 'box' or 'chest' for burial of the dead. G.

Make frutefull Lord! my barren heart
therein,
Shield me from storme of still assailing sin.

SON LIX.

WHILST in the vale of carnall sense I dwell,
—Foule Sodome, sinke of sin and badge of
shame—
Of whose polluted nature I do smell,
And aptly bend my selfe to them to frame:
Sent by thy mercie Lord! Thy angels came,
And did vouchsafe, a harbor to accept
Within my soule, which did professe Thy name;
But Satan who a watch on me had kept,
When as these guests within my conscience slept,
Inuironèd with lust my harbor weake;
For sorrow of this sin my soule it wept,
Whilst violently my bodie's bands they breake.
But strike Thou blinde their fury, them
expell,[1]
Take me Lord! from the flame of burning hell.

SON. LX.

MY bodie Lord! infected long with sin,
Whose running issue is almost past cure,

Which helpe, my humane phisicke cannot win,
And without comfort cannot long endure,
By viewing mercies Thine, becommeth sure,
If but Thy gracious hem, my hand may reach,
That loue in Christ my pardon shall procure,
And reunite in strength health's former breach.[1]
Through presse of worldly lets[2] faith shall me teach,
To seeke my safetie in Thy promise true,
Vouchsafe Thou eke repentance so to preach,
That—I no more offending—health insue
Thy vertue Lord!—which bidding me be cleane—
To yeeld me health of soule, is readie meane.

SON. LXI.

Now that I see O Lord! my open shame,
Conuict of sin and voyd of clothing pure,
Which couer might my soule which naked came
Of grace, and me from storme of world assure:
I do mistrust my selfe long to endure,
The heat and cold, which feare and frailtie bring;
And clothing of my owne workes to procure,

[1] St. Matthew, ix 20. G. [2] Hindrances. G.

I finde in deed to be a frutelesse thing;
To hide my selfe vnder Thy mercie's wing,
I therefore hasten now, in hope of grace:
Grant I beseech, the world no more me wring,
Out of Thy hands, but let me see Thy face,
With faith and comfort, clothèd by Thy hand,
And Christ Thy Sonne in my defence to stand.

SON. LXII.

WHILST Thou the chosen chieftaines of Thy word,
Do bend their power, by preaching to subdue
The fleshly Canaan, and put sin to sword,
And giue the soule to be possest a new
With righteous Israel, vnto Whom of due
Those earthly blessings rather do pertaine:
They send two spies[1] my secret thoughts to vew,
The Law and Gospell, which discouer plaine,
My fainting force, in feare for to remaine
Where yet repentant Rahab readie is
To lodge them safe, while Satan seekes in vaine,
To slaie these messengers of heauenly bliss:

[1] Joshua vi. 23. G.

I craue therefore sweet Sauiour for a sine,
Faith-bearing frutes, as pledge of safetie
mine.

SON. LXIII.

How oft, O Lord, with more then tender care,
Hast Thou by prophets cald me to repent;
How great Thy loue by Sonne, which didst not
spare,
To staie me back from hell, whereto I went?
Who to that end from heauen to Earth was sent,
Whose graces daily preachèd, offred peace,
And sought to stop my course to ruine bent,
And me from guilt of death for to release:
Like as the henne, whose voice doth neuer cease,
To clocke[1] her tender chickens vnder wings,
When furious foules on silly pray[2] do prease,
And would deuour—alas!—the helplesse things.
Such Lord Thy care I feele, and loue of me,
That thrall to Satan wouldst not haue me be.

---

[1] = cloak, with reference to the hens call, cluck, cluck. G.

[2] Prey. G.

SON. LXIIII.

WHILST with the wholesome food of heauenly truth,
—The manna which Thy written word doth giue—
Thou soughtst O Lord! to feed my wandring youth,
That it in plenteous peace by grace might liue,
By lust, lo! Satan sought my soule to driue,
To breake obedient bands vnto Thy law,
Which my offences—I protest—do griue
My helplesse heart, the which delight did draw:
The memory of Egypt's store I saw,
Of vanities—which carnall senses feed,—
Made me to wish, to fill againe my maw
With dishes such as to destruction lead:
Wherefore in wrath with quailes[1] thou cloidst me so,
That plagu'd with sin, my error now I know.

SON. LXV.

SINCE Thou hast raysed my poore abiected spright,
From threshing floore, where captiue I did stand,

[1] Psalm cv. 40: cf. Numbers xi. 20. G.

And callest me Thy battels for to fight,
Gainst sin—the Madianite which wastes Thy Land,—
Giue me a token by Thy mightie hand,
—O Lord!—whereby my faith may be assurde,
And be to me a pledge of former band,
That victorie by me shall be procurde :
Let heauenly deaw by praier be allurde,
To moysten this my freewill fleece of wooll,[1]
Then dry the dregs thereof to sin inurde,
Whose heauy waight makes grace and vertue dull;
And offring mine—of prayers to Thy name—
Accept, and with a holy zeale inflame.

SON. LXVI.

Whilst that in wealth and ease I did possesse
The empire of Thy many blessings sent,
I tooke in hand pure vertue to suppresse,
And pride with lust my powres they wholly bent,
To conquere reason, which Thy grace hath lent,
And quite forgetting world's late floud, for sin,

[1] Judges vii. 36-39. G.

To build a tower of trust, wherein I spent
The strength of flesh and bloud, high heauen to win :[1]
As though in Nature's strength the force had bin,
To shield themselues from floud or heauenly fire;
But now confusion iust my soule is in,
Makes labouring flesh from folly such retire,
And craues alone within Thy Church to dwell,
Whose wals of faith and truth may death expell.

SON. LXVII.

The temple Lord of this my bodie base,
Where Thou vouchsafst to place my soule to dwell;
And promisedst to make Thy chosen place,
Whence sacrifice of praises Thou wouldst smell,
Behold against Thy lawes doth now rebel,
By worldly vanities thereto allurde,
Where couetise and pride their packe doth sell
At such a price, as flesh and sin affoord:
But since O Lord! Thy promise hath assurde

[1] Genesis xi. 4. G.

My soule, that Thou art alwaies prest to heare
The plaints of penitents, which hath procurde
Thy Sonne Himselfe in temple this t'appeare,
Whip forth, fling down, this worldly wicked pack,
Fro out my soule! repell Thou Satan back!

SON. LXVIII.

WITHIN Thy house this bodie base of mine,
It pleasèd Thee, O Lord! my soule to plant,
A steward of the gifts the which were Thine,
And nature fild with measure nothing scant,
Of bodie or of mind, no blessings want,
And Fortune's fauours sharde with me no lesse,
In such proportion Lord, I needs must grant,
As Thou doest giue, when Thou doest vse to blesse:
But wantonly I wasted, I confesse,
Thy treasure put into my hands of trust,
And now alas!—though late—I seeke redresse,
Wise-steward-like to liue, when dye I must:[1]
I cast my count by Christ my debt to pay,
And frutes of faith from hell my soule shall stay.

[1] St. Luke xvi. 8. G.

SON. LXIX.

Now that it pleaseth Thee Lord, of Thy grace,
To plucke me forth of sinfull Sodom's lake,
Where I haue dwelt alas! this life long space,
Since I of holie Abram leaue did take;
Vouchsafe I pray Thee for Thy mercie's sake,
To graunt Thy Church be refuge for my life,
The Zoar where I may my dwelling make,
Safe from reuenging angel's bloudie knife;
And though the frailtie of Lot's ling'ring wife
Looke backe, with loue, on sinfull world's delight,
—Which common weakeness to all flesh is rife—
Yet keepe me constant by Thy heauenly might,
And let me not grow drunke with blessings Thine,
To procreate from lustfull daughters mine.

SON. LXX.

WHILST in this worldly wildernesse about,
For want of faith I backe am forst to go,
—Affraid of sinnes which giant-like are stout,
And foule affections, which like cruell foe
Of Esawe's race, their might and powre bestowe,
—To stop my passage to the promist land—

I gin to faint and to repine also,
Against the powre of Thy most mightie hand,
For which the serpent Satan now doth stand,
In readinesse my silly soule to sting,
And close me vp in death's eternall band,
Vnlesse to me Thy mercie succour bring,
That brazen serpent Christ nayld on the tree,
Whose sight by faith alone is cure to me.

SON. LXXI.

WHAT am I else Lord! but a sinfull wretch,
In sin and in iniquitie begot,
In conscience guiltie of the common breach,
Of euerie law, that may my honor spot:
Thy blessings gui'n me, I regarded not,
Thy threatned iudgments I did not esteeme,
My vowes to Thee I almost had forgot,
My sinnes no sinnes to hardned heart do seeme;
Like to my selfe I did Thy power deeme,
Because Thou didst forbeare Thy rod a while:
I sought by idols'ayd to heauen to clime,
Whilst world's delight my sences did beguile:
But helplesse now, alas! I turne to Thee,
To stay my race; let grace Lord! succour mee.

SON. LXXII.

Thou formedst me at first out of the clay,
Vnto the image of Thy glorious frame,
—O Lord of might—Thou shewdst to me the way,
To magnifie Thy pure and holie name;
Like potter's vessell first my modell came,
Out of a rude vnformèd lumpe of earth,
To holy vse it pleasd Thee me reclaime,
Before my life tooke vse of carnall breath;
Thou fedst me in the common humane dearth
Of knowledge of Thy will, with such a tast
Of pleasing fruite, as fild my soule with mirth,
And readie makes me now, no more to wast
Thy offred mercies; which, so blesse in me,
Of glorie that I may a vessell be.

SON LXXIII.

A seruant Lord euen from my day of byrth,
I vowèd was by parents vnto Thee,
A Nazarit I liuèd on the earth,
And kept Thy vowes as grace did strengthen mee,
Till Satan made me world's deceipt to see,
And trapt my sences with forbiden lust;

As Eue did tast of the restrainèd tree,
So fond affections did me forward thrust:
A sinfull Philistine—of faith vniust,—
To like, to loue, to craue, to wed, to wife:
Thy grace, my strength, to her reueale I must,
Till she to Satan sell my slumbring life:
A prisoner I, thus scornd and voyd of sight,
Sinne's house to ouerthrow, craue heauēly might.[1]

SON. LXXIIII.

Whilst in the plentie of Thy blessings sent,
I sought to solace Lord! my selfe secure,
And gazing on world's beautie long I went,
—In pridefull tower which did prospect procure—
I saw the baytes of sin, which did allure
My idle thoughts to follow wicked lust;
My kindled passions could not long endure,
But vnto furious flames breake forth they must;
I did pollute my soule, by fraude vniust,
And rest[2] Thy grace from his true wedded wife:
And that I might away all 'mendment thrust,
I did bereaue my knowledge of this life:

[1] Samson: Judges xiv-xvi. G. [2] = Wrest. G.

Whose bastard frutes slaie Lord! but let her liue,
That penitent we may Thee prayses giue.

SON. LXXV.

A seruant sold to sin O Lord! I am,
Whom Satan—Syrian proud—doth sore assaile,
Nine hundred chariots of desire there came,
Armèd with lust, which sought for to preuaile:
And to subdue by strength they cannot faile,
Vnlesse Thou raise my fainting strength by grace;
Let constant faith the flying furie naile
To ground, where grouelling is his resting place:
Then shall my soule with Debora imbrace,
In thankfull wise Thy mercies I receiue,
And so pursue the fleshly Canaan's race,
Till I the furie of the same bereaue.
And with my song Thy seruants shall accord,
To yeeld due praise to Thee the liuing Lord.

SON. LXXVI.

My soule like silly[1] Joseph[2] Lord, was sold,

---

[1] = innocent, G, [2] Genesis xxxvii. 28. G.

By fleshly brethren his,—vnkind alas!—
To vanities—the merchants—which behold.
From far they saw to Egipt which do passe.
A seruant vnto Ismael's seed it was,
And sold from sin to death, and so to hell:
Of humane frailtie Lord, a looking glasse,
In which all foule affections long did dwell:
Yet lo! alas! when sin seekes most t'exell,
And haue my mind consent to traitrous lust,
With grace O Lord, that enemy repell,
And heare my praiers, who in Thee do trust;
Who though a space in bodie's prison staies,
Yet Lord at length vouchsafe to heauen to raise.

SON. LXXVII.

So blinde O Lord haue my affections bin,
And so deceitfull hath bin Satan's slight,[1]
That to giue credit I did first begin,
To pride, and lust, as heauenly powers of might:
I offred all my sences with delight,
A sacrifice to feed those idols vaine, :
Of all the presents offred day and night,
Nought vnconsumde I saw there did remaine;

[1] Sleight. G.

Till that Thy prophets by Thy word made plaine
The falshood, by the which I was deceiued,
How Satan's kingdom made hereof a gaine,
And wickednesse my hope and faith bereaued;
But now the sifted ashes of Thy word
Bewraies Bel's prists: slaies dragon without sword.

SON. LXXVIII.

A wicked theefe that oft haue robd and slaine,
Thy graces of their frute, my selfe of blisse,
Now on the crosse of conscience I remaine,
To die the death the which eternall is:
I see no way to quit my selfe of this,
Vnlesse Thou Lord whose kingdom is aboue,
Remember me, and cansell life amisse
Out of Thy memorie, through Christ Thy loue:
Who in my flesh with me like death did proue,
That guiltlesse He, might guilties ransome bee;
Loue to my soule it was, that did Him moue,
The bands of death to bide to make vs free:
Blesse Thou my tong, increase thou faith in mee,
This night to be in paradise with Thee.[1]

---

[1] St. Luke xxiii. 43. G.

SON. LXXIX.

In bondage long to Satan haue I bin
  A maker of the bricke of Babell towre;
  By birth, a thrall to grosse and filthie sin,
  Whom Lust's taskmasters doth attend ech houre;
Affection to the flesh doth cleane defloure
  The memorie and loue of promist lands:
  The fiend—euen Pharo—seeketh to deuoure
  My soule, and chaine me to His dreadfull bands:
But Lord receiue me safe into Thy hands,
  Protect me from the rigor of his might,
  Quench Thou the force of Lust's inflamèd brands,
  In my defence giue me true faith to fight:
    Send Moyses, Lord, with powre of heauenly sword,
    And Aaron to direct me by Thy word.

SON. LXXX.

A Moabit I was of cursèd kinde,
  Unkinde vnto Thy Church Lord, and to Thee,
  Who sought by ayde of foolish Balaam blinde,
  To captiuate the soule that should be free,
Incestuous frutes of that high climing tree,
  Which doth subdue all reason and all grace;
  A carnall kinsman by a neare degree
  Vnto the soule, the which I haue in chase.

Whom I with lothsome sin sought to deface,
  And bastardise with carnall, fond[1] affect,
  Whose ofspring Thou vnto the tenth man's race,
  Didst once out of Thy sanctuary reiect.
    Yet now by faith made free of Iury land,
    A suter here before Thy Throne do stand.

SON. LXXXI.

Lo! how I groueling vnder burden lie,
  Of sin, of shame, of feare Lord of Thy sight,
  My guilt so manifold dare not come nigh
  Thy throne of mercy, mirror of Thy might:
With hidden and with ignorant sinnes I fight,
  Dispairing and presumptuous faults also ;
  All fleshly frailtie on my backe doth light,
  Originall and actuall with me go.
Against a streame of lusts my will would roe
  To gaine the shoare of grace, the port of peace,
  But flouds of foule affections ouerfloe,
  And sinke I must ; I see now no release,
    Vnlesse my Sauior deare this burden take,
    And faith, a ship of safetie for me make.

---

[1] = Foolish. G.

SON. LXXXII.

FROM Iuda wandring Lord to Jericho,
From holie law of Thine to carnall lust,
Whilst midst the prease of lewd affects I go,
I robbèd am of raiment pure and iust,
And wounded lye Lord, groueling in the dust,
Not any passer by can giue me aide;
In fleshly strength or friendship is no trust;
By highway seene, to helpe me few haue staide:
But since my Sauiour Christ on crosse hath paide
A ransome rich to cure my bleeding sore,
By faith to craue the fruites, I'm not affraide,
In hope my health thereby for to restore:
Binde vp my wounds with balme, leade me to rest,
Giue me such gifts of grace, as like Thee best.[1]

SON. LXXXIII.

This slender citie—Lord—of strength behold,
Wherein I dwell, Bethulia my bower
Of flesh, whereto sin laies a batryt bold,
And seeks with sword and dearth my soule's deuower:

[1] St. Luke x. 30. *et seqq.* G.

Suppresse Thou hellish Holofernes power,
Who prides himselfe in praie of children Thine ;
I haue no trust in mountaines, wals, nor tower,
For want of faithe's—true fountaine—we shall pine ;
Raise vp this female couragde heart of mine,
Strengthen my hand to reue this monster's hed,
Let me not taste deceiptfull follie's wine,
Nor be polluted with world's sinfull bed :
But constantly by faith fight in defence,
Of feeble flesh, and driue Thy enemies thence.[1]

SON. LXXXIIII.

Not that my faith doth faint a whit is cause,
That I so instant am on Thee to call,
O God of life ! but yeelding to Thy lawes,
Before Thy sight, my soule these teares lets fall,
Which in Thy bottle kept I know are all,
And quench the fury of Thy burning ire,
Which sin enflamde, and qualifie it shall
The quarrel which hath set Thy wrath on fire :
If feruently the childe due foode desire
Of father, he will not giue him a stone ;[2]

---

[1] Apocrypha : Jud. iv. 6 : xi. 9 *et alibi*. G.
[2] St. Matthew vii. 9. G.

If of the wicked, iustice man require
Importunely, some iustice will be showne :
More righteous iudge and father Thou to mee,
Art Lord indeed, and far more kind wilt bee.

SON. LXXXV.

The many trials Lord that I haue found,
Since out of Egipt darknesse I am brought,
Might witnesse well how in Thee still abound,
Powre, mercy, truth, wherby Thy workes are wrought.
But foule dispaire against my faith hath fought,
Amidst the wildernesse wherein I stay ;
And daintier food my fond affections sought,
Then manna, which Thou sentst me euerie day,
The desert Zyn, doth fountaine pure denay,
Of grace, wherewith to quench my fainting ghost ;
Eternall death expects my soule as pray,
And lust assaults me with a hideous host.
Stretch forth hād Lord, smite Thou my hart of stone
With rod of true repentance, griefe and mone.

212

SON. LXXXVI.

THOU hast O Lord of mercy, me enricht
With flocks of fauour, and of graces great,
Since I in Bethell first the pillar pitcht,
Of praises to Thy name and mercies seat,
Yet fleshly Esawe's foule affections threat,
A ruine to the frute faith forth should bring,
With pleasing humors him for to intreat,
I feare it be to soule a dangerous thing:
Shield me Lord, vnder Thy protecting wing
Of mercy, which may saue from Satan's rage ;
My heart and voyce shall still Thy prayses sing,
If Thou the malice of my foes asswage ;
In Sychem shall my heart an alter reare,
The mightie God to loue, to serue, to feare.[1]

SON. LXXXVII.

THE talent which Thou pleasedst Lord to giue,
To me Thy seruant that I should bestow,
Whilst in Thy seruice on the Earth I liue,
My diligent increase thereof to show,
I haue abusèd Lord—too long—I know,
And feare Thy comming to be nigh at hand ;[2]

---

[1] Abraham : Genesis xii. 6-8. G.
[2] St. Matthew xxv. 25-28. G.

I see for breach of dutie what I owe,
And of Thy iudgements do in terror stand:
Thy grace hath left me in a forreine land,
Where vnexpert of vertue I do straie,
I shall be throwne to Satan's thralfull band,
Voyd of Thy heauenly ioy and blisse for aye,
Vnlesse Thou helpe, for Thou doest vse to giue,
Grace vnto grace, and faith to faithlesse driue.

SON. LXXXVIII.

SINCE that it pleaseth Thee Thy selfe to show,
A iust reuenger Lord of heath'nish sin,
And bring the pride of foule Philistines low,
Who Thee defame, when holy arke they win;
Now that to fetch it home I do begin,
And in the temple of my heart to place,
Grant so I may Thy secrets see therein,
That plagues, for my presumption do not chase
It so from me, as they that fled the face
Of glorie Thine, which therein did appeare:
Let faith and loue draw home by trustie trace.
The constant cart,[1] whose carriage is so deare;

[1] 1 Samuel vi. 7-8. G.

And let me order so this holie worke,
That dregs of sin not in my deeds may lurke.

SON. LXXXIX.

In famine great of grace, and comfortlesse,
Thy seruant Lord, doth in Samaria dwell,
For Lord, fierce Aram doth with sin oppresse,
The citie where my soule to harbour fell:
I want the strength His armies to repell.
Of lust and of affections most vncleane,
My mind whose loue doth motherlike excell
Her children—thoughts of 'mendment—sees so leane,
That forst by famine, she can find no meane
To feed them long; her faith so poore is growne.
That nature pitie now secluding cleane,
Her greedie nature doth deuour her owne.
Releeue in time this siege, Lord cause a feare
Of Thee, this camp of cruell sin to reare.[1]

SON. XC.

On sweet and sauorie bread of wholesome kinde,
Which in Thy word Thou offrest store to mee,

---

[1] Kings xviii. 2 : xx. 1 : *et alibi*. G.

To feed vpon the flesh doth lothing finde,
And leaues, to leane—O Lord—alone on Thee.
The leauen of the Pharisies will bee
The surfet of my soule, and death in fine,
Which coueting to tast forbidden tree,
To carnall rules and reasons doth incline:
So lauishly my lusts do tast the wine,
Which sowrest grapes of sin filles in my cup,
That lo! my teeth now set on edge, I pine,
Not able wholesome food to swallow vp,
Vnlesse Thou mend my tast, and hart doest frame,
To loue Thy lawes, and praise Thy holy name.

SON. XCI.

Ovt of Thy flocke, O Lord, through my defect,
A silly sheepe my selfe—behold!—am lost,
To seeke me forth in time do not neglect,
Since I so precious price to Thee haue cost,
By many by-paths Lord, my feete haue crost,
And cannot find the way vnto Thy fold,
Through many stormes of deep despaire thus tost,
To craue Thy aide at last I now am bold:
If thou of silly groat that count doest hold,

That Thou doest search the house to find the
same,[1]
No doubt my soule to sin by nature sold,
May mercy find, by calling on Thy name :
The saints in heauen conuertid's gaine reioyce ;
On earth Thy praise is song, in heart and
voice.

SON. XCII.

BEHOLD amidst world's desert all alone,
Seducèd by the frailtie of the sprite,
Accompany'd with fleshly comfort none,
My soule wlth sin compellèd is to fight,
Where suddenly alas ! before my sight,
I Satan see, me ready to assaile,
By two, his seruants, which are most of might,
Presumption and despaire ; which seldome faile,
The best perfections of man's strength to quaile ;
By pride, or want of faith, or couetise,
By lust, or gluttony, or fainèd vaile,
Of vertue, which doth many sinnes disguise :
But chase him Lord away by written word,
Which is more sharpe than his two edgèd
sword.

[1] Luke xv. 9. G.

SON. XCIII.

THE dreame which Thou to Pharo[1] didst reueale,
Thou in my selfe hast made me see in deed,
The state—alas!—of man's weake common weale
Whereas affections of all sorts do feed,
The fruteful soyle of grace some whiles did breed,
Full faire effects in truth of heauenly kinde,
But many barren thoughts alas succeed,
And threaten famine to vertuous minde.
Store of such yeares are[2] yet I feare behinde,
Which Lord, will starue the comfort of my faith,
Vnlesse Thy mercy and Thy wisedome finde,
A storehouse to laie vp what Scripture saith,
In hope of which Thy goodnesse, lo! I liue,
Which of Thy grace Lord, do Thou to me giue.

SON. XCIIII.

THE seed which Thou the husbandman hath sowde
Within my soule—O Lord—by prophets hand,
Hath taken roote at last, by deaw bestowd

[1] Genesis xli. G. [2] Misprinted 'as'. G.

From heauenly grace, which fructifies my land:
But lo! I saw the world's deceipt to stand
In readinesse to mingle tares therein,
Whilst sleeping me, in vanities he fand,
He made my frutes to ouerflow with sin:[1]
But ere Thy haruest to approach begin,
Vouchsafe to weed these frailties so away,
That when Thy corne is to be gathered in,
I may be cleane, and in Thy garner stay;
Burne Lord with chastisement my fleshly lust,
And cleanse my life by faith, both pure and iust.

SON. XCV.

WHAT strength hath man? wherein may he repose
A power to stay him in a vertuous way?
To loue Thy flocke Thou Lord my soule hast chose,
Whom to obey my vowes and words did say:
But in my power alas! there is no stay,
For light temptations made me cleane forget
My dutie to my Lord, and to denay

[1] St. Matthew xiii. 25-26. G.

Him who thus long I haue too lightly set:
But now my heart with teares my cheeks doth wet,
In sorrow of my so inconstant faith;
Repentance hath my sin before me set,
And conscience now my error duly way'th:
Grant that Thy word crow thrise and thrise to mee,
And warne me of my dutie vnto Thee.[1]

SON. XCVI.

The malice of this monster auncient foe
Of man, and of the Church which Thou didst plant,
Euen Satan, Herod-like about doth goe,
To make my frutes of faith to grow more scant,
Whilst yet with weaknesse feeble youth doth pant,
And wanteth grace to strengthen their estate;
The motions of the mind doth straight recant,
To see soule's safetie, which sin faine would hate;
The counsels of affections do debate,
And do conclude to murder Vertue's breed:
Lust, pride, and enuy, open wide the gate,
To furious flesh, that doth the wicked deed.

---

[1] St. Luke xxii. 61. G,

My soule—their mother—mourns O Lord
their end ;
My future frutes of grace do Thou defend.

SON. XCVII.

So foolish Lord haue my affections bin,
So carelesse of the blessing Thou doest guie,
So prone my natvre vnto euerie sin,
So thanklesse of Thy grace by which I liue,
That violently Thy loue away I driue,
And sell the patrimony to ensue ;
I carry water in an open siue,
And change for lentil pottage birth-right due.
Too late—alas !—my folly I do rue,
Who world's delight preferréd haue so long,
Reiecting heauenly knowledge, treasure true,
Vnto my soule imposing open wrong,
Yet not so late—O Lord, I pardon craue—
But yet one blessing Thou for me wilt haue.

SON. XCVIII.

A sinfull Syrian Lord, my father was,
Exilde from Paradise by iust desart,
I wandred into Egipt, there alas!
To finde in world some food to please my hart :

Where seruile bondage vnto sin and smart,
I suffered so long through Satan's rage,
That heauenly aide I crau'd thence to depart,
Which only able was my griefe t'asswage :
From silly seruant and an abiect page,
Thou broughtst me forth to knowledge of Thy truth,
—The blessed land—and showdst me on a stage,
A patterne how to guide my wandring youth ;
Such frutes therfore as faithfull soile doth yeeld,
I offer here first crop of blessed field.

SON XCIX.

I see—alas !—proud Satan hath too long
Defrauded Thee, O Lord, of that is Thine,
And loue of world hath drawne me vnto wrong,
Whose heart Thy offrings to bestow repine .
My outward knees vnto Thee do incline,
My tong doth promise present of my store,
I say these gracious gifts are none of mine,
But will them all Thy aulter laie before ;
But vanities doth presse me euermore,
And want of faith to leaue some part behinde,
Although I see death readie at the dore,

My hollow heart and lewd deceipt to finde :
Grant that I may my soule, my power, my will,
Present O Lord ! to serue Thee onely still.

SON. C.

SINCE Thou by grace out of wilde oliue stocke,
Hast pleasd me Lord within Thy Church to plant,
And reckon me as of Thy proper flocke,
Who else all pleasant frute by nature want ;
Vouchsafe my thankfull frutes be not so scant,
As cause Thee to reiect me backe againe,
Of former bountie Lord do not recant :
But let me in Thy garden still remaine :
By mercy, not by merit, I attaine,
This blessing promisèd so long before,
Let not this gift of Thine returne in vaine,
But let Thy goodnesse multiply the more :
Make sweet the frutes which bitter are by kinde,
Increase thy grace in body and in minde.

CONCLUSION.

MOURNE thou no more my soule, thy plaint is heard,

The bill is canseld of the debt it owes,
The vaile is rent, which thee before debard,
And Christ, His righteousnesse on thee bestowes;
Thus comfort to the patient alwaies growes,
If they attend the time God hath assignde,
Our strength to beare, our Maker best He knowes,
And at a need is readie for to finde;
Our Sauiour is so mercifull and kinde,
Vnto our selues He will not leaue us long;
He castes our faultes through loue His backe behinde,
And turnes our plaints into more plessant song.
And when we are euen at the gates of hell,
His glorie, mercie, power, doth most excell.

The second Part of Christian Passions,

CONTAINING A HUNDRED SONETS OF COMFORT, IOY, AND THANKESGIUING.

PREFACE.

SOME men do mourne for suddeine ioy they say,
And some likewise in midst of sorrow sing;
Such diuers frutes do passion often bring,
As reason cannot course of Nature stay:
And happie sure he is—I not denay—
That both these motions hath from heart contrit,
When frailtie of his flesh appeares to sight,
And Mercy calling him backe from decay.
Who can behold the flesh and spirit fight,
The doubtfull issue and danger of the thing,
The losse whereto our nature might vs fling,
And gaine, which grace doth giue, through Sauior's might,
And not delight, to glorifie His name,
And yet lament his proper natiue shame.

SON. I.

As through a mist, or in a cloud a farre,
I see a glimse of heauenly grace to shine,
And to reuiue the fainting faith of mine,
And spirits, which with darknesse shadowed are.
The fleshly fog of sin did iudgment barre,
Of proper vse, of power, of reason sound,
—Which in first parents franckly did abound—
And better part of Nature's strength did marre;
But since my eyes of grace a sight haue found,
Of that eternall light which doth incline,
Fro out these fogs of feare I hope t'vntwine,
And force of fainting faith for to confound,
And on a ground more firme will build my trust,
And that in Christ Whose promises are iust.

SON. II.

CLENS'D[1] are the cloudes, and darknesse fled away,
And now in triumph doth my Sauiour ride,
Sin, hell, nor death, dare not His sight abide,
The world nor Satan can His progresse stay:
This piercing light of truth shall so bewray,

---

[1] Misprinted 'cleng'd'. G.

Ech stratagem their practise doth deuise
Against my soule, that there shall not arise
One cloud of care to darken this my day.
But that my thoughts—like to the pilate wise—
Shall looke about, lest that my heart should slide,
And by this sunne my course so constant guide,
That all their slightes shall not my soule disguise,
Which now espies the malice they me owe,
Which lōg they clothd with shade of plesāt show.

SON. III.

When as my conscience layeth forth before
My thoughts, the sinnes which daily I commit,
I thinke my selfe an instrument vnfit,
To witnesse forth Thy glory any more:
But when I see that sin was first the dore,
By which death entred and such hold did take,
That death did first our want apparent make;
And want first cause that man did ayd implore,
That praiers first Thy mercies do awake,
That mercies do renue our dullèd wit,
That ioyed heart should not vnthankfull sit,
And thanks to Thee doth fleshly glory shake;

It straight doth slake the fear which bad me stay,
And bids me still proceed to praise and pray.

SON. IIII.

SINCE to so holy vse I consecrate
That silly talent Lord thou lenst to me,
That it a trumpe vnto Thy praise might be,
And witnesse of their woe that Thou doest hate:
Doe Thou O Lord, forget the abiect state
Of flesh and bloud, base mettle of my frame;
And since that Thou hast sanctified the same,
Vouchsafe Thy grace my weaknesse may abate:
That Thou my former wandring will didst tame,
And me prepare in minde to honour Thee,
Canst giue me gifts the which thereto agree,
How ere my proper power be weake and lame;
So shall Thy name be precious in my sight,
And in Thy praise shall be my whole delight.

SON V.

WOULD God I were as readie to confesse,
And yeeld thee praise sweet Sauiour day by day,

As to craue my wants I am forward ay,
And feruently at need to Thee to presse,
To beg of Thee alone; Thou wilst no lesse,
Because Thou onely able art to giue,
And with each needfull thing by which we liue,
Thou promisest our prayers Thou wilt blesse;
But we with vse of them should not so stay,
And onely seeke to Thee when need doth driue,
—Whose blessings running through an open siue,
No praise for recompense vnto Thee pay—
But when we pray, we should Thee laud also:
Our thankfull hearts with bountie Thine should go.

SON. VI.

I haue begun, O Lord, to run the race,
Where flesh and bloud against the world must fight,
On heauenly kingdome gazing with my sight,
Where is appointed scope of resting place:
Wingd with the will of zeale of heauenly grace,
I do indeuor alwayes to proceed,
In constant course vnto the arke indeed,

Where, in Thy mercies, I behold Thy face;
A feruent faith, it doth my courage feed,
And make my heauie limbs become more light,
When in Thy Sonne I see Thy glorie bright,
The pledge vnto my soule that hope shall speed,
This blessed seed Thou hast Lord sowne in me,
And all the frutes shal to Thee offred be.

SON. VII.

WHERE shall I finde fit words or proper phrase,
Wherewith to witnesse all the loue I owe?
Whose gratefull minde in thankfulnesse doth grow,
And to the world Thy worthinesse would blase:
Vnfrutefully the greater sort do gase,
Vpon Thy works and blessings they receiue,
And carelesly Thy honor they bereaue,
And suffer chance or wit Thy fame to rase,
Whilst vnacknowledgèd Thy loue they leaue,
Forgetting all the gifts Thou doest bestow,
Whose blinded nature so doth ouerflow,
That most vnkind to Thee, themselues they show.
But since I know by grace Thy blessing great,
My pen Thy praises alwaies shall repeat.

SON. VIII.

THE more I seeke to dedicate my power,
In celebrating of Thy honour great,
—Whose throne is fixèd in Thy mercies seat—
The more my dutie groweth euerie hower;
Some times with eagle's flight aloft I tower,
And seeme to see the glorie of Thy sunne,
But ere my willing wings haue scarse begunne,
To mount, they droop with clog of heauie shower:
Vpon the hill of truth I footing wonne,
By faith, which laboureth with feruent heat,
Of worthie praises Thine for to intreat;
But ere I haue begune my worke is donne;
So farre I runne, in seeking to begin,
I cannot write, such maze my muse is in.

SON IX.

As fareth with the man the which hath bin
In perill but of late to haue bene drownd,
Though afterward he do recouer ground,
Knowes not at first the safetie he is in:
So when I thinke vpon the flouds of sin,
Wherein I was neare drenchèd ouer hed,
What time all hope of comfort cleane was fled,

And I into dispaire to sinke begin.
My fainting faith with feare euen well nigh dead,
My minde amazèd it doth so confound,
That though Thy mercies freely do abound,
In port of peace I am not free from dred,
But being led fro out the peril's sight,
I shall enioy more pleasure and delight.

SON. X.

Since Thou, O Lord, hast giuen to me at last,
The victorie against the deadly foe,
Who like a lyon roaring still doth goe,
My soule—poore Lot my kinsman deare—to wast:
Since grace at length his pride hath now defast,
And by the hand of faith he is subdude,
And that my strength by Thee is so renude,
That his affections almost are displast,
Since Thy high priest with present me pursude
Of bread and wine, of which He did bestow,
And with the same the blessings gaue also:
Whence life, whence libertie, whence health insude:
I haue indude as proper vnto Thee,
Thy Church, with tyth of faith, Thou gau'st to me.

SON. XI.

IF he to whom his Lord did but remit,
A silly debt, was thankfull to him found,
And that the more the sinnes forgiuen abound,
The more he loues that pardonèd is of it,[1]
Then sure it seemes it were good reason fit,
That I whose soule was sold to death and hell,
Whose sinnes in multitude did so excell,
With idle braine should not ingratefull sit:
But as the flowing fauors daily swell,
So should my voice Thy praises euer sound;
And since Thou hast powrde oyle into my wound,
I should not spare Thy mercies forth to tell:
And—so as well as Thou shalt giue me grace—
I will Thee laud, each season, time and place.

SON. XII.

Now that I haue some safetie Lord attaind,
Fro out the laberinth wherein I was,
Since grace as guide therein to me did passe,
And loue was line which me my issue gaind;
Since that my wandring steps faith hath refraind,
And that Thy word was Sybil's braunch to mee

[1] St. Luke vii. 47. G.

Through hell and death a way to let me see
To Elizian fields, where blisse for aye remaind,
I must not Lord so much vnthankfull bee,
To breake the vowes which once I made alas!
But I will show Thy mercies in a glas,
That by my words, men may acknowledge Thee,
The onely Hee hath any power to saue,
And raisd my soule fro out the verie graue.

SON. XIII.

I SHAME to see how large my promise are,
How slow my deeds that should performe the same,
I know the constant meaning whence they came,
But will and power are falne at strife and iarre,
What soule begins to do, doth bodie marre,
What loue would build, distrust would ouerthrow,
A plenteous offring, zeale doth bid bestow,
And fainting faith likes not to set it farre;
My will at least his good intent shall show,
Which Thou O Lord cause vnto better frame;
A free will offring Lord Thou wilt not blame,
Of such weake frutes as are on Earth below,

Which yet shal grow more fruteful by Thy
grace,
And as they be, wilt in Thy Sonne imbrace.

SON. XIIII.

THE end whereto we all created were,
And in this world were plast to liue and dwell,
—If we with iudgment do obserue it well,—
Was nothing else but God to serue and feare,
In which we badges of His glorie beare,
To yeeld Him right the most our weaknesse may,
Which—to our strength—we ought not Him
denay,
Who out of earth to heauen this dust shall
reare:
Which when within myselfe I deeply way[1]
I do condemne the dulnesse which befell
To me, whose gifts in nothing do excell;
By which I might His glorie great display,
On Whom do stay, all things that being haue,
Who to each creature all things freely gaue.

SON. XV.

As is the treasure frutelessse which is hid,

[1] = weigh. G.

And blisse no blisse a man doth not enioy,
—But rather is a meane to worke annoy,
To him that carefully preserue it did:—
So oftentimes the wisest sort haue slid,
Into like error, whilst they do conceale.
The gifts of grace, which God did them reueale,
And hide the talent, which is them forbid:
As frutelesse is it to the common weale,
That men respectiuely become too coy,
And triflingly their time away to toy,
And without good to others let it steale:
I therefore deale to world, and do impart,
These silly frutes which grow on feeling hart.

SON. XVI.

The pleasures of this new possessèd land,
Fore-promisèd long since to children Thine,
Whereto I haue arriuèd safe in fine,
And to enioy the same assurèd stand;
To paint with praises I would take in hand,
That so I might incourage many more,
To follow forth the conquest where is store,
Of corne, of wine, and oyle for faithfull band.
Our Jesus Christ Himselfe is gone before,
And showes the clusters of the healthfull wine,

Whereof who tasts, shall not with famine pine,
Nor starue when plentie is at citie dore :
Ne need deplore the strength of Anak's race,
For He the power of hell will cleane deface.

SON. XVII.

Be twixt two strong extreames my thoughts do flie,
Twixt heat and cold, twixt heigth and depth below,
And both of them from one desire to flow,
The surest way to sauing health to trie ;
Faith bids me mount unto the heauens hie,
Vpon the merits of my Sauiour deare,
A guiltie conscience bids me not come neare,
Lest in consuming iealousie I die ;
A heart contrite doth well me to appease,
With works of righteousnesse, true faith which show :
Faith saies, that God my strēgth and power doth know,
And that I cannot finde saluation here,
But bids me cheere my soule and nothing feare,
Loue in His Sonne will make Him me forbeare.

SON. XVIII.

FROM far I see the stars which guide the way,
From East to West, I find my Sauiour out,
I well might wander all the world about,
To seeke saluation and in one place stay:
I[1] shining truth did not His house bewray,
Which in His word points out His dwelling place,
By which directed, I will walke apace,
Whilst yet I do enioy the light of day;
And when I come before His blessed face,
To offer vp My presents will not doubt,
Although their basenesse all the world should flout,
So that my faith I may Him once imbrace,
Which giueth grace and makes accepted well,
Mean works, as much as those which more excell.

SON. XIX.

Now will I daunce[2] O Lord before the traine,
Of those which following Thee seeke home to draw
Thy holy arke, the terror of thy law,

[1] = aye (?) G. [2] 2 Samuel vi. 14. G

That it with vs may pledge of peace remaine;
I care not though the world my deede disdaine,
And think it not beseeming thing for me,
In such a worke an instrument to be,
Whose yeares they deeme more fit for other vaine:
For so I Lord Thy sauing health may see,
And 'scape the harme of cruell Satan's paw;
Though all the scorners of the world me saw,
Yet would I not ashamèd be of Thee;
For being free, of holie promist land,
I care not how my state on Earth do stand.

SON. XX.

No recompence O Lord is fit for Thee,
If duly Thy desert we do regard,
Ne hast Thou want or need of man's reward,
At whose command all creatures readie bee;
Yet if our thankfull minds Thy goodnesse see,
Confessing whence to vs these blessings flow,
And in the vse of them obedience show,
Although alas! it be in meane degree;
Thou yet doest frame Thy loue to vs below,
And as Thou findst the giuer's heart preparde,
—Who to his power his prèsent hath sparde—

So dost Thou cansell debt which he did owe,
And doest bestow more graces then we craue;
For which naught els but thāks Thou lokst to haue.

SON. XXI.

How precious are the praiers of Thy saints,
Which able were Thy threatened wrath to stay,
And make the sunne returne in pride of day,
When as Iosias heart for feare it faints;[1]
Thy fauor vnto Abram vs acquaints,
Of how great force repentant heart is found,
When—hauing vowd vile Sodom to confound[2]—
To staie at seruant's sute Thy wrath Thou daints;[3]
By prayer man hath powre euen death to wound,
By prayer he may moue a mount away,
A faithfull feruent prayer finds no nay,
If that the thing we craue be pure and sound:
Yea God hath bound Him selfe by them to man,
Whose worthie praise no tongue well vtter can.

---

[1] Joshua x 12. G. [2] Genesis xviii. G.
[3] = deignest. G.

SON. XXII.

THANKS will I alwaies studie Lord to pay,
To Thee, the giuer of all good and grace,
And thankfully Thy mercies will imbrace,
And witnesse forth Thy workes from day to day.
My heart, my mouth, my pen they neuer stay,
To take occasion freshly to renue,
The memorie of praises to Thee due,
Lest Nature's weakenesse let them passe away:
My frailtie—in this point—indeed I rue,
Who till I see new blessings in this place,
Forget the fauours late before my face,
And mercies Thine, from which such bountie grew;
For it is true so dull our sences are,
That oft Thy blessings do our iudgments marre.

SON. XXIII.

WHERE so I cast about my wandring eye,
By chance or choice, by hap or els by will,
Before my sight some obiect is there still,
Wherein Thy power and loue I do espye;
In view whereof, if I my thoughts do trye,
To raise my heart to ioy I matter finde,
And vnto Thee my loue so firme to binde,

That tong nor pen should neuer idle lye;
Whose grace vnto Thy creatures is so kinde,
As patrons of the same the world doth fill,
Who mad'st not onely, but doest still instill
Some feeling of the same vnto the minde,
Which is not blinde, or too much obstinate;
Which later nature chiefly Thou doest hate.

SON. XXIIII.

WHILST I do studie fitly to begin,
To vtter forth some part of my intent,
Which to Thy praise with zeale and loue is bent,
For freeing me from due reward of sin,
I finde a laberinth that I am in,
Of many merits which do me inclose;
Which, as this holie motion in me rose,
Of diuerse subiects for to treat do win;
Among the rest my heart hath chiefly chose,
To giue Thee thanks for comfort to me sent,
In staying me the wandring course I went;
And feeling faith, with knowledge where it growes;
And though I lose therwith the world's delight,
Yet will I joy in hope of heauenly sight.

SON. XXV.

SINCE Thou hast, Lord, vouchsaft to send me ayde,
By Holie Spirit Thine, in time of need,
—As Philip to the eunuch came indeed—[1]
Which in my wandring iourny me hath stayde;
Since He hath taught me what thy prophets sayde,
And what humilitie was in Thy Sonne:
—Whose patience like a lambe hath freedom wonne,
Vnto my soule, for which He raunsome payde—
I see no earthly things should stay vndone,
The duties which requirde of me I reed:
By faith vpon Thy promises I feed,
And to Thy sacraments for strength I runne;
And thus begunne, I will continue still,
To learne Thy lawes, and to obay Thy will.

SON. XXVI.

How can I limit well my tong or pen?
Within what bownds may I my selfe inclose?
Who such a theame to write vpon haue chose,
Whereon the more I muse, more grow'th it then.
It fares with me herein, euen right as when
A hastie mind forgetteth what to speake,

[1] Acts of Apostles, viii. 27-39 G.

When stammering words the perfect sence do
breake,
And makes vs not be vnderstood of men :
Such worthie matter in my mind there growes,
So plentifull, and I of skill so weake,
So pleasing to me, and so proper eake,
That in the choyce of them I iudgment lose ;
And euen as those want matter, silent be,
So plentie of Thy praise confoundeth me.

SON. XXVII.

Now that Thy mercies do so much abound,
As Thou vouchsafest Lord with me to dwell,
And glorious arke of hope, which doth excell,
Drawne home by hungry faith my heart hath
found,
Since power thereof, did sinfull Dagon wound,[1]
And yet disdaineth not my humble state,
I freely open Lord, my lowly gate
Of lips and tong, which may Thy praises sound ;
Thy blessings seem to flow to me of late,
Since in my soule Thy word I did embrace ;
My zeale refreshèd is with heauenly grace,

[1] 1 Samuel v. 3. G.

My comfort, wealth that hell cannot rebate;
In such a rate Thy fauour do I finde,
As bindes me loue a Father found so kinde.

SON. XXVIII.

What should I render Thee my Sauiour deare,
For all the gifts Thou doest on me bestowe?
Whose gracious measure so doth ouerflow,
As power of recompence cannot appeare;
I do imbrace Thy gifts with ioyfull cheare,
And to Thy alter speedily do runne,
To follow forth Thy praise—but new begunne—
Till all Thy people may Thy mercies heare:
Thy glorious image shineth in Thy Sonne,
Thy loue to man did his obedience show;
His loue and mercy vnto man hath wonne
The gifts of grace, whence faith and comfort grow,
Where-through we know that we are Thy elect,
And these our feeble frutes wilt not reiect.

SON. XXIX.

The powerfull pen the which records Thy praise,
O Lord of life, hath many volumes made;

Thy wondrous works each leafe doth ouerlade,
Which aye increase as growing are my dayes;
Vnsearchable indeed are all Thy wayes,
In multitude they number do exceed,
In glorie they do admiration breed,
Their goodnesse, power of recompence denayes.
The hungry, Thou with plenteous hand doest feed,
Thy fauour to Thy creatures doth not fade;
The more in view of all Thy works I wade,
The more I finde my sence confound indeed;
But yet in steed of eccho to Thy fame,
I will giue thanks and laud vnto Thy name.

SON. XXX.

This stately stage where in we players stande,
To represent the part to vs assignde,
Was built by God, that He might pleasure finde,
In beautie of the works of His owne hand;
All creatures of the ayre, the sea and land,
Are players at His appointment of some thing,
Which to the world a proper vse may bring,
And may not breake assignèd bownds or band:
Some do in ioy still forth His praises sing,
Some mourne and make their mone with heauy mind;

Some shew the frutes of Nature weake and blind,
Some shew how grace base sin away doth fling;
God—like a king—beholds; Christ doth attire
The plaiers with the shape, their states require.

SON. XXXI.

Who so beholds with constant fixèd eye,
The fauor and perfection of my choyce,
He cannot chuse but must in heart reioyce,
That mortall sight may heauenly blisse espie;
All earthly beautie he will straight defie,
As thing too base to occupie his braine,
Whose fading pleasures so are payd with paine,
That they true tast of pleasure do denie:
But who so can this perfect sight attaine,
Cannot containe, but yeeld with cheerfull voyce,
An eccho to the angels heauenly noyse,
Who to His praise do singing still remaine:
They then are vaine who fix their sight so low,
That such a glorious God they will not know.

SON. XXXII.

O heauenly beautie, of loue the fountaine true,
Whose shining beames do penetrate my soule,

With such a zeale as former thoughts controll,
And drawes, heart, powre, and will Thee to insue;
Thou mak'st my fainting sight for to renue,
And dazeling eyes new strength thus to attaine;
To Whom alone perfection faire is due,
Thou mak'st Earth's bewteous shadow seeme but vain;
Thy works of glorie, and of powre remain,
Ingrauen in thankfull hearts, which them inroll;
The loue and mercy made Thee pay the toll,
Which to our dying soules true life did gain,
Thy loue doth wain,[1] my thoughts frō baser loue,
And mak'st my heart and mind to soare aboue.

SON. XXXIII.

If beautie be as men on Earth suppose,
The comely shape and colours which agree,
In true proportion to the thing we see,
Which grace and fauor both do neuer lose:
If white and red be borrowed from the rose,
If bright and shining to the sunne compar'd,
If high and straight to goodlinesse w'award,

[1] = wean. G

And beautie haue such base descriptions chose;
Then let the wise this beautie true regard,
Where all perfections in one subiect be,
Surpassing frute of the forbidden tree,
Which—but to tast—man suffred death's reward;
Which is prepard, and offred to our sight,
In Christ to loue and feed vs day and night.

SON. XXXIIII.

How may this be, that men of searching mind,
Whose curious eyes in beautie do delight,
—The pleasing obiect of their fancie's sight—
In outward shape and colours, comfort find:
And yet the better beautie leaue behind,
Vnsought or vnregarded of at all,
Compard to which, none can it beautie call,
Vnlesse a buzzard whom affections blind:
This earthly forme of flesh it is so small
Of worth to charme the sence of noble spright,
As is a starre before faire Phœbus bright,
Whose glory doth their borrowed beauti'apall:
Thus wise men fall, whom carnall eies do guide,
Whose iudgement may not Vertue's sight abide.

SON. XXXV.

O HEAUENLY loue, with God Thou dwelst for aye,
Thou passest faith and hope in dignitie,
Thou keepst the law, thy feet step not awrie,
In all men's danger, thou the surest stay;
To our request, thou neuer sayest nay,
Ne wrath, ne enuy, moue thee ere a whit:
Thou multitude of sinnes in man doest quit,
Thou Law and Gospell both dost ouer sway:
Thou doest with God aloft in heauens sit,
With God in counsell thou art alwaies by,
Thou causest Christ man's weaknesse to supply,
And makest vs receiue the frute of it,
And euery whit of goodnesse that we haue,
Loue made Him send, Who loue therfore doth craue.

SON. XXXVI.

THE shining face of my faire Phœbus deare,
Whose glorie doth eclipse each other light,
Presents himselfe vnto world's open sight,
Their blinded eyes with ioyfull view to cheare:
But sluggish so the greater sorte appeare,
That—sleeping in self-loue and mind secure—
The cleare aspect of truth they not indure,

Nor of their blindnesse willingly would beare;
But so my sences do His beautie allure,
To gaze vpon His louely fauour bright,
That therein onely haue I my delight,
Where is all happinesse, I do assure;
He doth procure a plentifull increase,
Vnto my soule, of perfect loue and peace.

SON. XXXVII.

Avaunt base thoughts, incomber me no more,
By laying forth these earthly wants of mine,
As though Thou wouldst perswade me to repine,
Because of wealth I haue not needlesse store:
If Thou didst know thy nakednesse before
He cloth'd Thy soule, and fed Thy fainting minde,
—With righteousnesse and faith in Sauiour kinde—
Thou wouldst that former state much more deplore;
And then confesse, the comfort Thou doest finde,
By peace of conscience, in this flesh of thine,
Is greatest riches truly to define:
—So that contentment be not left behinde—

These gifts me binde to praise His holy
name,
And place chief wealth in knowledge of the
same.

SON. XXXVIII.

I will not feare with fervency of zeale,
To follow forth this faire affect of mine,
—To loue of Thee which doth my soule incline—
O Sauiour deare, who sure my griefe wilt heale:
Vnto thy proffred kindnesse I appeale,
Who of Thy selfe didst call me vnto Thee,
And promisedst I should Thy darling bee;
Made free within Thy Church and common
weale,
Disparagement there is not now in mee,
Ne shall distrust forbid me to be Thine;
But faith shall flie aloft to Thee in fine,
Where all Thy treasures safely I may see:
And happie hee bestows his loue so well,
Whose hope is payd with pleasures that excell.

SON. XXXIX.

Loue then I will, and loue Thee Lord alone,
For fellowship in loue there may not bee;

Loue for Thy loue—O Lord—shall be my fee,
For other recompence thou crauest none;
My vowes and deeds they shall be alwaies one,
All dedicated to adorne Thy name;
My heart, my soule, my strength shall do the
same;
Thy loue shall be my faith's true corner stone;
The loue of Thee shall my affections frame,
To follow that may pleasing be to Thee,
My eyes no beautie but in Thee shall see,
And Thy regard my wandring will shall tame,
Yea I will blame, and scorne each other thing
Saue what shall me vnto Thy fauour bring.

SON. XL.

FAINE would I praise Thee Lord with such a zeale,
And feruencie, as might my loue expresse;
Faine would my loue yeeld vnto Thee no lesse
Due praise, then Thou didst loue to me reueale:
But wanting power thereto, I yet appeale,
To that Thy goodnesse, which Thee first did
moue,
In fragil flesh of mine, the strength to proue,
Whose weaknes Thou by heauēly powre didst
heale:
Man's wit in words comes short in this behoue,

To recompence—nay only to confesse—
The many waies Thou doest our bodies blesse,
Much more our soules, which freely Thou didst loue;
Thy trustie doue, Thy holy Spright of grace,
Makes yet our weakenesse stand before Thy face.

SON. XLI.

O PERFECT Sunne whereof this shadow is,
A slender light, though it some beautie show,
On whom Thy influence Thou doest bestow;
Whose constant course still shines in endlesse blisse:
To scan Thy glorie, wit of man doth misse;
How far Thy mercie's beames abroad extend,
Tong cannot speake, nor wit can comprehend,
And humane frailtie is bewrayd in this;
The fire, ayre, water, earth they wholly bend,
The host of heauen, and creatures belowe,
To pay their dutie vnto Thee they owe,
Which didst their being and their vertue send:
And I intend with them—in what I may—
To witnesse forth Thy laud and praise for aye.

SON. XLII.

WHAT present should I bring of worthie prise,
To witnesse well the loue to Thee I owe?
I nothing haue but what Thou didst bestow,
Ne likest Thou the toyes of man's deuise;
I would not spare my powre in any wise,
No treasure seemes to me for Thee too deare:
The pleasures of the world the which are here,
Too base they are, how ere wit them disguise:
To yeeld Thee faith it doth the best appeare,
But mine is very weake—alas!—I know;
To yeeld Thee praise doth make a decent show,
But to Thy merit neither doth come neare;
With garment cleare, yet clothd of righteous
Son,
My selfe to offer vnto Thee, I run.

SON. XLIII.

WHO so beholds the works—O Lord—of Thine,
The stretchèd heauēs, the seat where Thou doest
dwel,
The Earth Thy footstoole, which dares not rebell,
Which all vnto Thy will do still incline:
The sunne and moone by day and night which
shine,
The changing flouds, the firme and frutefull land,

The planets, which do firme for euer stand,
All which gainst Thy behest dare not repine :
The host of angels in Thy heauenly band,
Th' infernall fiends with Lucifar which fell,
The fish, the foule, the beast agreeing well,
And all obedient to Thy heauenly hand,
May vnderstand Thy glorie, loue, and powre,
Without whose help, mā could not liue an howre.

SON. XLIIII.

As doth the moone by daily change of hew,
By growing, or decreasing, beautie show,
The influence, the greater lights bestow,
Whose absence, or whose presence, her renue ;
So must all flesh confesse, and thinke most true,
The faith or feare they haue for to proceed,
From heauenly grace, which heauēly gifts doth feed :
Without whose face, blind darknesse doth insue ;
Man's proper powre is so obscurde indeed,
With shades which rise frō earthly courts below,
That nothing but blinde ignorance would grow,
Vnlesse this sunne, did shining comfort breed,
Which serues in steed of fire vnto the same,
Fro whence this light of faith receiues his flame.

SON. XLV.

IF Saba queene[1] a iourney tooke in hand,
From South to North, wise Salomon to heare;
If humane wisedome was to her so deare,
That she did visit thus his holy land;
Then do I muse why men do idle stand,
In pride of youth, when wit and meanes abound,
Their tender braines to feed with wisedome sound,
Far passing that this queene in trauell found.
The error is the scarre of Adam's wound,
Who sought his knowledge not in fountaine cleare,
To whom forbidden skill did best appeare,
Neglecting graces him inclosing round;
But on the sound and written word I build,
Not Salomon such oracles could yeeld.

SON. XLVI.

How fond[2] a thing it is which men do vse,
To beat their braines, and so torment their hart,
In compassing the thing which breeds their smart,

---

[1] Sheba: 1 Kings x. 1-13. G

[2] Foolish, as before. G.

And do not know what is the thing they chuse :
They childishly the name of loue abuse,
And would define the nature of the same,
By passions which belong to hatred's name,
Wherein to pine with pleasure they do chuse.
Who euer saw that figs on thorne-tree came,
Or thistels roses beare, by any art ?
With pain, with grief, with shame, with losse impart
Their passions, which they for their loue do frame,
With iudgement lame; loue is a heauenly thing,
Where being plast, it perfect loue doth bring.

SON. XLVII.

Let earthly things in Earth their loue repose,
For flesh and bloud on faith they cannot feed;
It is a frute indeed of heauenly seed,
Which who disgesteth well life cannot lose;
The soule fro out of other mattter growes,
And vnto other matter turnes againe;
Immortally to liue in ioy or paine,
As grace to sundry vses it hath chose.

Then is it time my thoughts at length to waine,[1]
For laying vp my treasure for my need,
Where mothes and canker do so common breed,
As in the world whose wealth is meerely vaine;
If I attaine but wealth layd vp in store,
In Christ, my Sauiour, I desire no more.

SON. XLVIII.

Fye fainting Faith, disswade me not so much,
From following of my louely, heauenly choyce;
To thinke on Whom, I cannot but reioyce,
Whose name or memorie my heart doth touch;
What trauell ere befall, I will not grutch,[2]
Through fire and water I will Him pursue,
Whose sight my fainting soule doth straight renue;
His loue and mercy both to me are such,
If I should die for Him it were but due;
By Him I liue, and follow will His voyce,
Regarding lightly fame or common noyse,
Which threaten paine and trauell to insue,
There are but few that passe the narrow way,
But crowne of honor doth their trauell[3] pay.

[1] Wean, as before. G. [2] Grudge, as before. G.
[3] Travail. G.

SON. XLIX.

I FIND my heart is bent for to amend,
And follow Thee, forsaking wicked way,
From wickednesse my footsteps for to stay,
And to Thy will my works henceforth to bend :
But yet the cause which makes me this intend,
I finde is rather feare then loue of right.
Yet free-will offrings do Thee more delight,
And to such works Thou doest Thy blessing send.
It is not ill to set before my sight,
Thy heauie plagues for sin from day to day ;
And I had rather forth Thy fauours lay,
And for their loue in quarrell Thine to fight :
Which if I might by feruent zeale attaine,
Then should I hope the victorie to gaine.

SON. L.

No sooner Loue intirely me possest,
But see how Iealousie doth me assaile,
She seekes with deepe distrust my faith to quaile,
And to remoue from conscience, quiet guest ;
She telleth me my Lord doth sin detest,
And that my deeds they too vnworthie are,
That from His fauour they will me debarre,

Whose loue is fixèd onely on the best:
Feare had begun to worke in me so farre,
That to amaze my minde it could not faile,
Till to my Loue my state I did bewaile,
Who shining sweetly like the morning starre,
Did stay their iarre, and bid my soule to rest
In Christ, by whom I surely shall be blest.

SON. LI.

He is vnworthie to receiue a gift
From any man, that him mistrusts before;
I will not ought of Thee Lord doubt therefore,
Although no reason can my hope vp lift;
I know in deed it is slie Satan's drift,
To laie before me this my vile estate,
Which—being sinfull—Thou of force must hate,
And I reiected be without all shift;
But when I with myselfe Thy works debate,
Which haue examples of Thy mercie's store,
His reasons are of force with me no more,
Because that faith sets open wide the gate,
To me of late, which leads to treasure Thine,
Where—in Thy Sonne—Thou doest in mercy shine.

SON. LII.

FAINE would I follow Thee through sea and land,
My louely Sauiour, Whom farre off I see;
Zeale makes my mind with speed to hast to Thee,
But natiue weaknesse makes me doubtfull stand:
If to my ayde Thou gau'st not forth Thy hand,
And by Thy word encouradgst me to row,
I should so shun afflictions which do flow,
That feare should bend my faith like feeble wand;
But by Thy offred grace now strong I grow,
And through the troubles of the world will be
Bold to proceed, and faith shall succour me,
To witnesse the thankfulnesse I owe;
Thou doest bestow on me both power and will,
And with them both, I will Thee honour still.

SON. LIII.

As do the starres amidst the firmament,
With borrowed light beare record vnto Thee,
—O Lord of might—in which we men do see,
The image of Thy power to them but lent;

So when our weake indeuors Lord are bent,
To publish forth Thy praises, which excell;
These silly sparkes of light which in vs dwell,
Do shew Thy grace which vs this motion sent.
Although therefore no speech or tong can tell,
How infinite Thy glorie ought to bee,
—Which passeth human sense by high degree,
As wisest men to grant, they do compell—
Yet Thou lik'st well, we show herein our will,
Which I have vow'd vnto Thy seruice still.

SON. LIII.

CALL me O Lord, for lo! I do attend
To follow Thee where so Thou doest direct;
I know Thou wilt not my intent reiect,
Who gladly would proceed where so Thou send;
I doubtfull stand, which way my course to bend,
Because I finde such ignorance of skill,
To follow forth according to my will;
A frutefull course the which I did intend,
As Thou with forward zeale my minde didst fill;
So shew me Lord whereto I am select.
And I shall carefully the same effect,[1]

---

[1] = affect or choose? G.

And feruently thereto go forward still;
Depend I will, vpon occasion fit,
That faithfully I may accomplish it.

SON. LV.

Like silly babes, such must the seruants bee,
In innocencie and obedience still,
Vnto Thy holy lawes—O Lord—and will,
From wrath, pride, malice, lust, and enuy free:
With serpent's eyes of wisedome must they see,
And stop their eares, which Sathan would deceaue,
With charmes of pleasure, which a scar do leaue,
And onely lend obedient eare to Thee:
Yet with simplicitie of doue receaue
The yoke of law, whose rule they must fulfill,[1]
And suffer patiently, the word to kill
The force of sin, which would soule's health bereaue;
Such Thou wilt heaue, and hold in heauēly arme,
And with protecting hand, defend from harme.

---

[1] St. Matthew x. 16. G.

SON. LVI.

WHO so could like to Steu'n[1] behold and see,
The throne triumphant where our Sauiour sits
In maiestie aloft, as best Him fits,
A Iudge and Sauiour to His saints to be,
Coequall with His Father in degree,
Possessor of the place for vs prepard :
Who readie stands our weake works to reward,
And from the fury of the world to free ;
He were but base, if ought he did regard
This transitorie honour, which so flits,
Which to attaine so much doth tyre our wits,
And yet so niggardly to man is shard,
And afterward doth leaue a stinge behinde,
Of care of conscience, and of griefe of minde.

SON. LVII.

WHO seeketh not with all his powre and might,
To eternize vnto himselfe his state ?
That chance or time may not his blisse rebate,
Or death itselfe may not dissolue it quight ?
Thus some therefore for honour fiercely fight,
And some for wealth do trauell far and nigh ;
Some worldly wisedome with great studie buy,

[1] Acts of Apostles, vii. G.

To make them famous seeme in vaine world's
sight:
Which is the readiest way they do espye,
To keep their name from death, which so they
hate,
Yea all suppose posteritie the gate,
T'immortalize this flesh, whose floure must dye;
But all go wry, wealth, honor, wit haue end,
And children passe; faith onely life doth lend.

SON. LVIII.

What wealth may be to this alone comparde,
To be co-heire with Christ of Father's loue?
To haue our earthly thoughts so raysd aboue,
That world and worldly things we not regard?
To see by faith a kingdome rich preparde
For vs, which shall eternally remaine,
—Made free from worldly cares and troulbes
vaine—
Which is for children His, a due reward?
Who can discouragde be with earthly paine,
Or tedious combats which the flesh doth proue?
Since care of vs our partner Christ did moue,
To share our griefes, His ioy for vs to gaine:
Which thoughts should waine our wils frō
base desire,
And vs incourage higher to aspire.

SON. LIX.

If Paradise were such a pleasant soyle,
Where all things flourisht first and prosperd aye
Wherein who liuèd, neuer could decaye,
Till sin by Satan's slight[1] gaue man the foyle:
Which blessings afterward did cleane recoyle,
And left man naked, in reproach and shame,
To dust to turne againe from whence he came,
On barren Earth to liue with sweat and toyle;
Then is our state much better then that same,
Our paradise a place of blisse to staye,
Wherein our soules shall rest most free from blame;
Our Sauiour—Abram's bosome—doth desplaye,
Where He our name hath writ in booke of life,
To be exempt from feare of care, or strife.

SON. LX.

What is felicitie whereof men wright?
Which to attaine, our studies still are bent,
Which to procure, such time and paine is spent,
By endlesse trauell therein day and night;

[1] Sleight. G.

Sure if it be nought else but firme delight,
  And that delight consist in peace of minde,
  Then here on Earth this treasure none shall finde
  Whose pleasures vanish quickly out of sight:
The Earth doth chaunge, as seas do rise with tyde,
  And stormes insue[1] the calme before that went:
  This happinesse but for a time is lent,
  And payd oft times with penance more vnkinde,
    By fortune blinde. True blisse consists herein,
    To loue the Lord, and to abandon sin.

SON. LXI.

How many priuiledges great and rare,
  Do we enioy, that do Thy name professe;
  Euen many more by far,—I do confesse—
  Then we obserue, or how to vse be ware:
To giue Thy onely Sonne Thou didst not spare,
  Vs to redeeme from death's eternall wound;
  The sting of hell and sin He did confound,
  And way to heauen for vs He did prepare.
Yea so His mercies do to vs abound,
  That all the worldly creatures more and lesse,
  Yea heauenly angels do themselues addresse,

[1] = succeed, as before and frequently. G.

To serue man's needfull vse are readie found:
He doth propound, in Christ all these to man,
And hauing Him, no want annoy vs can.

SON. LXII.

By many gifts—O Lord!—Thou doest declare,
Thy mercies vnto man, whom Thou wilt saue,
The vse of all the which in Christ we haue,
By hand of faith, that precious blessing rare,
That doth His righteousnesse for vs prepare,
Our stubburnnesse with His obedience hide;
His patience doth our grosse impatience guide,
His temperance with our intemperance share;
His continence our frailtie lets not slide:
—For changing nature ours, His strength it gaue—
Our pride it hides, and hopes which faithlesse waue,
And shades our hart with loue, which still shall bide;
Thus euery tide, it readie is at hand,
For our defence a buckler safe to stand.

SON. LXIII.

How should the quiet mind in peace and rest,

Possessèd of the thing it most desirde,
—A thing so precious, none durst haue aspirde
To gaine, vnlesse the giuer had him blest—
How may it morne, how may she be opprest,
Who hath the bridegroome alwaies in her sight:
Who in her loue doth take so great delight,
As by His bountie hourely is exprest?
The dolefull darknesse fitteth blinded night,
The shining sunne hath cloudes of care retirde;
With heauenly heate my heart it hath inspirde,
Since in Thy sunne I saw Thy fauour bright,
The which did fight, as champiō strong for mee,
From cloudes of darknesse and from sin to free.

SON. LXIIII.

Who so of perfect temprature[1] is framde,
Must needs delight in heauenly harmony:
His sences so shall be renewd thereby,
As sauage beasts by Orpheus harpe were tamde;
Yong Dauid's harpe, Saul's furious spirit shamde,
And dolfins did Aryon's musicke heare.
Such sympathie in all things doth appeare,

[1] = temperament. G.

That neuer musicke was by wisdome blamde :
But he that could conceiue with iudgement cleare,
The sweet records that heauenly motions cry,
Their constant course that neuer swarues awry,
But by discords, whose concords after cheare,
Would hold so deare, the Mouer of the same,
That loue of Him should base affections tame.

SON. LXV.

Great is Thy powre, and more than we conceiue,
Thy glorie more then can discernèd be ;
Man's greatest gift is this, that he may see,
Or know, that vertue thine doth His bereaue :
His dazeling eyes each shadow doth deceaue,
His iudgement builded on inconstant ground :
His strength but weaknesse in it selfe is found,
His glorie, greater glorie must receiue
From Thee, in Whom all glorie doth abound :
What maiestie dare man compare with Thee,
To Whom all creatures bow obedient knee ?
Whose contemplations Thou doest cleane confound,
Vpon this ground. True blisse and wisdome stand,
To know, our wisedome floweth from Thy hand.

SON. LXVI.

As but vaine hope it is for man to trust,
To thing not promisèd, or not in powre
Of speaker to performe at 'pointed howre,
Which is the case of flesh and blood vniust:
So call that hope, no wise man can or must,
Which is performance of expected thing;
When as possession doth assurance bring,
Of thing whereafter we tofore did lust:
The saints in heauen in ioyful rest do sing,
Whom hope nor feare do raise or yet deuower,
But men on Earth haue hope a resting tower,
To shield them from despightfull Satan's sting:
Faith is the wing makes me to hope ascend,
And truth in Christ will make my hope haue end.

SON. LXVII.

Great are the gifts, O Lord, Thou doest bestow,
On sinfull man, by Thy abounding grace,
Who when they want, doest neuer hide Thy face,
But still a patron of Thy bountie show:
Which makes vs both Thy powre and mercy know,
And so with shame and sorow to repent,
Our thanklesse natures so vnkindly bent,

So slacke to pay the praises which we owe:
But when I do consider Thou hast sent
Thy Sonne Himselfe for to supply our place,
Whose patience did the death on crosse imbrace,
Those to acquite, who did with faith assent:
All speeches spent, seeme then to me in vaine,
And onely I admyring still remaine.

SON. LXVIII.

I haue beene blind, and yet I thought I saw
And now I see, yet feare that I am blind;
No blindnesse like to that is of the mind,
Which doth the soule to deadly danger draw:
My carelesse steps did stumble at a straw,
And yet supposd my walke had beene so ware,
That to haue err'd had bene a matter rare,
When euery thought did violate Thy law:
But since to search my selfe I do prepare,
So darke of sight my soule and sence I find,
That if Thy Christ—my loue—were not more kind,
Eternall death I see should be my share.
But now I dare, in spight of wicked foe,
A better course with constant courage goe.

SON. LXIX.

WHY should he faint or thinke his burden great,
That hath a partner to support the same?
Why coward-like should he his honour shame,
That hath a champion readie at intreat,
Who can and doth death and confusion threat,
To all impediments which stop our way?
On whom repose our trust we boldly may,
He being iudge, and plast in mercie's seat?
He sees our thoughts and knows what we would say,
He doth our mouthes to fit petitions frame,
He hides our errors if our faith be lame,
And He Himselfe doth also for vs pray,
We need but stay, and trust to His good will,
And we are sure He will our want fulfill.

SON. LXX.

ALTHOUGH the world do seek to stop my way,
By many stumbling blocks of feare and doubt,
And bid me seeke a further way about,
And on the staffe of carnall strength to stay;
Though sin, though hell, though death do me denay,

That any powre shall bridle their intent,
But would compell me walke as worldlings went,
The headlong path of pleasure to decay,
Yet will I not this purpose mine repent,
So long as faith will be my soldier stout,
To ouerthrow this fearefull thronging rout;
Whom to subdue, this grace was to me sent,
Ne shall be spent in vaine this paine of mine,
Hope against hope, shall be the field in fine.

SON. LXXI.

It were vnfit a concubine to keepe,
Or that her children should possession haue,
Among the frutes which lawfull wedding gaue,
By vertuous spowse, which in the soule doth sleepe;
And yet behold how shamefully do creepe,
Into possession of my powre and will,
These thoughts and works which motions are to ill,
And trench themselues in fleshly fortresse deepe:
Whose base societie will with vices fill,
The holy brood which grace would spotlesse saue;

In such a doubt[1] my yong affections waue,
That they consent I should them foster still,
But that would spill more vertuous heritage:
Therefore exilde these be, though hell do rage.

SON LXXII.

Sometimes my nature seemeth to repine,
To see the pleasure and the plenteous store,
The wicked do enioy for euermore,
Abounding in their corne, their oyle and wine:
But when I see my weakenesse so encline,
To the abuse of portion I possesse,
My heart with ioy, full often doth confesse,
Thy loue doth much in earthly scarstie shine;
These things are good and bad, as Thou doest blesse,
Which I dare not directly craue therefore,
Such danger followes them euen at the dore,
That plentie lightly doth the soule oppresse;
And as I guesse, contentednesse doth grow,
In gratefull mind, though state be neare so low.

---

[1] Misprinted, 'boubt.' G.

SON. LXXIII.

IF he vnworthie be the sweet to tast,
That shuns the sowre—as we in prouerbe say—
To honor, pleasure, profit, in the way
Great perill, paine, and cost, so often plast;
If as vnworthie health, he be disgrast,
That will refuse a bitter purge to take,
When he doth know it will his feauer slake:
So do temptations proue the mind more chast,
If we with courage do the combat make,
And to the end immoueable do stay:
The more that Satan doth his spight display,
The more the pride and powre of him we shake,
And he will quake, and sin shall haue a fall,
And faith in Christ shall triumph ouer all.

SON. LXXXIII.

So shun the rocks of dangers, which appeare
Amidst the troubled waues of worldly life,
Which in each company are alwaies rife,
Which with soule's perill most men buy full deare;
I feare almost to keep my course so neare,
The conuersation of such tickle tides,
And thinke him blest, that banishèd abides

In desert, where of sin he may not heare:
But when I note where so a man him hides,
That stil affections breed an inward strife,
That Nature beares about the bloudie knife,
And to the death the proper soule it guides:
That fancie slides away, and I prepare,
In combats of the world to fight my share.

SON. LXXV.

Were it not straunge, that members of the same
One liuing bodie, and one parent's childe,
Should by the other daily be defilde?
And of vnseemly thing should haue no shame?
And yet we which of Christ do beare the name,
And children of His father vs do call,
At discord with this parent daily fall,
And Christ our eldest brother do defame;
It seemeth well we be but bastards all:
Though stock be true, we be but oliues wilde;
Who thinks vs better, he is but beguilde,
Our frutes are bitter and increase but small,
And who so shall examine well his works,
Shall see, that gall in purest thoughts there lurks.

SON. LXXVI.

It is no light or curious conceipt,
O Lord Thou knowst, that maketh me to straine
My feeble powres, which blindfold did remaine,
Vpon thy seruice now at length to waight;
But onely shame to see man's nature fraight,
So full of pregnant speech to little vse,
Or rather oftentimes to Thy abuse,
Whilst to deceiue, they laie a golden baight;
And do not rather thinke it fit to chuse,
By praises Thine, true praise themselues to gaine,
And leaue those fond[1] inuentions which do staine
Their name, and cause them better works refuse:
Which doth abuse the gifts Thou doest bestow,
And oftentimes Thy high contempt do show.

SON. LXXVII.

For common matter common speech may serue,
But for this theame both wit and words do want,
For He that heauen and Earth and all did plant,
The frutes of all He iustly doth deserue:

[1] Foolish, as before. G.

No maruell then though apt my pen do swarue,
  In middle of the matter I intend,
  Since oft so high, my thoughts seeke to ascend,
  As want of wisedome makes my will to starue :
But Thou O Lord, who clouen tongs didst send,[1]
  Vnto Thy seruants, when their skils were scant,
  And such a zeale vnto Thy praise that brant,[2]
  As made them fearelesse speake, and neuer bend,
    Vnto the end, one iot from Thy behest,
    Shall guide my stile, as fits Thy glory best.

SON. LXXVIII.

How happily my riches haue I found ?
  Which I no sooner sought, but it is wonne,
  Which to attaine, my will had scarce begunne,
  But I did finde it readie to abound :
The silly faith I had was setled sound
  In Christ, although for feare it oft did pant,
  Which I did wish more constantly to plant,
  That it might all temptations so confound.
With feruency this little sparkle brant,
  Till it inflamde my zeale, and so did runne

---

[1] Acts of the Apostles, ii. 1-4. G.
[2] = burned, as in next sonnet. G,

Vnto the fountaine of true light—the sunne—
Whose gracious soyle to feed it was not scant:
Men find more want, the more they couet still,
But more man couets this, it more doth fill.

SON. LXXIX.

When desolate I was of worldly ayde,
Vnable to releeue my selfe at need,
Thou hadst a care my fainting soule to feed,
Because my faith vpon Thy fauour stayde:
My dying hope Thou hadst with mercy payde,
And as Thou didst releeue Thy seruant deare,
Elias, whom the rauens in desert cheare;[1]
So am I comforted, whom sin affrayde.[2]
The cries of little rauens Thine eare doth heare,
And slakst their hunger kindly—Lord—indeed,
When parents do forsake deformèd breed,
That so Thy prouidence might more appeare,
Which shineth cleare, in blessings euery day,
To me, much more than I can duly way.[3]

---

[1] 1 Kings xvii. 6. G. [2] = terrified. G.
[3] = weigh. G.

SON. LXXX.

AMIDST this pilgrimage where wandring I
Do trace the steps which flesh and bloud doth tred,
My comfort is, that aye mine eyes are led,
By gracious obiect which in faith I spy;
Whose brightnesse guides my steps, which else awry
Were like to slide, through Sathan's subtil slight,
'Gainst whom His holy angels alwaies fight,
And suffer not my strength too farre to try:
By day His word and works are in my sight,
Like to a cloud to comfort me in dread;
By fire through deserts and the sea so red,
His hand doth gouerne me in dangerous night;
His favour bright, conducting this my way,
An host of stops shall not my iourney stay.[1]

SON. LXXXI.

I SEE a storme me thinks approach a farre,
In darkned skie, which threatens woe at hand;
Vnto my tackle I had need to stand,
Lest sudden puffs my purposd course debarre:

[1] Exodus xiv. 20. *et alibi*. G.

These tempting thoughts full oft forerunners are,
Of fierce affections, which do moue the minde,
Which if resistance not in time they finde,
The strongest tackling they do stretch or marre;
I closely therefore will my conscience binde,
And arme my vessel with couragious band,
Of skilfull saylers, which do know the land,
Whose harbors for my safetie are most kinde:
And in my minde shall faith the pylot bee,
Whose skill shall make me wishèd port to see.

SON. LXXXII.

How is it that my course so soone would stay,
Before I haue begun the thing I thought,
If ease or pleasure I herein had sought,
I had not then made choyse of such a way:
More facill is the course vnto decay,
More fauour with the world it will attaine;
But I mislike the ioy requit with paine,
And faining words, not meaning as they say:
Men breake their sleeps some silly pelf to gaine,
With losse of life small honour some haue bought,
Yea philosophers, pleasure set at nought,
To win a name of vertue to remaine:

Then I will waine[1] my selfe from earthly rest,
With heauenly crowne and honour to be blest.

SON. LXXXIII.

When I begin to faint in my conceipt,
To see the little powre I haue to good,
How sin hath vertue in me still withstood,
And frailtie on my flesh doth alwaies waight ;
I am confounded and amazèd straight,
And readily could turne and flie the field,
And all my trauell to the tempter yeeld,
Before I would aduenture more to fight :
But when I duly note whereon I build,
My faith, which watered is with Christ, His bloud,
Of force sufficient to withstand the floud,
And me from perill and destruction shield,
I easily welde each burden on me layd,
And of my safetie nothing am affrayd.

SON. LXXXIIII.

The chastisements which often do befall,
Vnto the most belou'd of God, and blest,

[1] = wean, as before. G.

Doth breed vnto their soules both peace and rest,
And home from wandring thoughts their mind
doth call,
And sure are tokens not of fauour small,
Who father-like doth vs in time correct,
Who else the care of Him would soone reiect,
And haue no heed vnto our wayes at all.
The good phisition that would life protect,
Cuts of a limbe sometimes as it seemes best,
And yet the patient doth the same disgest,
Or any payne that worketh good effect:
Should God neglect vs then to exercise
With rods, wherby to make vs grow more
wise?

SON. LXXXV.

How should my feare or sorrow long remaine,
—Although the world did swell, and ouerflow
With danger, which nought else but death do
show—
When I by death do finde a present gaine?
Faith me assures that all assaults are vaine,
That seeke to seuer me from heauenly blis:
The loue of Christ assureth me of this,
That I with Him shall safely still remaine.

What though of earthly pleasures I do misse?
And though the care of them vnpleasing grow,
Yet this by good experience I do know,
All things turne to the best to children His:
I therefore kis the crosse with ioyfull cheare,
Because in chastisement doth loue appeare.

SON. LXXXVI.

Although those Gibeonites, the natiue borne
Of sinfull flesh, haue slily me beguilde,
When as I thought all lust to haue exilde,
By shewing faynd repentance raggd and torne:
Though flesh and bloud vnto this league haue sworne,
Not asking counsell of the Lord at all,
By which into a snare my soule did fall,
And deepe hypocrise my powre did scorne;
Yet meane I them vnto account to call,
And since they haue my holy thoughts defilde,
Accursèd I will hold them, and as vilde,[1]
Will hate their ofsprings all, both great and small,

[1] Vile. G.

And be they shall, but bondmen to my
soule,
Who daily may their proud attemps con-
trowle.

SON. LXXXVII.

When I began a conquest of my will
To make, and yeeld it vnto reason's law,
My reason to the rule of God to draw,
And by that rule to guide my actions still,
It had bene wisedome first the flesh to kill,
Who breeds affections, which do still withstand
The building of the worke I haue in hand,
And thornes are in my sides to worke me ill;
But now my error I do vnderstand,
And must—by feare of wrath—keep them in aw,
And by the chastisement of sin they saw,
Make them to yeeld vnto obedient band,
Then shall my land with faithfull souldiers be
Replenishèd and armèd strengthen me.

SON. LXXXVIII.

Not euerie one that with his lips doth pray,
Or praise Thy name, is gratefull in Thy sight;

Thy searching eyes haue not so much delight,
In those that cry, Lord, Lord, each houre of day
But such as in Thy bounds obedient stay,
And make Thy will a law vnto their mind,
That in Thy promises do comfort find,
And follow not the world's deceitfull way ;
To such Thou showest Thy selfe a father kinde,
And doest coroborat[1] their heart with might,
Against all powers wherewith they daily fight ;
Their sores Thou tak'st to cure, and doest vp bind,
Angels assignd, do them inuiron round,
And to their comfort, mercies do abound.

SON. LXXXIX.

How should I quicken vp my selfe indeed,
To true and faithfull loue euen as I ought ?
Vnlesse I call to mind whence I was brought,
And by Whose aide, Who did this kindnesse breed,
Which when I only waigh, my heart doth bleed,
To see that bountie of a God so kind,
And note the dulnesse of my nature blind,

---

[1] A noticeable early use of this word. G.

That should forget the Lord Who me doth feed.
When I was almost lost, He me did find ;
When I forgat Him cleane, on me He thought,
When I was sold to sinne then He me bought,
When I was wounded, He my sores bid bind,
Yea when I pind, He gaue me plenteous store :
Which gifts I will record for euermore.

SON. XC.

Why should I faint or feare, or doubt at all,
How fierce so euer fleshly combat show?
Since I so sure a succour readie know,
To shield me safe, what euer do befall?
If He haue such regard of sparrowes small,
As none of them—till God appoint—do dye,
If to our haires which fall, He haue an eye,
That none of them vnnumbred perish shall:
Why should I thinke him deafe when I do cry?
As though He had no care of vs below,
As though He would not needful things bestow,
Although our patience He delight to try ;
Who can deny but flowers that grow in field,
In glory staine the beautie pride doth yeeld.

SON. XCI.

How do God's blessings to His saints abound,
Whose gifts of grace, although they be but small
At first, yet more and more increase they shall,
As seed well watred in a frutefull ground;
The proof whereof I—sinfull—wretch haue found,
Whose faith nigh famishèd, He now hath fed
From heauen, with great increase of fish and bread,
Which strengthen dying soule with comfort sound;
His word for table He did open spred,
His seruants for to feed me, He did call;
Their dole so free, I finde more fragments fall,
Then in my basket, sences home haue led,
Yet He hath bed[2] to such more to bestow,
As greatest store of former treasure show.

SON. XCII.

I KNOW not Lord how to discharge aright,
The dutie that for graces great I owe;
No need Thou hast of me at all I know,

---

[1] St. Matthew x. 29—30. G. [2] = bade. G.

Yet in Thy seruice shall be my delight,
To publish forth Thy praises day and night,
To serue Thy saints with gifts I shall possesse,
Thy wondrous workes by all meanes to confesse,
I will imploy my substance, wit, and might.
The remnant of my life shall well expresse,
That—dead to sin—in Christ to life I grow,
Which shall to world, my mind regenerate
show,
Although that I cannot sinne cleane suppresse,
And will addresse my thoughts to Thee alone,
Because on Earth true ioy or blisse is none.

SON. XCIII.

If I did hope by pen to patterne out
The many merits of Thy majestie,
—Which of Thy mercies we do daily trie—
And endlesse matter I should go about,
But I—alas!—my strength so much do doubt,
That nothing lesse than such a thought I haue,
To point foorth others to a thought I craue,
Whose confidence in skill is much more stout.
Yet dare I say that nature neuer gaue.
The power to flesh and bloud to looke so hye,
Nor gifts of grace, full few there are apply,

To giue Him laud aright, that did them saue.
How to behaue my selfe herein I learne,
And wish my will might others likewise
warne.

SON. XCIIII.

WHAT tongue or pen can shew itselfe vnkind,
Vnto a Father full of mercy so,
Who freely doth such benefits besto,
And of our case hath such a carefull mind ?
Before we were, a way He forth did find
Whereby to purchase vs in heauen a place ;
When natiue strength our glory should deface,
A remedie therefore His loue assignd :
He giues vs knowledge of the same by grace,
Which offerd is to them the which will go
Vnto the Word, where sauing health doth grow,
And faith, through which our Sauiour we im-
brace,
And being base by birth, and thrall to hell,
He vs adopts in childrens roome to dwell.

SON. XCV.

WHY should this worldly care haue now such
power

To quench the comfort which the soule shall
find
In this our God, who is to vs so kind,
The memorie of which should feare deuoure?
If faith were watred well with heauenly shower
Of grace, and knowledge of our happie state,
It would the force of all assaults abate,
And be a bulwarke strong, at trial's hower.
If we the world and flesh did truly hate,
And made His will a law vnto our mind,
If doubt of power or will, did not vs blind,
Which to distrust, sets open wide the gate,
Then would this rate of worldly care be lesse,
And He our faith with fauour more would
blesse.

SON. XCVI.

How loath this flesh of mine remaineth still,
To part from sinne, his old companion deare,
Of death or of a change, he would not heare,
But would imbrace him aye with his goodwill;
The very thought of death his thought doth kill,
The very feare thereof his sorrow brings;
So sweet the pleasures seeme of earthly things,
That nought else can our fond affections fill.
But who is wise, fro out the snare he wrings,

Before perforce, death doth approch him neare;
That abstinence no vertue doth appeare,
When want of power subdues affections stings,
But who so flings, from them when they pursue,
To him, pure name of vertue indeed is due.

SON. XCVII.

Who so would liue, of force he first must die,
Death is the doore which leadeth vnto life,
Life which shall be deuoyd of change and strife,
Whose comfort shall our teares of sorrow drie;
The way is straight the which man must go by:
If to the heauens he purpose to ascend,
His grosse corruption must to graue descend,
And dead the power of sinne therein must lye:
If he to be regenerate intend,
First must he mortifie the motions rife,
Of lust, which kill the soule with cruell knife,
And eke his ruine presently pretend,[1]
For God will send a happie change indeed,
As haruest paies with plentie plow-man's seed.

---

[1] = portend. G.

SON. XCVIII.

When I with griefe sometimes to mind do call,
The wofull losse that sinne to man hath brought,
And want which to all creatures it hath wrought,
By Satan's slight,[1] and Adam's fearefull fall;
I find no comfort in world's vse at all,
But wish to be dissolu'd, with Christ to dwell,
From Whom all blessings flow, and do excell,
In thought whereof my comfort is not small:
Yea I do grow by thinking thereof well,
Into a doubt, if that in truth I ought
More sorrow parent's fall, which death hath brought,
Or ioy the life through Christ to me befell;
Yet truth to tell, I finde the change so good,
Our state is better now then when we stood.

SON. XCIX.

If I can speake and like a coward crake,[2]
If I can tell the thing the which is best,

---

[1] Sleight, as before. G.

[2] Boast, as in Spenser:

............She was bred and nurst
On Cynthus hill, whence she her name did take:
Then is she mortall borne, howso ye *crake*."
(F. Q. VII. vii. 50.) G.

If I in muster seeme in battell prest,
And yet shrinke backe when I should triall
make,
If I endeuour others to awake,
Fro out the deadly slumber they are in,
And yet my selfe cannot reuolt from sin,
But in the pride thereof do pleasure take,
By all my trauell I no gaine shall win;
Although my paine shall proue to others blest,
But—as the symbal's sound doth to the rest—
I might haps morne, when others mirth begin;
The feast but thin, would be vnto my share,
Though many dishes to the guests I bare.

SON. C.

Fortune and chance, blind guides to blisse fare-
well,
Vpon your leasures I no more attend;
I not regard what good or ill you send,
Nor in your tents of pleasures wish to dwell;
A greater blisse then ere through you befell,
Ye made me to neglect, I now do see,
Whose hope from feare could nere continue free,
But aye distrust did 'gainst my faith rebell:
The Earth's delight the which ye promist me,
Could not my soule from sorrow ought defend,

Your sweete with sower was mixèd in the end,
So vaine and variable both they be,
Then happie he that seeketh blessed rest,
In Christ alone, and doth the world detest.

CONCLUSION.

Words may well want, both inke and paper faile,
Wits may grow dull, and will may weary grow,
And world's affaires may make my pen more slow,
But yet my heart and courage shall not quaile;
Though cares and troubles do my peace assaile,
And driue me to delay Thy prayse awhile,
Yet all the world shall not from thoughts exile,
Thy mercies Lord, by which my plaints preuaile.
And though the world with face should gratefull smile,
And me her pedler's packe of pleasures show,
No heartie loue on her I would bestow,
Because I know she seekes me to beguile,
Ne will defile my happie peace of mind,
For all the solace I in Earth may find.

Finis.

Sundry Affectionate Sonets of a feeling Conscience.

PREFACE.

WHERE hast Thou rangd my retchles[1] soul so long?
How too securely hast Thou luld my mind?
In so long space, no cause or meanes to find,
To—once againe—renue Thy vowèd song.
Be not too bold, thinke not thy perill past,
May be, thy iourney is but new begun,
Pleasures do vanish, dangers fly as fast
To stop thy course, if slowly thou do runne.
Thy vowes are made, they may not be vndonne,
And cause thou hast—if blessings not thee blind—
To keepe thy promise to a God so kind,
By Whom alone, thou freedome's rest hast wonne:

---

[1] Transition-form of 'reckless', = careless, negligent. G.

To Him—nay to thy selfe—then do not wrong,
To Whom thy hart, powre, will, by vow belong.

SON. I.

Of Thee and of Thy prayse—Lord—will I sing,
Who rid'st on wingèd chariot of the skie;
Whose throne is plast aboue the thrones most hie,
Whose will doth forme and change ech formèd thing:
To Thee the offerings of Thy bounties gift,
To Thee the due of my attaynd desire
I will present, and with a voice vplift,
Contend to cause the world Thy name admire.
Thy prayses do not mortall praise require,
For lo!—alas!—they no way can come nye
Vnto the holy hymmes Thy saints apply,
And angels sing, inflam'd with heauenly fire:
Yet shall my soule, such zealous present bring,
As shall record my loue to heauen's high king.

SON. II,

Exild be mortall cares, raysd be my song,

To treat—with stile condigne[1]—Thy honor still,
O mighty Ioue, Who heauen and Earth dost fill
With myrror of Thy power : to Thee belong
All powers and wils, of body and of mind,
Thou mak'st and blessest with Thy prouidence ;
Thy bountie to the needy is so kind,
As nought but mercie and loue proceedeth thence :
At our right hand a readie safe defence,
If Satan's practise once assaile vs will ;
Thou holy motions dost in vs distill,
And dost illuminate our dullèd sence :
Thou dost redeeme, fro out the enemies throng
The innocent, whom worldlings vse to wrong.

SON. III.

Fro out what dreame, what sleepe, what charmèd rest
Rouse I my selfe? who too too long haue stayd,
—With worldly cares aud vanities dismayd —
And cleane forgot almost soule's solace blest ?
My greedy nature quaffèd ouer much

[1] = worthy. G.

Restrainèd poyson—potions of delight—
New libertie did former dyet grutch,
Though life the one, death other show'd to sight;
Nature, gainst grace prouoketh still this fight,
World to our wils doth yeeld accursèd ayd,
Satan our senses dulles, that not affrayd,
We worke our wracke with greedy force and might:
But waken me—O Lord—I Thee request,
With pleasure, paine, welth, wo, as likes Thee best.

SON. IV.

What is thy measure full? dost thou suppose
Of strength, of perfectnesse, of plenteous store,
Of frutes of faith profest; that now no more
Thou carest, albeit thy tree true beautie lose?
It can not be, whilst life and sap remaine,
That barren branch, so holy plant should beare:
A faire greene tree of goodly leaues were vaine,
Vnlesse that kindly frute also there were.
Words are but leaues, works fruits that should be there,
Shew that thou liu'st, by charitie therefore;
True holinesse doth teach a righteous lore,

Whereby to neighbor's good, our thoughts we
reare;
Vaine is our knowledge and our holy showes,
If in our life the fruite of loue not growes.

SON. V.

How can I hope for all my forward speed,
My fresh incounters of the riuals first,
My bold intent and zeale, which venter dirst
To runne so hard a race, and long indeed,
To win the prize? if past the greater paine,
I faint or do begin, my speed delay,
Or trusting ouer much the goale to gaine,
Let euery leaden heele, leade me the way.
In race of soule to heauen, light many a stay,
And fainting body doth for pleasure thurst:
The world strowes golden fruits — of tast
accurst—
Which toucht with loue, we lose to soule's
decay:
Then let me still runne on, so haue I need,
For constancie stands most the soule in steed.

SON. VI.

All will not serue, the more I would beware,

The more I headlong fall and drowne in sinne :
So farre vnlike the victorie to winne,
That to His building morter I prepare.
One thing I say, another thing I do,
One showe of worke I haue, an other deed :
I runne cleane from the marke I looke vnto,
With one hand quench the fire, with 'other feed.
One error doth a hundred errors breed,
If one I cut, to grow do ten begin.
This fleshly laberinth that I am in,
Is of the sinnefull race of Hydra's seed,
But yet my trauell still I will not spare,
Because I know, God hath on me a care.

SON. VII.

Faine would I bring some fruit of sauorie tast,
For offering of freewill and of my zeale ;
But I do feare my weakenesse to reueale,
—Like new wine in a crazèd vessell plast—
The vessell yet—not liquor—being mine,
And it fild in by master of the store,
I hope He will not at my gift repine,
But—if it faile—will it replenish more.
My weakenesse I do oftentimes deplore,
And for reliefe, to Him I do appeale :
Yet ioy, the bounty, that He daind to deale,

And halting hast, to those that go before.
In hope that my—nay His gifts—shall be grast,
Through loue vnto His Sonne, whom He imbrast.

SON. VIII.

I MARUELL much sometimes to see my will,
Contraried by my selfe with hart's consent;
To see me crosse the course my purpose ment,
And yet th'euent thereof proue better still.
I am by nature vnto euill prone,
And that pursue, with forward fleshly ayd:
Straight way my mind is chāgd—by means vnknown—
And heart consents, my former will be stayd.
The cause hereof, and issues I haue wayd,
And find them strange, yet bending in intent
Vnto my good—sometimes though ill I ment—
And fayld of plots, my greatest wisedome layd:
Which doth my soule in fine, with comfort fill,
To see God's prouidence, my purpose spill.

SON. IX.

I now begin to doubt my present state,
For that I feele no conflict in my mind;
A settled concord, needs must be vnkind,
Twixt flesh and spright, which should ech other hate;
They neere agree, but to their common woe,
And that through sin which luld them both a sleepe;
A warfare in this bodie would I goe,
Lest fraud, or treason in through rest should creepe.
The practises of Sathan are so deepe,
Armèd with flesh and lust—whom prone we find—
That hardly can the soule his freedome keepe,
But that these fiendes would him with frailty bind.
Vnlesse with heauenly weapons at debate,
With them we stand, and fight both rare and late.

SON. X.

When I remember, with what speed in post
The Iewes—return'd from bondage—tooke in hand

Their temple to ɪestore, and armèd stand,
In breach of wals to build, what enemies crost.
When I their bountie note, in offering store,
All freely giuen, and more then they could vse ;
How true their treasures were that would no more,
Their workmen's faith—accounts whilst kings refuse—
How these our latter times—which we accuse
Of ignorance, through fraud of Balaam's band—
Did yet powre forth the plenty of the land,
To holy vse, which other did abuse ;
I sorrow much to see true zeale cleane lost,
And pure religion shakt for sauing cost.

SON. XI.

What loue is this whereof the world doth tell,
Which they to God confesse and men admire ?
Loue hath his lawes, and doth effects require
Of charitie—to neighbour—to excell.
For as the members of one bodie bee
Partakers of the passion others haue,
And speedily concurre to helpe we see,
Because—thereby—the bodie's good they craue.
So if their loue to God they freely gaue,

And held Him head, their zeale would burne
like fire
To serue His saints, the needy to attire,
And home the stray to call, the lost to saue.
For how can they th' inuisible God loue
well,
Whē they neglect their neighbors, neer that
dwel?

SON. XII.

Who so will serue the Lord, he must bestow
The whole—not part—of body or of mind:
If in his heart dislike hereof he find,
His soule not yet regenerate we may know.
Betwixt two stooles no sitting safe there is,
And kingdomes so deuided cannot stand:
We must imbrace and loue or that or this;
And not looke backe, if plough be once in hand.
If God's we be, we Beliall must withstand,
We cannot Him well serue and Baal blind:
To Balak—Balam's kindnesse of such kind—
Did draw him to accurse the blessed land,
Whereby his asse did master's blindnesse show;
And still bewrays, weak faith, where this shal
grow.

[1] St. Matthew, vi. 24: St. Luke, ix., 62: Numbers xxii., 25. G.

SON. XIII.

GIUE all to Him that all did giue to thee:
More then His due thou hast not to bestow:
By yeelding all, thou thankfulnesse mayst show:
The more thy store, the more His gifts would bee.
A chearefull giuer God doth best accept,
Though He doth giue that gift thou dost present;
His blessings must be vsde and not be kept,
—Like fruitlesse tallents,—not to profit spent.
Thy soule and bodie both, since God hath lent,
The vse of them—entire—to Him should grow;
What is our power and strength, He well doth know:
And giues the will; which—vsde—He is content.
But for to share a part, that scorneth Hee
Who knows our thoughts, and secret hart doth see.

SON. XIIII.

BVT will you know—indeed—the surest way,
To make the child of God a loathing find

Of sinne—which doth infect both heart and
mind—
And vs the grace of God doth so denay?
Let man but see the fierce and angry face,
Let him behold a man deuoid of grace,
Whom euery thought and deed to death doth
wound.
Let him—if euer grace did so abound
In him, as he found God a father kind—
But call to mind how much it should him bind,
And how saluation standeth on that ground:
Then will he in his conscience surely say,
I will dwell no more in sinne, nor mends
delay.

SON. XV.

SOMETIMES cleane tyr'd, or sham'd of sinne at last,
—If not for loue of good, or feare of hell—
I seeke to stay affections which rebell,
And how to quench their heat my wits I cast:
I find euen while the thought is in my head,
A liking thought thereof doth me possesse:
From thoughts to liking are my humors led,
And liking longs againe to worke no lesse.
My laberinth felt, I seeke in vaine t' expresse,
An idle thought can not such thoughts expell:

I thinke to exercise my time so well
In some good work, as may vaine thoughts suppresse;
But I do tyre, ere litle time be past:
Prayer alone withstands the greatest blast.

SON. XVI.

Me thinkes sometime, I muse and much admire,
The dulnesse of the Iewes, who daily saw
The powrefull workes of Christ, which well might draw
A stony heart, to loue of Him t'aspire:
Much more I maruell that the words He spake,
Seem'd parables, and darke vnto His owne
Disciples; who His scholars He did make,
To whom all secrets should by time be knowne;
But when I find the wonders on vs showne,
Vnnoted or acknowledgéd, by awe,
Vnto His will, or word, or holy law,
And common ignorance by most men showne:
It makes me feare we want the holy fire
Of faith, loue, zeale, which dutie would require.

SON. XVI.

What vaine lip-labour is it men do vse

To speake of God, His name in word confesse?
When as in life no dutie they expresse
Of godlinesse, but fleshly freedome chuse:
Not euery one that cryeth often Lord,
Shall enter to possesse eternall rest:[1]
Vaine ostentation was—we see—abhord
In Pharise, whose speech and showes were best:
Hypocrisie the Lord did aye detest,
And chiefly that in them, His name should blesse,
As Anany, with Saphira[2] no lesse
Do witnesse by their death, at hand addrest;
Let vs therefore this babbling forme refuse,
Of boasting holinesse, which doth abuse.

SON. XVIII.

I goe about full oft—like Iewes most blind—
To offer vp to God a sacrifice
Propititiatorie, gratefull to His eies,
Thereby remission for my sinnes to find:
But lose my labour whilst I cleane forget,
First with my neighbour to be reconcild,[3]
A heape of rankor doth my conscience let,[4]

---

[1] St. Matthew, vii. 21. G. [2] Acts of Apostles, v. 5. G.
[3] St. Matthew, v. 24. G. [4] Hinder. G.

From looking for remorse in Father mild.
The mercies on the which my hopes should build,
My owne malicious purpose me denies;
For how should I that grace to gaine deuise,
Which from my neighbour's sutes I haue exild?
At temple dore my offering stayes behind,
Henceforth therefore, till malice leaue my mind.

SON. XIX.

O HAPPIE Simon of Syren,[1] art thou,
Who chosen wert that office to supply,
To beare part of the crosse, on which should die
Thy Sauiour,—world's new life and comfort true:—
Not wood I meane so much, which thou didst beare,
But that remorse, which thereby I suppose,
—Through shame and sorrow, pittie, care, and feare—
Which for His innocencie in thee rose,
Such crosses and full many more then those,
—Euen for my sinnes and for my selfe—wish I
As many as on fleshly strength might lye,

[1] St. Matthew xxvii. 32. G.

Or grace would aide, ere faith did comfort lose :
That for His seruant so He would me vow,
And try and vse me as He best knowes how.

SON. XX.

What are our senses drownd and past recure ?
Are rest and ease—the needfull aides of man,
Without vicisitude of which none can
Continue long—become by peace impure ?
Shall blessings proue our curse, desire our bane ?
Shall wish attaine his will ? Will worke our wo ?
Shall profit be our losse ? losse turne to gaine ?
Shall God's great goodnesse be requited so ?
Should father's kindnesse make a child a fo ?
—O God forbid !—our vowes were other, whan
Our tyrèd soules, our prayers first began
To send, as suters to our God to go.
His loue to vs did our desires procure ;
Let our desires His growing loue allure.

SON. XXI.

When I do see the mercies manifold,
Which God doth vse t'extend to His elect,
Whose actions alwaies He doth so direct,
That loue and fauour in Him they behold :

How things restrainèd vnto them are free,
  And all things holy to the holy are :
  How priuiledgd in euery thing they bee,
  And nothing from His loue can them debarre.
My mind from common comforts flyeth farre,
  And findes—on earth—no true ioy in effect;
  On God alone, I place my hart's affect :
  Where peace is perfect, without strife or iarre,
    And through these worldly cares I wander—
      bold,
    Secure—in courage, more then can be told.

SON. XXII.

Come to the councell of your common weale,
  Ye senses mine (which haue confederate bin
  With world and Satan, to infect with sin
  My soule, whose harbour in your house befell—
Thinke ye your safety great, when he is thrall ?
  That ye can scape, if soule once captiue bee ?
  That plagues she feeles, shall not on ye befall ?
  And ye with her, bring endlesse woe to mee ?
What earthly beauty can eyes brightnesse see ?
  What melodie heare eares ? what likèd smell ?
  What vnloathd tast, or feelings please so well,
  That are not often noysome vnto yee ?

Then—since such hazard great, short ioy ye
win—
To watch with me gainst common foes begin.

SON. XXIII.

In midst of plentie, and of happiest state,
Wherein by nature all men do delight,
Me thinkes I see, most cause of feare and
fright,
Most perils, and most dangerous growne debate:
A masking rout of treacherous bayted hookes,
Cast forth by Sathan for to choke the mind,
By euery sense, where so the thought but
lookes,
To draw vs to destruction, wretches blind:
It was graue prouidence of Iob I find,
—Fearing the charmes and dangers like to
light
On feeding children—praying day and night,
To mollifie the wrath of God most kind.[1]
Which would to God were vsd by vs like-
wise,
So should lesse euill of our mirth arise.

---

[1] Job i. 5. G.

SON. XXIIII.

How little comfort do I find—alas !—
In these vaine pleasures, which my flesh desireth ?
The vse of them full soone me cloyes and tireth,
And solace gone as thing that neuer was :
I striue sometimes to tast the same content,
In mirth and company that others find ;
Yet seldome tast the blisse I not repent,
And leaues no bitter sting or griefe behind :
In fine I finde the bodie is too blind
To iudge of happinesse, since it admireth
A shadow, which from memory retyreth,
And therefore chuse hencefoorth to feed my mind,
With some such solace, as that will not passe,
And I with comfort see, in faithfull glasse.

SON. XXV.

Well if I find no greater be my powre,
But yeeld and reele with euery puffe that blow'th,
And that my nature still such frailtie show'th,
As that my constant purpose fayles each howre :
If I can not approach or see the tree

Of fruit forbid, but needs I must it tast,
If lust unlawfull so abound in mee,
That headlong I must needes to ruine hast:
The readiest way to keepe my conscience chast,
Must be to shun occasions, where do grow
The rootes whence fruits of deadly poyson flow,
And therein only think my safeguard plast:
For—if I see—I hunger to deuowre
The bayt—soule's bane—and dwell in sinfull bowre.

SON. XXVI.

Who toucheth pitch shall therewith be defilde,
—The prouerbe saith, and practise sheweth plaine—
The purest conscience custome soone will staine,
And wisest wits, by boldnesse be beguilde:
We therefore warily had need to walke,
And stop temptations when they first do rise;
For euill deedes insue of euill talke,
And euill company polutes the wise.
We know that Sathan alwayes watchfull lies,
By many meanes, vs to his will to gaine;
If we a little yeeld, it is in vaine
For safe retreat to hope, or to deuise:

Vnlesse God's grace the bulwarke stronger build,
By which hel's powre is quencht, and he exilde.

SON. XXVII.

He that to do no euill doth intend,
He must do nought that may thereto belong;
He that is purposèd to do no wrong,
To thought or speech of ill, he must not bend:
Sinne is a theefe, and searcheth euery part,
And powre of man, to find a harbor fit;
He can disguise his purpose well by art,
And in a trap vs vnawares can git.
If we but kindly talke—to practise wit—
He soone can frame the minde to pleasing song:
The mind, the bodie soone can draw along,
To yeeld consent vnto, and practise it:
In fine he can vs teach sinne to defend,
And—noozled once therein—to find no end.

SON. XXVIII.

When I looke backe vpon the slipperie way,
Wherein my youth with other worldlings past,
I half amazèd do remaine, agast

To see the ruine wherunto it lay ;
So many by-pathes, crooked and vniust,
So many stops and stayes, and wayes impure ;
So little hold of helpe whereto to trust,
So many blockes my perill to procure :
Such flattering traines to ruine to allure,
As had not grace the gracelesse stayd at last,
I had my selfe to hell, euen headlong cast,
There to remaine without remead or cure :
I then—compeld—with thankes to God do say,
That in man's proper strength there is no stay.

SON. XXIX.

Among the many fierce assaults we haue,
To me impatience seemes most strong of all,
Which makes vs from our best defence to fall,
Of wisedome, reason, faith, which all do waue :
Our temp'rance thereby we do quickly loose,
Humilitie and loue we oft do shake ;
From law and reason we our eares do close,
And bit in teeth—like stubborne coltes—we take :
Of heauenly promist ayde, no count we make :
Of our deserts we take no heed at all ;

For vengeance we with fury onely call,
Or with dispaire we comfortlesse do quake;
When we—like Dauid—should lewd Simei saue,
In feare least God forth His commission gaue.[1]

SON. XXX.

Who seeketh ayde his frailties to withstand,
He may be sure he shall not deadly fall;
Who but for grace, to God doth truly call,
He shall find comfort doubtlesse out of hand:
To see his sinnes, to feare their vengeance due,
To call for grace, to seeke the same amend;
Of God's elections, tokens are so true,
That such—as His—He doubtlesse will defend.
If that his humbled heart, his soule do bend
To will of good, though fruit there be but small;
He cannot fruitlesse said to be at all,
Because His merits Christ to him doth lend:
And he as free shall be of promist land,
As those in whō more righteous worke He fand.

---

[1] 2 Samuel xvi. 9—14. G.

SON. XXXI.

It is not causelesse, Christ did vse compare
Man's mind vnto the soile that tillèd is;
They both fulwell indeed agree in this,
Vntillèd, they vnfrutefull are and bare:
Such seede as is bestow'd, they do receaue,
And both yeeld frute as God doth giue increase;
Some seed is spilt, some Sathan doth bereaue,
Some prosper, and produce a plenteous peace:
And as deuouring fowles do neuer cease,
Ne wormes, ne swine, to seeke do neuer mis,
Each one to spoyle a part, whilst plow-man his,
Due recompence of paines cannot possesse;[1]
So doth the soule, though tild with studious care,
Gret store of weedes bring forth, good frutes ful rare.

SON. XXXII.

If wo there was by Christ pronounst indeed,
Against Corasin and Bethsaiday,
Because vnpenitent they sluggish lay,
And to His preaching gaue not carefull heed;[2]

---

[1] St. Matthew xiii. 18-23. G.

[2] St. Matthew xi. 21: St. Luke x. 13. G.

Then woe and double woe I feare—alas !—
Belongs to vs, who scornefully reiect
The same word preachèd, which vnheard doth pas,
Or vnobayd—at least—through foule neglect :
Our liues, our double hearts, doth well detect,
Our want of charitie, selfe loue bewray ;
Our pride, our lusts, our couetous denay,
That eares haue heard, or hart doth grace affect :
Then woe is me that woe ourselues we breed,
And that for feare of woe, our hearts not bleed.

SON. XXXIII.

It should not seeme, that we do sinne detest,
As we professe, and make the world to thinke ;
When we not only at foule faults do winke,
But rather at the doers make a iest :
How could a thing displeasing mirth produce ?
Or heartie laughter grow, by heart's displeasure ?
To laugh at others fall doth shew an vse
Of our like guilt, who sinne so slightly measure,
The mouth doth speake from hart's abounding treasure,
The heart delights, when mind consent doth bring ;

The mind—polluted once by bodie's sting—
Infects whole man; on whom sinne then hath seasure,
And when—thus—sinne hath built a place of rest,
He makes vs euery euill to disgest.

SON· XXXIII.

THE fatall haps, and iudgements which befall
On others and on vs, remorse should breed:
For warnings of our selues they stand in steed,
And vs unto repentant feare do call:
They are not alwayes worst, who do sustaine
The greatest plagues, ne yet the others free
Of guilt—howbeit vnpunisht they remaine—
But rather for the more part worse they bee:
Christ's holy iudgement teacheth this to mee,
By fall of Sylo towre—the which indeed—
Slue not the worst;[1] and euen the best had need,
Their due deserts in others doome to see.
Let one man's wo, be warning then to all,
And life reformd, amend sinnes great and small.

[1] St. Luke xiii. 4. G.

SON. XXXV.

I often times endeuour to prepare
My mind, to beare with patience Nature's due,
Death, which—though fearefull—must perforce insue,
And which no humane flesh did euer spare:
I therefore when I see the many woes
That others do sustaine by liuing long;
The sicknesse, want, dishonour, spight of foes,
Which most men must sustaine by right or wrong:
The hazards which on earth to vs belong,
The doubtfull hopes and feares which aye renue;
Ten thousand fainèd pleasures—for one true—
And care to compasse them we haue among:
I grow to graunt, that life is but a snare,
Death, way to life, a life deuoyd of care.

SON. XXXVI.

Who sees the seed that in the ground is cast,
Cleane frō all weeds, without both chaffe and straw,
Yet afterward when haruest neare doth draw,
Shall see the weeds, increase therein so fast:

Who sees the trauell to receiue againe,
The corne from chaffe, and stubble cleansèd made,
May see corruption in the soule remaine,
Which so with drosse, the slender crop doth lade.
And in the soule may see like daily trade,
—By Nature's weakenesse, which vs keepes in awe—
So much, that though we heare and feare the Law
And Gospell, and in them a while do wade :
We bring few fruits—and them most bad—at last,
Which Sathan, world, and flesh, with sin haue blast.

SON. XXXVII.

Though lawfull many things indeed I find,
To such as do them with a conscience pure ;
Yet like I not my selfe, for to inure
To things, not pleasing to the weaker mind ;
And many lawfull things there are beside,
Which be not yet expedient to be done ;
A Christian's actions, must the tutch abide
Of such, as by example will be wonne.

For why, the ignorant do blindfold runne.
The trade that others tread, as way most sure,
And memory of ill, doth more indure
Then good, wherefore we warily should shunne
The action which may chance insnare the blind,
Although the wise from hazard safely wind.

SON. XXXVIII.

VAINE are the brags, and faith but fruitlesse is,
Of such who bost of vertue and holinesse,
When as profanèd speech doth yet expresse
A hollow heart, by tongue that talkes amisse.
The tongue declares th' abundance of the hart,
And by our speech we vse t' expresse our mind,
A truly touchèd soule, with wound doth smart,
When vaine or fruitlesse speech to rise they find:
But nature—forst—will soone returne to kind,
And who his seemelesse speech will not suppresse,
Vaine and deceitfull must his brags confesse,
And that delight in sinne is yet behind;
Who therefore hath no care at all of this,
His knowledge, zeale, and life receiues no blis.

SON. XXXIX.

I OFTEN others heare lament, and say
They cannot see the fruit they do expect
By prayer; and my selfe feele like effect,
Because indeed, I vnpreparèd pray.
Not that my knees with reuerence do not bow,
Or that my tongue, it doth not craue reliefe;
Or that my heart, my words doth not allow;
But charitie doth want, and firme beliefe,
Which to true praiers are assistants chiefe,
Both which—for most part—man doth vse neglect,
For want of either of which we are reiect,
And to our weaknesse addeth double griefe:
Who doth till reconcilement, offring stay,
His faithfull lawfull prayers, find no nay.

SON. XL.

THE season of the yeare, the natiue kind
Of euery creature to produce some thing,
Into my conscience doth this motion bring,
To God and Nature not to be unkind:
Two soyles I haue, and both vnfruitfull be,
Through weedes—of sin—which both them ouer grow:

The body barren and the soule I see,
Of vertuous fruits, which God and world I owe:
Vouchsafe yet Lord—Phauonean breath—to blow,
With heauenly grace inspiring so my mind,
That soule regenerate, in body find
Reformèd life, true life in me to show:
For fleshly fruits—too rife—to hell do fling,
Soule's blessed seed, ascends on angel's wing.

SON. XLI.

All men by nature greedy are to know,
And—knowing much—the more they do contend
—To draw vnto true knowledge perfect end—
By practise to the world, some fruits to show:
What knowledge is there then in heauen or earth,
—For one of wisedome great—so high and fit,
To trauell in, euen from the day of birth,
As that is gathered out of holy writ?
Therein is matter for each kind of wit,
Strange, ancient, pleasing, subtle, for to spend
The finest wits, and make them stoope and bend,
Whilst weakest braines, find skill and ioy in it.
Though high it reach, it beareth fruit below,
Which—tasted once—makes stomack strōger grow.

SON. XLII.

STRANGE are—in truth—the fruits that man doth
win,
And plentifull by vse of studie indeed,
Which appetite and matter still doth breed,
If but to gather them we do begin :
But heauenly studie much more copious is,
Contayning all that humane art doth teach :
And—not alone it feeds our minds with this—
But soule's true solace it doth further reach :
It doctrine supernaturall doth preach,
And doth diuinely sow the sacred seed
Which shall our soules with lasting comfort
feed,
And worldly skill, of ignorance appeach :[1]
That is the studie we should neuer lin[2]
To spell, read, conster, and to practise in.

SON. XLIII.

DOWNE let vs fling the battlements begonne
Of sinne, which in our soules so fast are built;
At first, or not at all it must be spilt,

[1] Transition form of 'impeach.' G.

[2] = cease. G.

Or else his fort—once made—the field is wonne.
If we neglect our watch, and not preuent
His practises but euen a little while,
Our trauell afterward is vainely spent,
And he our best attempts will soone beguile :
If we at lust's assaults but seeme to smile,
—Though lowly first he creepe, yet straight on stilt—
He will vpstart, and make vs yeeld to gilt,
And we ourselues soule's slaughter be the while,
Because we stay not sinne till it be donne,
But—rather—after it do fondly[1] runne.

SON. XLIIII.

There is great ods we see and must confesse,
Betwixt the speaker's and the doer's faith,
Words well, but deeds much better man bewraith,
And both conioynd, do dutie best expresse.
One promiseth to come—as was requir'd—
To feast ; the other it denyeth, but went : [2]
The first he did neglect what was desir'd,
The latter's deedes, do show he did relent :
He had the prayse and feast, who did repent,

[1] Foolishly. G. [2] St. Matthew xxi., 28-31. G.

His words, his blame, who breaking promise
stayth.
Whose life doth not confirme what tongue it
sayth,
—For all his brags—in end shall sure be shent,[1]
But who doth tongue and hart to God
addresse,
His deeds—be sure—with grace He still will
blesse.

SON. XLV.

Haue we not cause to blush full oft for shame,
To see how we neglect our neighbour's need?
How slow to helpe, where we might stand in
steed,
How slight excuses we do vse to frame:
When yet our Sauiour seemeth to respect,
The silly oxe which in the ditch doth lye,
Whose aide a stranger ought not to neglect,
If—but by chance—he saw it passing by:[2]
But if our brother readie were to dye,
—For very want necessities to feed—
We let Him sterue, and take of him no heed,

[1] Punished. G. [2] St. Matthew xii. 11.

Yea—though he craue—we stick not to deny,
As though it vs suffisd, to beare the name
Of Christians, yet in life deny the same.

SON. XLVI.

Not onely doth the Lord repute as good,
The deedes which He in vs Himselfe hath wrought;
—Yea though our wils 'gainst Him in thē haue fought,
And He perforce—by grace—our powers withstood—
But if we euill do, by stubborne will,
And seeke indeed no good at all thereby;
But euen our lewd affections to fulfill,
—So that all grace in vs do seeme to dye—
Yet euen in them, this good we shall espy,
—If we His children be whom Christ hath bought—
That He permits vs not to fall for nought,
But that our frailtie and our wits we try:
And so more earnestly vnto Him pray,
And find that pretious frute a Christian may.

SON. XLVII.

We had not need in idlenesse to spend

The dayes—both few and euill—which we haue :
The reason, powre, strēgth, helth which God vs gaue,
To some good end—no doubt—he did vs lend :
Full many businesses shall we find,
Enuironing our life on euerie side,
Which if they were retaynèd still in mind,
In watch and trauell they should cause vs bide :
The worldly cares of all men well are tride,
The daunger of the soule I seeke to saue ;
A world of lusts attend vs to the graue,
And Sathan lyes in waite to leade vs wide
From heauen, whereto true wisedome wils vs bend ;
Thinke then if man haue need watch to the end.

SON. XLVIII.

Since it hath pleasd the Lord, to set such store
Of blessings to the bodie, that it may,
In peace and plentie spend one ioyfull day,
—Which many want, and it long'd for before :
I not repin'd that it the same should vse,
But feard the frailtie of the flesh—alas !—
Which made my soule, for safest way to chuse,
—With Iob—in feare and care my time to pas :
For sacrifice, my soule there offered was,

Thy Holy Spirit, the priest, my will did slay;
His zeale inflam'd the thoughts which prostrate lay,
And quencht Thy wrath with teares like fluent glas,
So that—though Sathan readie was at dore
Me to accuse, and try—I feare no more.

SON. XLIX.

WHAT miracle so great hath euer bin
So farre from reason's, or from Nature's bounds?
What thing God's glory and His prayse resounds,
More then His mercie in forgiuing sinne?
If things contrary to their natiue kind,
—To ioyne accord, producing strange effects—
Do admiration breed in euery mind;
What thing so much God's glorie then detects,
As this, to see, how daily He protects
And blesseth vs in whom all vice abounds?
How He doth hide our faults which so Him wounds,
Supplies the want, which proper powre neglects.
Then—since distrust His miracles keepe backe—[1]
Let vs be sure, that we true faith not lacke.

[1] St. Matthew xiii. 58. G.

SON. L.

As those whose skill with colours life-like draw
 The portraitures of men, with shadowes rare,
 Yet shapes deformèd, they ne will nor dare,
 To shew to others, as themselues them saw :
So when I make suruay—by rule of truth—
 Of all my actions, and my soule's estate,
 I am asham'd to see the 'scapes of youth,
 And feare to looke on that I lou'd of late :
And as I do my selfe euen for them hate,
 So feare I others could no more me spare,
 If I should shew myselfe naked and bare,
 Who with these fowle affects held no debate ;
  Yet since they are but breaches of the Law,
  The Gospell will me shrowd from Sathan's paw.

SON. LI.

Among the many trauels of the iust,
 The last, which holy Iob—alas !—sustaind ;
 I thinke his soule and bodie most it paind,
 And like thereto—vs likewise martyr must,
When we—vpon vs—feele God's heauie curse
 For sinne, from which no one of vs is free ;
 That comforters should seeke to make vs worse,
 And friends like foes, should our tormentors bee.

To hud-blind[1] vs when most we need to see,
By colouring sinne, which ought to be explaind,
Or amplifying errors which are faind,
To make our soules and bodies disagree:
All these he felt by friends he most should trust,
To hell by pride, or by dispaire to thrust.

SON. LII.

Slow is our God—indeed—and very slo
To wrath, and that the wicked dearly find;
His children sooner feele correction kind,
And so repent, whilst sinfull forward go.
Slow though He be, yet sure His iudgements are:
They are deferd, they are not cleane forgot;
He tries our natures, letting raines so farre,
Lose to our wils, that we regard Him not:
But when we furiously to hell do trot,
He stayes our steps, and wils doth gently bind,
Whiles He the reprobates the more doth blind,
Till they—through sinne—do fall to Sathan's lot:
By God's correcting hand and patience so,
The one to sinne inclines, the other fro.

---

[1] Transition-form of hood-wink. G.

SON. LIII.

When I consider of the holy band,
Of loue and mercie with the Iewes was made,
The heauenly and earthly blessings which did lade,
Their soules and bodies, whilst in grace they stand.
When I examine cause of this their change,
And note in soule and bodie wofull fall;
How exiles—comfortlesse—the Earth they range
Depriu'd of knowledge, glory, hope, and all:
When I—as cause hereof—to mind do call,
Their stubborne, faithlesse, and ingratefull trade;
—With which the prophets did them oft vpbrayd,
And causes were of wrath from heauen not small—
Methinkes I see like iudgement neare at hand,
For trespasse like, to punish this our land.

SON. LIII.

O that we could be rauishèd awhile,

[1] Bond or covenant. G.

Fro out these fleshly fogs, and seas of sin,
Which grosse affections daily drench vs in,
And do the tast of perfect sense beguile :
That so whilst selfe-loue slept, true loue might show ;
That pride might so put on an humble mind,
That patience might insteed of rankor grow,
And naked truth, from craft might freedome find :
That vertue had some harbor safe assignd,
And reason had his scope, and did begin
—Of these fowle fiends—a victorie to win,
And them in bondage to the soule to bind :
Then should we see how farre they do exile
Our perfect blisse, whilst thus they vs defile.

SON. LV.

LIKE master like the seruants proue—say we—
We therefore are—of like—of Sathan's traine,
His auncient lesson which did parents staine,
We learne as yet, and lie as fast as he.
False are his rules, himselfe an old deceiuer,
Vntrue he is, vntruth he first did teach ;
God being truth, nought can so soon disseuer,
And no one sin to more offence doth reach :

Sathan himselfe can not God's lawes appeach[1],
To be vniust, nor say we iust remaine,
But by new names doth his fraile scholars gaine
To follow follies which affections preach;
Lust, wrath, and couetise, pride cald we see,
Loue, value, thrift, and clenlinesse to bee.

SON. LVI.

We may reioyce, but yet in Christ alone:
Alone in Him is cause of true joy found,
All other ioy is but indeed vnsound,
Perfection or continuance elsewhere none:
If man with Salomon the hap might haue
To tast each earthly pleasure he desir'd,
He would but giue that prayse the other gaue,
That—once possest—their pleasure straight retir'd:
From Earth to heauenly knowledge he aspir'd,
And humane wisedome he did throughly sound;
In which he saw calamities abound,
And did neglect as vaine, things most admir'd.

[1] Transition-form of 'impeach,' as before. G.

In this alone, contented ioy is showne,
To loue, feare, serue, this Christ our corner
stone.

SON. LVII.

Wise Moses and graue Talion's law[1] seuere,
Do well agree to reason naturall :
And God in like sort, lets his iudgements fall,
So that our sinnes their proper vengeance beare :
As eye for eye, and tooth for tooth was due,
So Nature doth our faultes for most part pay,
With pennance by it selfe which doth insue,
As we shall find if we our actions way :[2]
And God Himselfe doth on th' adúltrer lay,
On wrathfull, couetuous, and proud men all,
Shame, bloud, want, scorne, vnlesse in time they
call
For grace, which only can their ruine stay :
Whereby we see, whom men keepe not in
feare,
God makes—by Nature—badge of trespasse
weare.

---

[1] Lex talionis. G. [2] = weigh. G.

SON. LVIII.

It seemeth strange since death so common is,
That daily we experience thereof haue,
By rich, and poore, wise, fooles, that go to graue;
That we so little heed do take of this:
Since nought so much contrarie to our will,
Doth flesh befall, or Art doth seeke to shun;
That yet we headlong hast to ruine still,
Of soule and bodie, which to hell would run.
Scarce we so soone to liue haue but begun,
But—drenchèd in affection's[1] fearefull waue—
We seeke to slay the soule, we wish to saue;
And no outrage in bodie leaue vndone:
So that if God did not—of mercie His—
Perforce our wils restraine, we heauen should mis.

SON. LIX.

Who would not craue to haue his wounds be heald?
Who can be heald that will not shew his griefe?
Who—senseless of his paine—would know reliefe?

[1] = evil affection or passion. G.

Who can giue cure, whilst truth is not reueald?
Who can be iudge of ill, that knowes no good?
Who can know good, that shuns to learne the same?
Who can it learne, that selfe-loue hath withstood?
Who can condemne himself, that knowes no blame?
Knowledge must first our minds more lowly frame,
Through lowlinesse will feare and sorrow grow;
Feare will seeke forth a pledge for debt we owe,
And pledge and portion find in Christ His name:
Thus knowledge of our state, and pride repeald,
Is way to sauing health, by Scripture seald.

SON. LX.

The weapons which I did vnwieldy find,
Of natiue strength, and powre of flesh and bloud,
—With like whereof Goliah me withstood—
And I for changèd sling—left once behind—
By God's good grace—Who courage gaue and strength—
Is now become a sword more fit for mee,
Who—practisd in His battels now at length—

The vse thereof, find not vnfit to bee :
For since to Him it dedicate I see;
And I refreshèd am with holy food,
My courage makes me hope I weare it shood,
And cause my soule's great foe therewith to flee.
For humane arts and knowledge of the mind,
Do serue the saints, though worldlings they do blind.

SON. LXI.

It is not rest from trauell and from paine
Alone, that in the Sabboth is requir'd ;
Not abstinence from meat, that was desir'd
So much, when Ionas did his fast ordaine,
As rest from sinne, and inward meditation
Of God's great workes, and mercies which abound ;
As feeding of our soules with recreation
Of heauenly doctrine, in the Scriptures found :
As by prostrating humbly on the ground,
Our stubborne hearts puft vp and almost fir'd
With wicked lusts,—with vanitie attir'd—
Festerd with all affections most vnsound ;
A Sabboth or a fast so spent, is gaine,
Whē flesh beat down, the sprite doth raisd remaine.

SON. LXII.

WHAT is the cause that men so much eschue
The reading of the sacred written word?
For nought else sure but that—like two-edg'd sword—
It separates and shewes the faults from true:
Ne sentence in it read or truly wayd,
—Or by the preacher vtterd—turnes in vaine,
But woundes the soule with sorrow, which affrayd,
—If God's it be—to grace it cals againe:
But such as Sathan's be, to heare refraine,
The heauy iudgements that they haue incurd;
And—faithlesse—thinke, God can ne will afford
To them, the blisse that children His attaine.
It is a signe therefore, grace neuer grew,
In such as shun to heare, and learne anew.

SON. LXIII.

WHEN I do heare sweet Musick's pleasant sound,
By which the angels' records are exprest,
—Who sing to God due prayses without rest—
Me thinkes to pray with them my selfe am bound:
When I the concord sounds of true consent,
Do note, which by their different voice is bred,

It makes my hart to melt to see man bent,
By discord to dissolue the blisse, that led
To heauenly comfort, which the angels fed,
And is of Christian loue perfection best;
Whose vnitie in Christ hath made them blest,
To liue in Him when law had left vs dead:
The saints therefore on Earth should aye be found,
With thankfull, ioyfull hearts of loue t'abound.

SON. LXIIII.

As doth the fire, which imbers[1] ouer-spred,
And powder in the cannon rammèd hard,
—By which his furies but awhile debard,
When they breake forth—procure more feare and dred:
As aire in cloud, or earth restrainèd long,
Doth by his nature in the end preuaile:
And—in reuenge of his so sufferèd wrong—
Doth earth-quake breed, or thūndring firebolts haile:
So when increasing sins, afresh asaile,
Our God of mercie, then is He prepard,

[1] Embers. G.

Our insolencies fiercely to reward
With double ruine, which He will not faile
To terrifie those that in sinne are dead,
Whilst His to liue—reseru'd—thereby are lead.

SON. LXV.

When I do see a man of loftie mind,
Delighting in the pompe he doth possesse;
A ruine or a shame at hand I gesse,
For which effect God doth His iudgement blind:
For as most daintily we vse to feed,
The beasts to slaughter that we haue ordaind:
So surfet of delights, a feare should breed,
Least sowrer penance afterwards remaind:
The proofe hereof hath still the godly waynd,[1]
From pride, or too much trust in happinesse;
Which do not still God's fauour firme expresse,
But vsd as trials are, of conscience faynd;
We therefore cause of care in plenty find,
To moue vs pray, and watch the end behind.

---

[1] Weaned. G.

SON. LXVI,

As doth the morning comfort to vs bring,
By giuing light to guide vs in our wayes;
As sun-shine beames his beautie then displayes,
To solace, feed, refresh each earthly thing:
So should—me thinkes—a thankfull heart thereby,
Be mou'd, to waigh the fruits by them we haue,
And by that light a greater light espy,
Who these—for bodie's good—vnto vs gaue:
Like light vnto his soule forthwith to craue,
Whereby it sleeping—void of holy rayes
Of grace—in sinne doth spend away the dayes,
Which Christ our Sauiour died, the same to saue;
Vnto Thee Lord—Creator, powrefull king—
With birds by break of day they prayse shold sing.

SON. LXVII.

I LIST[1] not iudge or censure other men:
As I do iudge, so iudge me others will,
And God Himselfe that part can best fulfill:
With others faults I will not meddle then,

[1] = choose. G.

Vnlesse so farre as dutie doth desire,
Which is with loue to warne them of the way ;
Whose weaknesse doth our louing aide require,
To stay their steps wherein they are astray :
But I must iudge myselfe—doth scripture say—
And that I will, but not by natiue skill :
The Law and Gospell they shall try me still,
And their true touch, shall my estate bewray :[1]
My conscience witnesse more then thousands ten,
My hart confesse my faults with tongue and pen.

SON. LXVIII.

I SEE sometimes a mischiefe me beset,
Which doth amaze me much, and griefe procure ;
I haue a hope or hap I wish t' endure,
But it doth vanish straight, and I do fret.
I craue sometimes of God with feruencie,
A thing—me thinkes—which might worke to my ioy,
My prayers yet He seemeth to denie,
And by the contrary doth worke my'annoy :
I find at length the thing I scorn'd—as coy—
Fall to my profit, and doth me assure,

[1] = choose or reveal. G.

That God by this His goodnesse doth allure
Me to depend on Him, and not to toy
—By natiue reason guided,—but to let
His prouidence haue praise, and honor get.

SON. LXIX.

How should I vse my time henceforth the best?
The little that remaines ought well be spent:
Too much lost time, cause haue I to repent,
Best mends must be, well to imploy the rest.
To pray and prayse the Lord is fit for me,
To craue things needfull, and His mercies tell;
My spirituall wants and carnall plenties be,
As many yet His blessings which excell:
But multitude of words please not so well,
He knowes the heart, which righteously is bent:
All holy actions are as prayers ment,
And He is praysd, when sinne we do repell:
Then if my life, the world and flesh detest,
I pray and prayse, and shall finde actions blest.

SON. LXX.

Good words are praisd, but deeds are much more rare:

One shadow is, the other substance right,
Of Christian faith — which God and man delight—
Without which fruits our barren tree is bare :
Deed[1] well done, is more comfort to the soule,
More comfort to the world, to God more prayse,
Then many learnèd words which sinne controule,
Or all lip-labour that vaine glorie sayes.
Who in a holy life doth spend his dayes,
And still maintaine gainst sinne a valiant fight,
He preacheth best, his words are most of might,
He shall conuert men most from sinfull wayes :
Such shall haue honor most—affirme I dare—
With God and man, and lesse of worldly care.

SON. LXXI.

SINCE we by baptisme, seruants are profest
To Christ, Whose name we—as an honor—beare,
It is good reason, we His liuery weare,
And not go ranging vainely with the rest:
Since we do feed—by bountie of His hand—
On precious food, which He doth giue and dresse ;

---

[1] Misprinted 'once'. G.

—Who at the well of life doth ready stand
Vs to refresh, if thirst do vs oppresse.—
We are too slow our selues to Him t'addresse,
To craue and vse these gifts in loue and feare:
His righteous liuery we do rather teare,
Then whom we serue by vse thereof expresse:
Little he got that was such bidden guest,
And how can thanklesse seruants then be blest.

SON. LXXII.

SINCE shame of men much more then godly feare,
Restraineth vs from sinne, as proofe doth preach;
Since more we after name of vertue reach,
Then to the truth thereof we loue do beare:
It were a part of wisedome to deuise,
To vse our nature—of it selfe so vaine—
From so base custome—euen for shame—to rise
To actions good, which might true honor gaine.
The best remede[1] I therefore find remaine,
To purchase prayer, and vertue's habit teach,
Is to professe the same in speech, whose breach
In life we should refraine, lest we should straine

[1] = remedy. G.

Our name, which would at length our liking
reare,
To loue of God indeed, and sinnes forbeare.

SON. LXXIII.

The difference is right great—a man may see—
Twixt heauen and earth, twixt soule and body
ours,
Twixt God and man, heauen's powre and earthly
towres :
As great the difference, in their vse must bee.
By high, ambitious, and by wrathfull sword,
Are earthly , transitory kingdomes gaynd ;
Humilitie with patient deed and word,
To heauenly crowne and honour doth attaine :
Man will his conquest with vaine glory staine ;
Heauen's kingdom former pride forthwith
deuours,
It equals all estates, sects, skils, and powres,
And makes the bodie well vnite remaine,
Whereof the head is Christ, the members we,
And held coheires of heauen with Him we be.

SON. LXXIIII.

For vs who do by nature still incline
Vnto the worst, and do the best forget,

Who do all passèd benefits lightly set,
And so vnthankfully gainst God repine:
It were great wisedome dayly to obserue,
Such sundry haps as do to vs befall,
By which to learne, how much God doth deserue
Who those, and passèd benefits gaue vs all.
And since there is not any blisse so small,
But for the which, we ought acknowledge debt,
On each occasion we should gladly get,
A meanes our mindes to thankfulnesse to call.
For nought God craues, ne we can giue in fine,
But drinke with thankes His cup of sauing wine.

SON. LXXV.

THE parable of seed well sowne on ground,
Which did according—as the soyle did sarue—
Some neuer bud, some bloome, some straight-way starue,
Some grow, and in His crop so much abound:
Doth well describe—as Christ full well applyes—
The nature of the word, the which is sent
By written Gospell and by preacher's cryes,
Into the heart, which—hearing—it doth rent:

And—as well tild—sometimes begins relent,
And yeeldeth blessed fruit, and prayse desarue;
As God the showres of grace doth freely carue,
And diligence in weeding it is spent:
For many times such sinfull tares are found;
As good has bin the seed in sea had drowned.[1]

SON. LXXVI.

I cannot chuse—but yet deuoyd of pride—
To note the happie and the glorious time
Wherein we liue, and flourish in the prime
Of knowledge, which those former dayes not tride:
For all preheminences which are read,
—Forespoke of latter age by prophets all—
As happie were perform'd, as promisèd,
When Christ those mysteries did on Earth vnfold,
And those accomplish which were long foretold:
The same, yea more by farre—we dust and slime
Vnworthy wayers of Thee, high we clime—
Enioy, through preachèd truth more worth thē gold.

[1] St. Matthew xiii., 3 *et seqq.* G.

But woe is me, this grace is vs denyde,
We—to our selues—haue not the same applyde.

SON. LXXVII.

If thou do feele thy fleshly thoughts repine,
When thou dost beare the crosses God doth send,
And that thou under burden of them bend,
And out of due obedience wouldst vntwine:
Remember when as yet a child thou wast,
Thou sufferedst patiently the parent's rod,
Because thou knewst his hatred could not last,
Though he thee punisht, doing thing forbod:
And wilt not thou much more yeeld vnto God
Obedience, who thy good doth still intend?
Whose fatherly protection doth defend
Thee from His wrath, when sinne had made thee od:
The father to thy soule He is in fine,
His wrath asswag'd, His loue doth soone encline.

SON. LXXVIII.

True is it sure, and none will it denay,
That faith inableth man to be more fit

For heauenly knowledge then a humane wit:
To which, hid secrets God will not bewray.
But what is faith, and how it may be knowne,
How best attaynd, in that most men mistake:
In iudgement of the same would care be showne,
And of true faith from false, this difference make;
If worldly strength and wisedome man forsake,
If he by humble prayers seeke for it,
If of God's promises he doubt no whit
In Christ, but for his strength that rocke he take,
It builded is on ground which still shall stay,
From fleshly bondage free, at latter day.

SON. LXXIX.

What high presumption is there growne of late,
In abiect shrubs of Sathan's darnell seed?
That—bramble-like—sinne thus aspires indeed,
To top the cedar, that his pride doth hate?
I graunt the fault in suffering him so long,
In humble shape to creepe and clime so hie;
Sinne—poyson-like—with age becomes more strong,
And crokadell-like doth slay with teares in eie:
But since therefore no other shift I spy,

I like and will my loftie top abate,
My prostrate soul, may so restraine the state
Of his increasing powre, whereby that I
In building of God's house may serue some steed,
And sinne confounded lie, like lothsome weed.

SON. LXXX.

Who sees in common view of humane kind,
The exild captiue-state of sinfull man,
Sold vnto death—which onely ransome can,
Appease the wrath for fall of parents blind—
May,—if he be of faithfull number,—proue
A greater comfort then he can expresse,
To see himselfe, whose sinnes these plagues do moue,
Freed from th' eternall death, whilst nerethelesse
The wicked reprobate, who not confesse
Their fall, nor feele the fauours Christians wan,
Headlong proceed, in path first parents ran,
And to the double death, themselues addresse:
But happier he ten thousand times shall find,
His weakest state, then their great gifts of mind.

SON. LXXXI.

WHO giues may take, we ought not to repine:
Both wealth, and ease, yea life also by right,
God giueth all, all things are in His might,
And He can send and will, good end in fine,
Why should we then grudge any thing to beare,
That He doth send? or nigardly bestow
Our liues or goods? since to that vse they were
Giuen vs, as Nature teacheth vs to know.
The greate increase of fruite the same doth show,
Which from one graine producéd is in sight,
Which as thing cast away appeares to light,
Till He—by blessing His—doth make it grow—
Which should our hearts to faith in Him incline,
And not distrusting seeke for farther signe.

SON. LXXXII.

OVR blinded natures that cannot foresee,
Th' effect of nature, or what may succeed
Of actions ours, this error forth doth breed,
That we th' euent, by chance suppose to bee:
To vs they may indeed by hap befall,
—As things beyond our skill and powre to stay—
But—as God's works—chance can we not them call,

Or fortune's deed, or hap as we vse say :
God doth foresee, and guide each thing the way,
It shall proceede, and He doth giue the speed,
That doth insue, and present are indeed,
Things past and future, as they stand or stray :
Him as true cause of all things wee agree
To be, and from all chance and fortune free.

SON. LXXXIII.

It is a thing we lightly do neglect,
And yet a thing—me thinks—we most should feare,
As which within our conscience still doth beare
A witnesse of our guilt, and soule infect :
When we by fame do find our spotted name,
—The greatest plague a man on Earth may find,
The hardest witnesse of our worthy shame,
And sorest censurer of deed or mind,—
Yet so selfe loue—doth iudgement often blind,
Or ignorance our natiue reason bleare,
That what is said or thought, by whom or where,
We little care, but let it passe as wind;
Though prouerbe truely say, by fame's affect,
God's iudgement lightly doth a truth detect.

SON. LXXXIIII.

If common fame be lightly, likely found,
And fame for ill be such vnhappinesse,
Then this—me thinkes—a man must needs confesse,
That ill report—from person's good—doth wound.
If by report, much more if poore opprest,
If innocents, if they to God complaine,
If vengeance they do call, to haue redrest,
The griefes and agonies they do sustaine:
If God—as so He hath—hath witnest plaine,
That He will heare their cries whom men oppresse,
And will His care of them herein expresse,
That their complaints and cryes turne not in vaine;
What yron age is this, that such a sound
Of cryes against oppression doth abound?

SON. LXXXV.

My younger thoughts do wish me to withstand
The graue aduise, which grace with loue doth lend,
Their rash decrees to tyranny do bend:

These wish me—wisely—note the cause in hand;
The safe possession of a crowne in peace,
By abstinence a while, and patience vsd:
Sinne's power to shew, the others vrge, ne cease
To say, that pleasures should not be refusd:
The worser part my soule had almost chusd,
And for the pleasures which an hour doth send,
—And to eternall bondage after tend—
I bin by law and reason both accusd:
But since Thy goodnesse Lord gaue blessed land,
Keepe in Thy lawes my fleshly subiect's band.

SON. LXXXVI.

Alas! how watchfull and how diligent
We are to further euerie fond desire:
How slow againe to thing God doth require,
And how against the haire, good motions went.
Full many more solicitors we find,
To satisfie each trifle flesh doth craue,
Then to the things good conscience would vs bind,
And which—as duties—God in law vs gaue:
The wit, will, memorie, we ready haue
To blow the bellowes of affection's fire;

The soule may drenchèd perish in the mire
Of fleshly thoughts, ere any seeke to saue,
Or spare one minute—which is fondly spent—
To succour it, though it to good were bent.

SON. LXXXVII.

We haue bene babes, babes yet by nature we,
Vnskilful, ignorant of heauenly law,
And babe-like should be then in feare and awe
To God, by Whom create and rulde we be:
Weake food best fits weake stomacks—as is sayd—
And charitie would wish true weaknesse beare;
Like strength to all God's wisedome hath denayd,
But by long sucking t'were fit we stronger weare:
Nothing to beare away, though much we heare,
To speake of faith, which forth no fruites can draw,
To feed with greedinesse the bodie's maw,
And yet no spirituall strength to let appeare,
Is signe the soule is dead, in thee or mee:
For liuing trees, by kindly fruit we see.

SON. LXXXVIII.

Not euery action which to happie end
  A man doth bring, is token as I find
  Of goodnesse in the doer, though our mind
  And common sense some reason so pretend:
The deed which meriteth—for vertue—prayse,
  Must be premeditate in will before,
  Indeuour'd lawfully, and which bewrayes,
  No priuat obiect or respect we bore;
And God Himselfe things iudgeth euer more,
  Not by effects, as men of wisedome blind,
  But by intentions faithfull, honest, kind,
  Of such as doing them His aide implore:
    He issue doth to actions different send,
    As He to greater good—euen[1] ill—will bend.

SON. XLIX.

If God should measure vs as we deserue,
  —For each offence requiting equally—
  His iustice we with horror should espie,
  From which excuse—to shield vs—could not
    serue:
But iustice His by holy bounds restraind,

[1] Misprinted 'euer'. G.

Of mercie, which doth weigh our weake estate,
A proper counterpoise for vs hath gaind,
Whilst iustis' wrath, Christ's mercy doth abate;
His Sonne our Sauiour, doth set ope a gate
To safetie, by the pardon He did bye,
With bloud most innocent, lest we should die,
Guilty of sin, which iustice needs must hate.
Thvs we—by faith—cannot be said to swarue,
Our faults are His, of merits His we carue.

SON. XC.

It is a custome that deserueth blame,
And ouer common with vs now a dayes,
That euery man his fault on other layes,
And some excuse for euery euill frame,
And rather then we will the burden beare,
We lay on God—Whose prouidence rules all—
The cause of what our wicked natures were
Producers of, with wilfull bitter gall.
Thus from one sin to other we do fall,
And haires[1] herein our nature vs bewrayes,
Of parent first, who his offence denaies,
And rather God, wife, serpent guilty call,

[1] = heirs. G.

Then to confesse his proper free-will lame,
And by repentance praise God's holy name.

SON. XCI.

How can He be the author held of ill,
Who goodnesse is itselfe, and onely true?
To Whom alone perfection still is due,
And all the world, with goodly workes doth fill?
It is not God, it is our selues alas!
That doth produce these foule affects of sin,
Our sickly nature first infected was,
And lacking tast of truth, delights therein:
Our deeds in vs, how fowle so ere they haue bin,
What good soeuer of them doth insue,
That part is God's, our corrupt nature drue,
The worser part; and flesh, death, snares did spin,
And euen our deeds, the which our soules do kill,
Are good to God, and worke His glorie still.

SON. XCII.

Doth any man desire his life to mend,
And that of sin he might a lothing finde?
Let him but on his actions looke behinde

Forepast, and see where to they most did bend :
Let him on others' looke with equall view,
And note deformitie of lothfull sin,
Let reason—not affections—tell him true,
The brickle[1] state himselfe to fore was in ;
As doctrine, that to penitence doth win,
And true repentance, one of honest mind,
When he in other sees affects so blind,
As he in reason thinks could not haue bin :
Such as himselfe ashameth to defend,
And to be guiltlesse off, he would pretend.

SON. XCIII.

I haue desir'd, and held as chiefe delight,
To lead my life, where mirth did alwaies dwell,
From soule, so sorrow thinking to repell,
In feast and sport so past I day and night :
But if—as oft there did—a dismall chance
Befall, whereby I found some cause of griefe,
I was amaz'd, dispair'd, and as in trance,
No comfort found, or meanes to giue reliefe ;
My former ioyes prouokèd sorrow chiefe,
I loathd the thoughts before did please so well,

[1] = brittle. G.

My meditations then of death befell,
And of world's pleasures, which were vaine and chiefe,
Which made me chāge my former humor quight,
For teares, cares, sorrows, still to be in sight.

SON. XCIII.

SINCE we are found—if we our selues do know—
To be a barren ground, and good for nought,
Vnlesse by husbandrie we will be brought,
To aptnesse for some good whereon to growe:
Since preachers are the husbandmen ordaind,
And preaching of the prophets, is the seed,
By whose indeuours onely fiute is gaind,
Of holy life, the which our faith doth feed;
Me thinkes it should a greater aptnesse breed,
In tennants to this soule, which Christ hath bought,
To haue it so manurde and daily wrought,
As it might grow to betterd state indeed,
And yeeld some crop of goodnesse which might show
The thankfull hearts, which we to God do owe.

SON. XCV.

When I behold the trauell and the payne,
Which wicked men in euill actions bide,
What hazards the assay to goe aside,
When with more ease, they vertue might attaine:
How theeues and murtherers such boldnesse vse,
Such watchfull painefull meanes their wills to win,
As euen religious men do oft refuse,
To tast of like, though they would faine begin:
I finde too true, that we are sold to sin,
And that the bodie doth the spirit guide,
That reason yeelds to sense, and sense doth hide
Lust in his liking, which doth forward slide
From ill to worse and neuer doth refraine
Sin, which may sin; nor paine, which paine may gain.

SON. XCI.

Since nothing is more certaine then to dye,
Nor more vncertaine, then the time and howre,
Which how to know, is not in Phisicke's powre:
Yet Nature teacheth it, to be but nie;
For that death stealeth on vs like a thiefe,

And nothing liuing is exempt therefro :
His malice to preuent is wisedome chiefe,
That vnprouided he not take vs so :
As that on sodaine he appeare a foe,
And vs compulsiuely he do deuowre,
That God by him in wrath doe seeme to lowre,
And that to death,—not life—we seeme to goe ;
So let vs liue that death we dare defie,
Since heauen's eternall life, we gaine thereby.

SON. XCVII.

GREAT are the graces God in man doth show,
All tending chiefly to soule's proper gaine,
That by some meanes at length He might attaine
To higher thoughts, from earthly base and low :
Yet since no benefits we do receaue,
Can so assure vs of His loue indeed,
That loue of world and Earth they can bereaue,
And make our minds on heauenly ioy to feed ;
Much lesse a new desire in vs can breed,
To win the heauens by losse of life so vaine,
This common way by death He made remaine,
Ineuitable to all humane seed ;

By force those heauenly ioyes to make
vs know,
Which after death in lasting life shall grow.

SON. XCVIII.

Might Elizeus wish allow'd be,
And prayer blest, which Salomon did make,
And canst thou then thy trauell vndertake,
For worthier prize then they haue showne to
thee?
Sure heauenly wisedome earthly wisedome
teacheth;
Such wisedome findeth grace with God and
man,
Who seekes these first, God plenteously him
reacheth
All other earthly gifts he wisht or can:
That will I seeke, that will I studie than,
No plenty shall my thirst thereafter slake,
With Elizeus will I alwayes wake,
And watch the prophets wayes and manner
whan
My Sauiour doth ascend, that I may see
His glory, and He His grace redouble in
mee.

SON. XCIX.

LONG do the wicked runne a lawlesse race,
Vncrost and vncontrollèd in their will;
Their appetites at pleasure they do fill,
And thinke themselues to be in happie case:
But stay awhile, and let me see the end,
—Which crowneth euery good and perfect deed—
And you shall find their slipperie way to bend
To ruine, if in time they take not heed:
To earthly ease security doth breed,
Securitie the soule doth lightly kill,
It breeds forgetfulnesse of God, and still,
Doth quench the spright, and bodie pampering feed;
Who therefore doth delights too much imbrace,
Among the blest, may hap to lose his place,

SON. C.

LIKE as the sunne whose heat so needfull is,
Produceth daily different effects,
According to the nature of obiects,
Which hardneth that, yet molifieth this:
So doth the Gospell preachèd euen the same;
It makes some to repent and melt in teares,

Some stubborne hearts repine, and cauils frame
To quarrell at, and scorne such needlesse feares.
The lowly heart, in ioy and hope it reares,
The haughty mind, as low assoone deiects ;
In zealous hearts it neighbour-loue reflects,
Whiles other conscience, spight and rankor beares :
The natiue powre it keepes of perfect blisse,
And holy heat, consuming all amisse.

Epil[ogue.]

Tempt me no more to dwell in cedar tents,
Pauilions of princes and of pride ;
My tickle strength is dayly like to slide,
And makes my bodie do what soule repents,
My yeares forwarne me to forbeare annoy,
In likèd things, which do the sences feed,
In costly colours, gems, or games to ioy,
Or stately troopes, or honor's fruitlesse seed.
For passèd vanities my heart doth bleed,
And vowed hath the resting time I bide,
—If God in constancie my heart shall guide—
Some ryper frutes on former soyle to breed ;
Which graunt me Lord, that so Thy seruant I,
May in Thy courts remaine, and flesh defye.

An Introduction to Pecoliar Prayers.

To Thee—O Lord—who only knowst my sin,
And only able art, my state redresse,
To Thee alone my plaints directed bin,
To Thee my guilt alone I do confesse:
In hope Thy gracious aide at neede to win,
Who giuest me grace, these prayers to addresse:
My words can not expresse my inward griefe,
My deedes declare too well my true disease,
Yet doubt I not to craue of Thee reliefe,
Because Thy Sonne did first Thy wrath appease:
These are my wants, and many more then these,
But of them all, vnfaithfulnesse is chiefe:
Yet as repentant thiefe, on crosse found grace,
Vouchsafe my plaints with mercie to imbrace.

SON. CI.—*Craues grace to pray.*

O Powrefull God in Christ our Father deare,
Who mad'st and rul'st all things euen by Thy will,

Whose truth and loue, the heauens and Earth do fill,
Vouchsafe my will to frame, and prayers heare,
Touch Thou my heart, my blinded iudgement cleare,
That sorrow for my sinnes may teares distill:
Let true repentance kill all carnall lust,
Let purpose to amend, my soule direct,
To craue Thy aide, Who only canst protect
Man's feeble strength from thoughts, words, deeds, vniust:
Fraile is man's powre and will, his substance dust,
His purest actions, hourely it detect;
Yet do Thou not reiect Thy worke in me,
Who craue a will to pray, and faithfull be.

SON. CII.—*Salutation of the Church.*

HAILE sacred seate of God's eternall peace,
Where all His blessings kept in treasure are,
Twixt soule and bodie, which accords the iarre,
And causest cumbers of discord to cease;
From wandring worldly thoughts Thou doest release
My doubtfull hope, which sought for help from farre:

In Sathan's fiercest warre, a bulwarke strong,
In Nature's hote assault, a sure defence,
An arke of safety for our feeble sence,
A watchman's towre to those to Thee belong.
A harmony of heauenly musick's song :
Kind Shepherd to the soule, which strayes not thence :
For still with sweet insence[1] Thy lights do flame,
And Christ thy Priest and Captaine gards the same.

SON. CIII.—*For Constancie.*

Alas! O Lord, how fraile the flesh I find;
How readie to reuolt vnto distrust;
How willing to seeke helpe in flesh vniust;
Vngratefull fruit of gracelesse humane kind,
Which harboreth such monsters in the mind,
As soule and bodie both needs ruine must :
Like wauering sand or dust, with winds which moue,
From good to ill, from ill to worse we fall,
We haue not sooner grace for helpe to call,
And budding faith Thy mercies for to proue,

[1] = incense. G.

But weary long to seeke our ioyes aboue,
We quench this spright, and haue no helpe at all :
The perill is not small—Lord—I am in,
Inflame the faith, and zeale Thou didst begin.

SON. CIIII.—*For faith.*

Since thus my selfe I find to be vncleane,
Vnfit to bide before God's iustice throne;
Who recompence for sinne accepteth none,
But to the rigor of desert doth leane;
To fly to Thee my Sauiour Christ I meane,
Who paydst my debt sufficiently alone :
I need but make my mone to Thee I know,
For Thou art readie to relieue my want,
Thy Father's loue, and Thy obedience brant
With zeale, Thy mercies on vs to bestow :
Whereof since faith the vse to vs must show,
And as it is more feruent or more scant,
More powrefull is to dant Death's bitter sting,
Graunt faith may prayers frame, and comfort bring.

SON. CV.—*For grace to iudge of good and euill.*

Amidst these dangerous dayes wherein I liue,
Poore silly orphane distitute of skill,
By parent's fall forlorne, by nature ill,
Craue grace of Thee, O Lord! and therwith giue,
Powre to my weaknesse sin away to driue,
That so I may Thee serue and honour still:
Reforme my feeble will, and it incline,
To haue henceforth a wise and solide tast,
Of truth and falshod; let my choyse be plast
On perfect patterne drawne with vertuous line:
With serpent's wisedome let my iudgment shine,
To shun the snares whereto my lust would hast:
Vouchsafe my sute be grast, with help from Thee,
Thy Word the lampe of light vnto me bee.

SON. CVI.—*For innocencie in euill.*

Since so simplicitie, Thy word doth prayse,
—O Lord—as that Thy Sonne example gaue
By all His life and workes, that He did craue,
His seruants wherein to direct their wayes,

Like to the babe on mother's breast that stayes.
And sylly lambes and doues which no guile haue.
Since He is prest to saue, and to imbrace
The lame, blind, naked, leaporous reiect;
Since to yeeld health to all, and such protect
As simply do with faith approch the place,
When He in mercie's seat doth shew His face,
And prayers heare, and needfull suites effect:
Lord do me not neglect, poore, silly, blind,
Who meritelesse, yet mercy hope to find.

SON. CVII.—*Shame of sinne.*

How could I Lord, but be asham'd indeed,
To lift my eyes to Thee, to craue for ayde;
When I of thought, word, deed haue sins displayd,
With multitude of monstrous ofsprings breed;
The true portrait of Adam's carnall seed,
Which made him hide himselfe when he it wayd:
I therefore am affrayd, and shun to show
Vnto the world, the shamefull brood I beare,
Which thoughts do hatch, and vile affections reare;
Too hatefull for a Christian soule to know,
And do so hastily to hugenesse grow,

As vaine it is a figge-tree leafe to weare :
I know no other where my shame to hide,
But with Thy merits ; or Thy wrath to bide.

SON. CVIII.—*Against defection.*

When I—O Lord—vnto my minde do call,
The fearefull records of the patriarkes best,
In whom great gifts of grace did seeme to rest,
And yet to foule and fearefull sinnes did fall ;
I do deplore the frailty of vs all,
And feare defection euen in those are blest.
And since I am the least, O Lord—alas !—
Of many, that in word professe Thy name,
And I some feeling tast haue of the same,
Which doth not forward to perfection pas ;
It makes me see—as in a looking glasse—
The feeble strength of this my present frame,
Which clogd with sin is lame, and wold look back
To hell—from which I fly—if grace should lack.

SON. CIX.—*Not to trust in flesh.*

What trust may I, O Lord ! on flesh repose ?
Whose mould is earth, whose substance is but dust,

His thoughts vncleane, his actions all vniust,
As is the stocke of parents, whence it growes ;
Whom fraud, vntruth, pride, lust, distrust
inclose,
By which—by nature—rul'd wee are and must :
I know the feeble trust, I may expect,
And safety which on such a frame is found :
Where weake foundation is the sand vnsound,
Which may not byde the brunt of stormie day,
When as temptations shall their powre display,
Or yet affictions vs enuiron round,
Vpon a surer ground, faith must me build,
And Christ my Sauiour so my soule may
shield.

SON. CX.—*Prayer for humilitie.*

SINCE Thou, O Lord and Sauiour ! doest confesse
Thy selfe a true Phisition vnto those,
Who with humilitie their griefes disclose,
And vnto Thee for ayd, by prayers presse ;
Vouchsafe Thou so my heart to Thee addresse,
That on Thy helpe alone my faith repose :
Vouchsafe my sight vnlose, make me to see
The naked show of Nature's powre and shame ;
Let me behold my workes, weake, lewd, and
lame ;

And let my heart with sorrow piercèd be,
And pressèd downe, procure such mone in me,
As may in fine repentance truely frame,
That humbly so Thy name, I may adore,
And faithfully in fine Thy health implore.

SON. CXI.—*For comfort in affliction.*

Leaue me not Lord, most humbly I Thee craue,
In this distresse, whereto my sins me bring,
Which headlong vnto hell, my soule would fling,
And make me thinke, there were no powre could saue
My wretched state from Death's eternall graue,
Which poysoned is by Satan's deadly sting:
But teach Thou me to sing, O Lord Thy praise,
Amids Thy saints, which see Thy mercies still;
With ioy and comfort do my courage fill,
Once Lord my soule, which yet in terror staies:
Make me to bend vnto Thy will my waies,
And frame my powers, vnto Thy holy will:
The powre of Satan kill, and so increase
My soule with comfort of Thy lasting peace.

SON. CXII.—*In prosperity not to forsake God.*

The more, O Lord, I see before my face,
The daily blessings, which Thou doest bestow,

On me, vnworthie wretch, who well do know,
How farre affections vile in me haue place:
The more I see, iust cause to call for grace,
Lest for abuse of them, Thou vengeance show;
For then most soone we grow, for to forget
The Giuer, when the giftes we once haue gaind;
Ingratitude our natures so hath staind,
Thy greatest blessing we most lightly set:
So farre we are from paying praise for debt,
We do forget the nurse vs fed and wainde:[1]
As Israell not refraind, Thee most t'offend,
When most Thou them didst feed and comfort send.

SON. CXIII.—*Man's sorrow for sin.*

I MUST commend the thing the world doth hate,
And like the thing that flesh and blood detest;
The cares and griefes by which I was opprest,
Which made me see and know my wretched state:
Wisedome is dearely bought, but not too late;
Who tasts true frute of care, knowes cumfort best:
Make me then Lord, disgest each bitter pill,

[1] = Weaned. G.

Which for correction of my sin is sent:
Purge Thou thereby, my drosse, make me repent
Each lewd affect[1] offensiue to Thy will:
A new and better nature Lord instill,
Which to Thy seruice alwayes may be bent:
With sorrow often rent my hardoned heart,
And let repentance purchase, cure of smart.

SON. CXIIII.—*For true feare.*

FEARE is a frailtie known to humane kind,
Which witnesseth a guilt where it doth dwell:
Since Adam's fall, his ofspring knew it well,
And euery man in conscience doth it find;
It takes possession in a troubled mind,
And—if grace want—dispaire driues downe to hell:
Yet these Thy praises tell, O Lord, they shall,
Who danted for their frailties, doe require
Grace to resist their lustes, and do aspire
For strength of true perfection for to call,
And haue a feare of sin—though neare so small—
For loue of right, as well as shunning ire,

[1] = affection, passion. G.

Kindle their loue with fire, sprinkle it with
feare,
That incense of obedient smoke it reare.

SON. CXV.—*Sorow for coldnesse of compasion.*

I FEELE, O Lord, and sorrow for the same,
The slender feeling, and compassion small,
The which I haue of neighbour's case at all;
Which to assist their states, my heart should
frame,
Who with my lips, professe a Christian name,
But stop my eares when they for helpe do call,
So easily we fall, and do forgett,
The lesson which our Maister Christ vs gaue,
Who vs with mourners, to lament would haue,
And on our brother's good, chiefe care should
set:
But selfe-loue and cold charitie, doth let
No frute of faith proceed, though neighbour
craue:
Yet Thou didst freely saue me wretch
cleane lost,
Whose life the blud of Thy deare Sonne hath
cost.

SON. CXVI.—*For Patience.*

When I, O Lord, in troubles sore opprest,
My heauie state with carefull thoughts do way,[1]
Which hope of happie issue doth denay,
And frailtie of the flesh can scarce digest;
I onely find therein at length some rest,
When on Thy mercy promisèd I stay;
And when from day to day, I see with shame,
My new offences, which do trespasse Thee,
And note how long Thy iudgements sparèd me,
Which iustly might burst forth in vengeance flame;
Yea when my Sauiour's sufferings show the same,
Which ought a rule to His elect to be:
I craue that I might see, like fruites of grace,
So that impatience hold in me no place.

SON. CXVII.—*For continuance of God's Word.*

The greatest plague that I see cause to feare,
To such as I, who haue so carelesse bin,
By reading and by preaching, for to win

---

[1] = weigh. G.

True knowledg, which our harts to Thee might reare
Is, lest Thy prophets' sound should so forbeare
To preach Thy word, that we should dwell in sin:
And wallowing therein, we should delight,
In ignorance—the headlong path to hell—
And wickedly in carnall tents to dwell;
And so surcease with sinne, or lust to fight:
Grant therefore—Lord—Thy sword may alwaies smight
My soule, till sinne it from me cleane expell:
Let prophets alwaies tell to vs Thy will,
And keepe vs vnder Thy obedience still.

SON. CXVIII.—*For grace to bring forth fruits.*

Although—O Lord—I do as truth confesse,
No powre in humane art that can Thee please;
That all polluted are with first disease
Of sinne originall, which did transgresse
By parent's fall, and workes in vs no lesse,
On whom by iust succession sin doth cease:
Yet since Christ doth appease the penance due,
By bearing burden on His backe for me,

And faith herein sufficeth me to free ;
Which faith must fruitfull be if it be true,
And workes of grace regenerate insue,
Which perfect pledge of safetie ought to bee :
I craue—O Lord—of Thee from day to day,
To guide my steps into a righteous way.

SON. CXIX.—*Aide in conflict with sin.*

WEAKE are my chāpions, Lord, which fight with sin ;
I meane my will and powre, which take in hand
The furie of their assaults for to withstand,
And victory of him do hope to win :
Some signe it is of courage, to begin
To fight, but cowards part to leaue the land.
I faine would come in band, and leige[1] would make
With Thee my Sauiour, ere I be assayld :
No other comfort man euer auayld,
But trust in Thee, when troubles them did take ;
Thou helpst Thy flocke, Thou dost not them forsake,

[1] = league. G.

If so their faith in Thee be nothing quayld:
No sillable is fayld of all Thy word,
Thy truth subdues the force of wrathfull sword,

SON. CXX.—*Comfort in affliction.*

Why do we not reioyce, whilst Christ we haue
Our Bridgrome, wedded sure to faithfull band?
His owne free-liking made our merit stand,
And by His word His loue to vs He gaue;
First pledge whereof was baptisme, which forth
draue
Our feare, and lent a gracious helping hand.
And that in sacred land we might be free,
And there possession haue of endlesse rest,
His Testament He made, and with the blest,
Our heritage—by faith—He made vs see:
He signd the writ with His assurance best,
Of bread and wine, which might a simboll bee,
His corps nayld on the tree for our dis-
charge
From sin, hell, death, which sets our soule at
large.

CONCLUSION.

Though long—my soule—thou banishèd hast bin,
From place of thy repose, by tyrant's might;

By world and worldly cares, by flesh, wherein
Thy wandring thoughts haue dazeld iudgemēt's
sight:
Learne yet at length to guide thy course aright,
Unto that end which must begin thy rest;
Learne once for shame, so constantly to fight
Against affections, which please fancie best,
That all vnfruitfull thoughts thou maiest detest,
And hold those common pleasures combers
great:
Whose issue, age and time with ruine threat,
When death vnlookt for, seemes a fearefull
guest,
Retire thyselfe as wise Barzilla[1] did,
From worldly cares thy purer thoughts to
rid.

---

[1] 2 Samuel xix. 31, *et seqq*. G.

Extra-Sonnets.

Note.

The Sonnets that follow—with the exception of the last from King James's "Exercises" 1591—appear in only three of the known copies of the complete volume, viz, the Bridgewater, Bodleian and our own. They are not in the British Museum copy. It does not appear that there ever has been a separate title-page for these Sonnets: only the heading as in our reprint, and without pagination—(15 leaves.)

S. W. SINGER, Esq., in annotating the Satires of BISHOP HALL (Satire VII: lines 1-6) observes: "The innumerable quantity of "excellent conceitfull" amatory sonnets, poured forth at that period, might well call forth the animadversion of the satirist: volumes teeming with the praises or complaints of the would-be lover and poet to his Celia, his Diana, his Diella, &c. But, perhaps, this points more particularly to Henry Lok's Love Complaints, then just published, with the legend of Orpheus and Eurydice. Lok is thought to be the subject of Hall's satire in other places." (Peter Hall's edition of Bishop Hall, Vol. XII. pp. 167-8). This is blundering through and through. Apart from the inaccurate citation of the title of the "Legend of Orpheus and Eurydice" (which it is'nt worth-while correcting here) the Legend itself, even had it consisted of Sonnets (which it does not) was not the production of Henry Lok, the H. L. being the initials of the publisher Humphrey Lownes, not of the Author, who remains anonymous. Then it is plain that Mr. Singer had never seen or at least read Lok's Sonnets, as he had never read the "Legend"; for they are in no respect, love-sonnets "excellent conceitfull" or otherwise. Not of earthly but of heavenly 'love' is his singing. Bishop Hall nowhere refers to our Worthy. Equally ignorant and second-hand is the criticism that represents these extra-sonnets as 'fulsome' and ultra-laudatory. For the period they are exceedingly subdued in their praise: and seem chiefly to have been inscribed in gift-copies of "Ecclesiastes." Throughout we have annotated the series of the Sonnets, helped herein especially by Colonel Chester. G.

Sonnets of the Author to Diuers, collected by the Printer.

AND FIRST TO THE LORDS OF HER MAIESTIE'S PRIUIE COUNCELL.

To the right Ho. and most reuerend father in God, my Lord Archbishop of Canterbury his grace.[1]

If Dauid did in passion iust arise,
When he recorded his exilèd state,
Compar'd with happy swallowes, which deuise
To build their nests so neare the Temple gate :[2]
May I not mourne, to see the world alate,
So swarme with bookes, which euery wher do fly,
Whose subiects as most base, might merit hate,
—Though curious braynes their wits therein apply—

---

[1] John Whitgift : enthroned 23rd October, 1583 : died 29th February, 1603 and buried at Croydon, Surrey, 27th March following. G.

[2] Psalm lxxxiv. 3. G.

When better matters buried long do ly,
  For lacke of fauourers or protectors grace?
  May I not take occasion thus to try
  My pen, and craue that you the same imbrace?
    Yes sure, world knowes, you can and will
      protect
    The cause, why God and prince did you erect.

To the Right Ho. Knight, Sir Thomas Egerton,
  Lord Keeper of the greate Seale of England.[1]

  WHAT fame reports—by mouth of good and
    wise—
  It is not flattery to record the same.
  The publike eccho of your prayse doth rise,
  That you by Iustice' ballance iudgement frame:
Then may you not my pen of boldnesse blame,
  If it present to your impartiall eye,
  This holy worke, to shield it with your name,
  Which may among prophane in daunger ly.

---

[1] Lord-Keeper from 6th May, 1596 until 1603, when on the 21st July, he was created Baron Ellesmere, and three days after Lord Chancellor of England. On the 7th November 1616, he was advanced to the dignity of Viscount Brackley. He died at York House, in the Strand, 15th March, 1616-17, and was buried at Doddleston in Cheshire. G.

Wise Salomon, child's parent true did try,
And Daniell false accusers fraud bewray,
By searching hearts affects, and words, whereby
One's fainèd loue, the others guilt, to way :
So iudge this worke, and him shall it depraue,
So I desire, you iustice prayse shall haue.

To the right Hon. the Lord Burghley, Lord high Treasurer of England, one of the most noble order of the Garter,[1] &c.

If Romaines held Sibillaes[2] workes so deare,
Because they from deuining spright did grow ;
More precious present then, receiue you here,
Which God on king, king did on world bestow.
Our Sibill you, our Salomon we know,
And so your words and workes the world doth prise :
To vertue you, your selfe a father show ;
Hence honor yours, hence countrie's good doth rise :

[1] The famous William Cecil, first Lord Burleigh. He had been Queen Elizabeth's Secretary from her accession, and was appointed Lord High Treasurer in September 1572, which office he held until his death, 4th August 1598. G.

[2] The Sibylline books. G.

Then this—no fiction that man doth deuise,
But built on best experience life can bring—
With patience reade, and do it not despise;
Your wise experience can confirm each thing:
It is not rated as Sibillaes were,
But—priz'd by you—it will the value reare.

To the Ri. Ho. the Earle of Essex, Great Master of the Horse to her Highnesse, and one of the most noble order of the &c.[1]

Not Neptune's child, or Triton I you name,
Not Mars, not Perseus, though a pere to all;
Such word I would find out or newly frame,
By sea and land might you triumphant call,
Yet were such word for your desert too small:
You England's ioy, you en'mies terror are;
You Vice's scourge, you Vertue's fencèd wall:
To Church a shield, to Antichrist a barre.
I need not feare my words should stretch to farre,
Your deedes out-fly the swiftest soaring pen,
You praise of peace, th'vndaunted powre of warre,

---

[1] Robert Devereux, second earl of Essex, the celebrated but unfortunate favorite of Elizabeth: beheaded 25th February 1600-1. G.

Of heauen's elect, the happie loue of men:
Not knowing then, how to expresse my mind;
Let Silence craue this gift may fauour find.

To the Ri. Ho. the Lord Charles Howard of Effingham, Lord high Admirall of England, one of the most noble order of the garter,[1] &c.

When as wise Salomon's most happie raigne,
Is registred in bookes of holy writ,
His greatnesse seemes increase of honour gaine,
By store of worthy peeres his state which fit,
Whose excellence of courage and of wit,
His impery[2] causd with wealth and peace abound,
Whose heads and hands, do neuer idle sit,
But seeking commons good, through world around,
By sea and land their swords free passage found,
Which subiects safetie bred, and feare to foe.
Like fame vnto our prince, you cause to sound,
Both farre and neare, whilst you victorious goe:

---

[1] Sir Charles Howard, second Baron Howard of Effingham, created Earl of Nottingham, 22nd October, 1596, and historically immortal as having defeated the Spanish Armada, 1588. He died 14th December, 1624. G.

[2] = empire: later used by Milton. G.

For which her trust, our loue to you is due,
As pledge whereof, I this present to you.

To the Right Ho. the Lord Cobham, Lord Chamberlaine of her Maiestie's houshold, Lord Warden of the Sink ports, and of the noble order of the garter, &c.[1]

Giftes are not measur'd by the outward show,
Nor by the price of peeres of noble kind ;
They shadowes are the hart's intent to know,
And simple figures of a faithfull mind :
Then since your vertues high all hearts do bind,
To striue to testifie their grate intent,
Vouchsafe suppose, my powre cannot yet find
A present fit as will and heart was bent :
And what king—writing once—thought time well spent,
That reade you once, as thing of some regard :

---

[1] Probably William Brooke, Baron Cobham, who held both of the offices mentioned *supra*, and who is stated to have died in 1596. His son Henry Brooke, who succeeded to the title, was summoned to the Parliament 24th October, 1597, and was constituted Warden of the Cinque Ports, but does not appear to have held the post of Lord Chamberlain. G.

His mind ment well, that it vnto you sent,
Time not spent ill, in view thereof is spard:
If it more worth, I more loue could expresse,
My due regard of you should yeeld no lesse.

To the Right Ho. the Lord North, Treasurer of her Maiestie's houshould.[1]

I MAY not say, I shun to shew my want
Before your selfe, whom I true noble hold,
Since I to others haue not made them scant,
And may of meaner men be well controld:
This common guilt of mine, makes me more bold
To prosecute the error I begunne,
Who craue your fauour not my faults vnfold,
Although my folly ouer-rashly runne:
If with the best they haue a pardon wonne,
They may the boldlier passe the common view:
What princes like, the people hold well done,
And fame in passage doth her force renew:
Which good or bad, your censure is to make,
When now first flight it in the world doth take.

[1] Sir Roger North, second Baron North, constituted treasurer of the Household in 1597. He died December 3rd., 1600. G.

To the Right Honorable the Lord of Buckhurst.[1]

As you of right impart, with peeres in sway
Of common weale, wherin by you we rest:
So hold I fit to yeeld you euery way
That due, the which my powre affoordeth best.
But when I call to mind, your pen so blest
With flowing liquor of the Muses' Spring;
I feare your daintie eare can ill digest
The harsh tun'd notes, which on my pipe I sing.
Yet since the ditties of so wise a king,
Can not so lose their grace, by my rude hand,
But that your wisedome can conform the thing,
Vnto the modell doth in margent stand:
I you beseech, blame not—though you not prayse—
This worke, my gift; which on your fauour stayes.

To the Right Honor. Knight Sir William Knowles, Controller of Her Maiestie's houshold.[2]

Of auncient vertues, honor'd ofspring's race

---

[1] Thomas Sackville, created Baron Buckhurst June 8th 1567 and earl of Dorset, 13th March 1603-4. He was constituted Lord High Treasurer in 1599. He has an imperishable fame in our poetic Literature. G.

[2] Sir William Knollys, created Baron Knollys, 13th May,

Of true religions, you blest progeny :
—On which two pillers vertue built your grace,
And court by gracing you, is grast thereby—
Of such—since this worke treates—such worke do I
Well fitting hold, for you to reade and shield,
Whose wisedome, honor, vertue, doth apply
To true religion, on the which you build :
My selfe too weake so heauy a taske to wield,
—As was the treating of so high a stile—
At first attempt began to fly the field,
Till some—which lik't the theame—bid pause awhile,
And not dismay : the title would suffise,
To daunt the vaine, and to allure the wise.

To the Right honorable Knight Sir Iohn Fortescue, Chauncellor of the Exchequor.[1]

He who in dutie much to you doth owe,

1603, Viscount Wallingford, 14th November, 1606, and Earl of Banbury 18th August, 1626. He died 25th May, 1632. He was, at the date of the Sonn'et Comptroller of the Household, having succeeded his father in that office in 1590: dut in 1601 was advanced to that of Treasurer, which he held until 1616. The name is found in Victoria's Court. G

[1] Ancestor of the Earl of Clermont. He was consti-

In power is little able to present ;
For pledge of gratefull mind, is forst bestow
These ill limd lines, but signes of heart's intent :
The scope whereof by Salomon was bent,
To teach the way to perfect happinesse,
By me transformèd thus, and to you sent,
To shew that I do wish to you no lesse :
To wish well, is small cost I do confesse,
But such a heart as truly it intends,
Is better worth esteeme, then many gesse :
And for all other wants makes halfe amends.
Such is my heart, such be therfore your mind,
Then shall my mite, a million's welcome find.

To the Right Honourable Sir Robert Cecill, Knight, principall Secretary to her Maiestie.[1]

To you—my hopes sweet life, nurse to my muse,
Kind foster-father of deseruing sprights—

---

tuted Chancellor of the Exchequer in 1589, and held the office until Queen Elizabeth's death, when he accepted in exchange the chancellorship of the Duchy of Lancaster. He died 23rd December, 1607. G.

[1] Queen Elizabeth's renowned Secretary, appointed in

This poem comes, which you will not refuse
—I trust—because of blessednes it wrights:
Your aged youth so waind[1] from vaine delights,
Your growing iudgment farre beyond your yeares,
Your painefull daies, your many watchfull nights,
Wherein your care of common good appears,
Assureth him that of your fame once hears,
That you some heauenly obiect do aspire;
The sweet conceit whereof your soule so chears,
That Earth's bred vanities, you not admire:
Such is this theame, such was first writer's mind,
For whose sakes, I do craue, it fauour find.

1596—afterwards Earl of Salisbury and ancestor of the present Marquis of that name. He died 17th February, 1611-12. G.

[1] = weaned G.

To other Lords, Ladies, and approued Friends.

To the Right Honourable, the Earle of Oxford, Lord great Chamberlaine of England.[1]

IF Endor's widdow had had powre to raise,
A perfect bodie of true temperature,
I would coniure you by your wonted prayse,
Awhile my song to heare, and trueth indure :
Your passèd noble proofe doth well assure
Your blouds, your minds, your bodi's excellence
If their due reuerence may this paines procure,
Your pacience—with my boldnesse—will dispence:
I only craue high wisdom's true defence :
Not at my suit, but for work's proper sake,
Which treats of true felicitie's essence,
As wisest king most happiest proofe did make :
Whereof your owne experience much might say,
Would you vouchsafe your knowledge to bewray.

---

[1] Edward de Vere, 17th Earl of Oxford. He died in 1604, having succeeded his father as Great Chamberlain in 1562. See our Memorial-Introduction to the Earl of Oxford's Poems in Fuller Worthies' Library Miscellanies, Vol. III. G.

To the Right Honorable the Earle of Northumber-
land.[1]

WHO would intreat of earthly happinesse,
He need but take a pattern of your state;
Borne noble, learnèd bred; whose acts expresse,
That honor cannot Vertue's force abate,
In home—kind loue, abroad vnmenast[2] hate,
In bodie's value and in spright of mind:
You haue no cause to blame your aduerse fate,
Which such a great aspect, hath you assignd:
Yet that you yet more happinesse might find,
The common loue your countrey you doth owe:
To offer you, this meanes thereto doth bind
My will, which in this lowly gift I show:
Which yet accept, for worthy prince's sake,
Who of each point a perfect proofe did make.

To the Right Ho. the Earle of Shrewsburie.[3]

WELL placèd vertue in high honor's seat,
Well bending honour to a Christian's state,

[1] Henry Percy, ninth Earl of Northumber and, who succeeded his father of the same name in 1585. He died 5th November, 1632. G.

[2] = unmenaced. G.

[3] Gilbert Talbot, seventh Earl of Shrewsbury, who succeeded to the title 18th November, 1590. He died 8th May, 1616. G.

Vouchsafe my pen your pardon may intreat,
Who this my vowèd seruice offer late :
Your shining glory did my hope abate,
When first to seeke your sight my fancie ment;
Your fame for vertue, yet did animate
My pen, which vnto you this present sent:
Your true nobilitie, which seemeth bent
To foster innocents from powrefull foe,
Doth promise me, wisht fruit of heart's intent,
If vnder your protection it doth goe :
The rather since of honor I do wright,
And the happinesse which is your soule's delight.

To the right Honourable, the Earle of Cumberland.[1]

The crownèd honor iustly which befell
To valiant Iosua, and wise Caleb's race,
—Whose faith to fainting people did foretell,
The fruitfull spoyle of proud resister's place :—
Their natiue vertues which you haue by grace,
Whose sword doth fight the battles of the iust,

[1] George Clifford, third Earl of Cumberland, who succeeded to his title 8th January, 1569. He died 30th October, 1605. G.

Which makes our hemis-phere your fame im-
brace,
And feebled hearts on your stout courage trust,—
My confidence in you excuse they must,
Who do my poems muster in your train ;
Whose theme hath bin by wisest king discust,
And in your practice do of proofe remaine,
Which leade the way vnto the holy land.
For which—whilst here you liue—you fight-
ing stand.

To the Right Honorable the Earle of Sussex.[2]

THE skilfull pilots that the ocean haunt,
In stormes are found to be of merry cheare,
Whom fairest calmes, with feare and dread do
daunt,
Because a signe of change doth seeme appeare.
The expert souldiers vsèd to the warre,
In time of peace do arme them for the fight,
And carefull Christians will foresee from farre,
The fierce temptations may in pleasure light:
Then since no settled rule there can be here,
Whereby to know the issues growing are,

[1] Robert Ratcliffe, fifth Earl of Sussex, who succeeded to the title 10th April, 1593. He died in 1629. G.

But change of times may comfort, clipse,[1] or
cleare,
And so our present state, amend or marre:
Learne here—braue chapion—noble, vertuous,
wise—
To beare all brunts that may in life rise.

To the Right Ho. the Earle of Southampton.[2]

AMONGST most noble, noble euery way,
Among the wise, wise in a high degree;
Among the vertuous, vertuous may I say,
You worthy seeme, right worthy Lord to mee.
By bloud, by value, noble we you see,
By nature, and by learning's trauell wise,
By loue of good, il's hate, you vertuous bee:
Hence publike honor, priuate loue doth rise,
Which hath inuited me thus to deuise,
To shew my selfe not slacke to honor you,
By this meane gift—since powre more fit de-
nies—

---

[1] = eclipse. G.

[2] Henry Wriothesley, 3rd Earl of Southampton, succeeded to the title in 1581. He was attainted for treason under Elizabeth, but was restored in blood under James. He died in 1624. G.

Which let me craue be read, and held for true :
Of honor, wisedome, vertue, I delate,[1]
Which—you pursuing—well aduance your state.

To the Right Honorable the Lord Zouch.[2]

WHAT haue I done ? that I would take in hand,
To pick forth patrons should my worke defend,
When such a lordly troope of nobles stand,
As in the choyce of them I find no end ?
But hauing thus begun, I do intend,
To fawne[3] on those, whose fauors I haue found ;
Amongst the which I trust, you helpe will lend,
Because the building is on such a ground ;
I know your learnèd skill, and iudgement sound,
Which might deter it to approch your sight;
But whereas loue—they say—doth once abound,
There feare and all suspect is banisht quight :
Your vertue's loue, your honor bids me yeeld
To you, on whose kind fauour I do build.

---

[1] = dilate. G.

[2] Edward La Zouche, eleventh Baron La Zouche, summoned to Parliament from 2nd April, 1571. to 17th May, 1625, in which latter year he died. G.

[3] A noticeable use of the word before it became deteriorated. G.

To the Right Honorable the Lord Willoughbie of Ersbie.[1]

Might I forget the comforts of my prime;
Might I neglect the matter which I wright;
Might I not know the hopes of present time,
Forgetting you, I might myselfe acquight:
But parentes fauors, once my youth's delight,
Your selfe a patterne of a happie peere,
Whose proofes of vertue publike are to sight,
Might me vpbraid with peeuish silence here,
If I should hold so meane a gift too deare,
For one—whose ancient—debter yet I rest;
For whom my poeme doth so fit appeare,
Since you, our Age recordes among the best;
Then thinke not I by slight[2] would kindnes gaine,
But hold this due, if honest I remaine.

To the Right Honourable, the Lord Burrowes.[3]

I not intend by present of a booke,
Which for the title most men will allowe,

---

[1] Peregrine Bertie, tenth Lord Willoughby de Eresby, who claimed the ancient barony, and was summoned to Parliament 16th January, 1580-1. He died in 1601. G.

[2] Sleight. G.

[3] Thomas Burgh or Borough, sixth Baron, who was

For equall praise—with first true author looke—
Because I newly it transformèd now:
Not for my owne presume I it to'avow,
—Vnworthie herald of that prince's says—[1]
Which duly to deliuer few know how,
And I—of all—most weake by many ways:
Yet since your high praisd bountie not denays,
A great acceptance of a kindly gift;
Vpon that hope my present boldnesse stays,
Who in my purpose haue no other drift,
But let you see, Earth's vaine, heauen's perfect blis,
Which with my heart I wish you tast in this.

To the Right Honorable the Lord Mountioy.[2]

To YOU the noble light of happie Ile,
In whose most vertuous breast the holy fire
Vnquenchèd liues, when all the world the while

summoned to Parliament 11th January, 1562-3. He died 14th October, 1597. G.

[1] Sayings or saws. G.

[2] Charles Blount, eighth Baron Mountjoy, who succeeded to the title in 1594. He was created Earl of Devon 21st July, 1603, and died 3rd April, 1606, when all his honours became extinct. G.

Nigh drownèd lyes in dreames of vaine desire;
Whose holy zeale the godly do admire,
Whose worthie constancie the wise commend,
For whom heauen's glorie waights, as vertuous hire,
To whom the hearts of men with honour bend,
Who do pure vertue to your powre defend:
Whom vaine delights of Earth cannot defile,
Whom—to protect religion—God did send;
Vouchsafe to listen to my song a while,
Which right true tidings to the world doth bring
Of what obseruèd was, by wisest king.

To the Right Honorable the Lord of Hunsdon.[1]

Of good king Dauid's holy and carefull bent,
Of wise and happie Salomon's desire,
Their liuely patterns, here I do present,
To you braue Lord, as kind deserts require:
Your gifts of nature rare, I not admire,
—Since heire you were vnto so noble a father,
Whose wisdome to true honour did aspire—
But gifts of grace, which by your life I gather,

[1] George Carey, second Baron Hundson who succeeded to the title 23rd July, 1596. He died 9th September, 1603. G.

And for the which you reuerenc't are the rather,
As heire to both those kings in common care,
Of God and realme, gainst which most lewd deprauer
Is forst his poysoned tongue for shame to spare.
As for that good to me by you hath flowne,
Was but one frute of many vertues knowne.

To the Right reuerend father in God, Toby, Bishop of Duresme.[1]

If double cumber of the people's care,
Of Paule's and Peter's sword and keyes may rest,
I would intreat you some small time to spare,
To view the face of your inuited gest:
Of all men you haue cause to vse him best,
Because you more than halfe the father are;
To you therefore, I haue him first addrest,
To haue his grace ere he proceed too farre:
Your count'nance may his progresse mend or marre,
Because—as of you first his life did grow—

[1] Tobias Matthew, elected Bishop of Durham in 1595: in 1606 he became Archbishop of York, and died 29th March, 1628. G.

So must his course be guided by your starre,
Which him first hope of heauenly light did show;
Vouchsafe then to bestow, one reading more,
To welcome him, or thrust him out of dore.

To the graue and learned Sir Iohn Popham, Knight, Lord chiefe Iustice of England.[1]

O WOULD I might without my heart's deepe griefe,
—For common crosses, following men opprest—
Record your worth, whence many find reliefe,
Which makes you iustly chiefe of all the rest:
Your carefull thought and bodie's paine addrest,
To reconcilement of contentious mind;
Your vniuersall loue to truth profest,
By which the desolate do fauour find,
Doth—as me seemes—in common dutie bind
My pen to chalenge you, truth's true defence,
Though dull my poem be, my sight not blind,
That sought to take his priuiledge from thence:
You—chiefe of Iudges—best of truth can treat,
To you therefore, I truth of truth's repeat.

[1] Appointed Lord Chief Justice 2nd June, 1591. He died 10th June, 1607. G.

To Sir Edmond Anderson Knight, Lord chiefe
Iustice of the Common pleas.[1]

Your eares so daily exercis'd to heare
The plaints and the petitions sutors make;
Make you most fit of many to appeare,
My selfe and workes, protection both to take:
Not for my selfe, but for the commons sake,
I presse thus into your presence now,
Whose theame may hap some drowsie heads awake,
To chalenge, if I dare this worke avow:
But if that you, whose wisedome best knowes how,
That lawfull make to speake, what Scripture taught,
I know the common sort dare but allow
My publishing, what from wise king I brought:
Then you the common shield to guiltlesse wight,
Vouchsafe this worke find fauour in your sight.

---

[1] Appointed Chief Justice, second May, 1582, and held the office until his death, first August, 1605. He was ancestor of the Baronets of this name and of the earl of Yarborough. G.

To Sir William Perriam Knight, Lord chiefe Barron of the Exchequor.[1]

Thou kind accorder of the dreamt discord,
Twixt law and conscience, God's and man's decree,
By whom oppression and brib'rie are abhord,
The common poysons of land's peace that bee:
I not vnfitly do direct to thee
These monuments, of wisest king's experience,
Them to allow, if you them worthy see;
Me to reproue, if I haue made offence:
I no man craue to stand in wrong's defence,
I may—as all men do—some weaknesse show:
If great my fault, spare not; if small, dispence,
Because it did not of meere malice grow:
This will you do vncrau'd; that done, I pleasd,
Both God and man submission hath appeasd.

To the valorous Knight, Sir William Russell, Lord Deputie of Ireland.[2]

If iustly Dauid did by law ordaine,

[1] Sir William Peryam was appointed one of the Justices of the Common Pleas in 1580, and Chief Baron of the Exchequer, 13th April, 1593. He died 9th October, 1604. G.

[2] Youngest son of Francis, second earl of Bedford.

That they an equall part of spoyle should
haue,
Who—when he fought—behind did still re-
maine,
The carriage from the spoyle of foes to saue:
Doth not your merits by more reason craue,
To be recorded in my Kalender?
By whose blest worke, God of His goodnesse gaue
Part of our peace, amidst such threatned warre?
In worthy vertues, most men's peere you are,
In true religious zeale, by none exceld;
Your noble house—like to a blazing starre—
Hath showne, wherein true honour euer dweld:
Then share with worthies all in blessed fame,
And reade this worke, which treateth of the
same.

To the valorous Knight, Sir Walter Rawleigh, Lord Warden of the Stannerie, and Captaine of the Guard,[1]

Of happinesse when as I hapt to write,
Me thoughts did make a period—Sir—in you,

He was constituted Lord Deputy of Ireland in 1594: created Baron Russell in 1603, and died 9th August, 1613. G.

[1] The 'immortal': beheaded 29th October, 1618. See

Who being sworne to Mars and Pallas knight,
They both with equall honor did endew,
And therefore might become a censurer trew,
Of greatest blessings men propound or find;
Vouchsafe you then this tract thereof to vew,
As if that Salomon had it assignd:
Whose interest in you expects your kind
And grate acceptance of his graue aduise,
From whom—though many other men were blind—
He chalengeth a doome right godly and wise:
But as for me his messenger, suffiseth
The prayse, to truly speake what he deuiseth.

To the valorous Knight Sir Iohn Norris, Lord Generall of her Maiestie's forces in Ireland.[1]

Among the blessed worthies of our time,
Your flickering fame aloft I do espy,
Whose toylsome trauell, such a pitch doth clime,
As euery auncient worthy came not ny.

Dr. Hannah's admirable collection of his Poems (1870.) G.

[1] Younger son of Henry, first Baron Norreys (or Norris) of Rycote, and brother of the first earl of Berkshire, of that family. He was subsequently President of the Council of Munster, and died in Ireland, unmarried. G.

The moderne Marses did your vertues try,
Whilst you, the proud Iberian forces quayld,
In Britany, and in Netherland, whereby
With equall armes they seldome haue preuayld:
The trecherous practise, wherewith they assayld
Th' inconstant humours of the Irish foes,
Your pollicies haue stayd, when force hath fayld,
Whereby your merit's measure daily growes;
So that I must of due, make roome for you,
Though twise nine worthies shold be coynd anew.

To the valorous Knight Sir Francis Veare.[1]

My pen was chang'd but purpose stay'd anew,
So soone as I amidst the noble traine,
Of worthy knights, did cast a thought on you,
Who yet—vnus'd to—did for grace remaine:
If you I win, I shall not litle gaine,
Because both much you can, and much you will
For wisedome, vertue, honor, sure sustaine,

[1] Younger son of Geoffrey de Vere, third son of John, fifteenth earl of Oxford. He was distinguished for his military services and was sometime Governor of the British forces in the Netherlands. He died 28th August, 1609, and was buried in Westminster Abbey. G.

Which haue bene your supporters hereto still:
I need not then perswasiue lines to fill,
The matter will suffise to moue your mind,
If that my hand the beauty of it spill;
Then let my loue of good, your fauour find,
Whose wisedome can, whose goodnesse may excuse
The faults, which—want not malice—made me muse.

To the worthy Knight Sir Iohn Stanhop, Treasurer of the Chamber to her Maiestie.[1]

No common thing it is to find —I graunt—
Humilitie and honour both in one:
Who loueth vertue, of them both may vaunt,
True honor still hath mild and vertuous showne;
Then since this worke of vertue treats alone,
—For sure true wisedome doth pure vertue teach—
It shall offensiue be—I trust—to none,
Their words of fauour for truth's shield to reach.

---

[1] Younger son of Michael Stanhope of Shelford, Notts. He was constituted treasurer of the Chamber 1696: created Baron Stanhope, of Harrington in 1505, and died 9th March, 1620. G.

Much lesse a shame, what mighty king did preach.
The same to suffer passe them vncontrold ;
But now adayes, men euery worke appeach,[1]
As barren, borrow'd, base, or ouer bold :
This makes me craue by you, wise, noble, good,
My wrong deprauer's malice be withstood.

To the worthy knight Sir Edward Dyer, Chauncellor of the most Honorable order of the Garter.[2]

Not last nor least, for common good desarts
I you repute, though fortune point your place :
Your loue to Vertue winneth many harts,
And Vertue's followers do your loue imbrace.
I know my argument requires no grace ;
Because grace it doth send, it brings delight :
For both all sue, all loue their pleasing face,
Yet vainely world, for both of them doth fight.
To make more plaine the way for euery wight,
This princely moderator paines did take,
Which—to your equals—men of learnèd sight,

[1] = impeach, as before. G.

[2] The friend of Sir Philip Sidney and Lord Brooke. He died in 1608. See our Memorial-Introduction to his collected Poems in Fuller Worthies' Library Miscellanies, Vol. III. G.

A full accord — if well iudg'd worke—will make:
You then kind courtier and sound scholler knowne,
Accept, reade, and protect these as your owne.

To the worthy Knight Sir Henry Killegrew.[1]

The natiue dutie which of right I owe,
To you good knight—for many fauours past,
To me and mine—do will me now bestow
Some token of my thankfull mind at last:
Which I more fitly no way then can show,
Then by presenting of this volume small,
Which from repentant heart of king did flow,
And many a warning too vnto vs all,
Who daily into new temptation fall,
And daily need assistance gainst the same:
In such respect this worke you well may call,
An antidote a happie life to frame:
Whereto since hitherto your vertues bend,
You will accept I trust—the gift I send.

---

[1] Closely related to the baronets of this name of Arwenwick, county Cornwall, and a well-known Elizabethan courtier. He died 1603. G.

To the vertuous gentleman Robert Bowes Esquire,
Embassador for her Maiestie in Scotland.[1]

As painters vse their tables set to show,
Of euery sight, ere they perfected bee,
By others better skill the truth to know,
Of faults which they themselues could hardly see:
And as best drugs on meanest shrub and tree,
By skilfull simplers gathred are sometime:
As gold in sand, as pearles in shell-fish wee
Do find, and amber in the sea-shore slime:
So vnder this ill-couchèd raggèd rime,
Which to your clearer sence I do present,
It may appeare how high his thoughts did clime,
That first to frame the same his studie bent;
And I excusd, who only do bestow,
What I to you, by auncient promise owe.

To the Vertuous Gentleman Fulke Greuill Esquire.[2]

Who can of learning treat, and you forget?

---

[1] Younger son of Richard Bowes, of Aske, county Durham, Esq., by Elizabeth, daughter and co-heir of Sir Roger Aske, Knight. He was ambassader to Scotland with his elder brother, Sir George Bowes. and was ancester of the family of Bowes of B.rnes. G.

[2] Consult our Memorial-Introduction to his collected Works: Vol. I. G.

Who may of vertue talke, and you neglect?
Who would true fame, from your due praises let?
Who should not—knowing you—your loue affect?
I therefore forcèd am in this respect,
To offer publikely for you to reed
The thing, the which vncrau'd you would protect,
If—by malignor's blame—it stood in need:
In diuerse, diuersly this worke will breed
I know, an humour in the censurer's braine;
The wisest, on the best contents will feed,
The curious—for some 'scapes—count all but vaine:
But of the better sort true prayse must grow;
The prayse of some is meere disprayse I know.

To the reuerend Doctor Andrews, professor in Diuinitie.[1]

I would not flatter Court, the Church much lesse,
But honouring both, I would them homage yeeld:

[1] The venerable and ever-to-be-revered Bishop Lancelot Andrews, then a Prebendary of St. Paul's and chaplain in ordinary to the Queen. He died 26th September, 1626. G.

In courts I liu'd, in Church—do I confesse—
I wish to die, and on that hope to build:
Then maruell not, I also seeke to shield
My bold attempt, with fauour of your wing,
Since your diuine conceit, can easiest wield
The burden, which this waighty theame can bring.
I meant in English dittie only sing,
The tragike notes, of humane well-away,
But waightie matter of so wise a king,
Compeld me yet a greater part to play:
Wherewith—halfe fainting—for your aide I craue,
Well meaning mind, from fearèd blame to saue.

To his especiall friend Richard Carew of Anthony, Esquire.[1]

As parents of their children fond appeare,
Oft times because with trauell them they bare,
Which makes them prise thē sometimes ouer deare,

[1] The celebrated Antiquary, Sheriff of Cornwall in 1586, and M.P. for Saltash 1589. He died 6th November, 1620. G.

When others see small cause for them to care.
As such likewise are oftentimes to spare,
In care of children that themselues haue none :
So is it like—with this my worke to fare—
With many readers when they are alone,
Who senslesse of my trauell like a stone,
—As neuer hauing yet so tride their braine—
Will think I cocker[1] this my brood, as one
Growne proud, that I some issue do attaine :
But you whose painfull pen hath shown you skill,
Can iudge my part, and it well conster[2] will

To his louing brother in law Robert Moyle, of Bake, Esquire, and Anne his wife.[3]

If like the world a while I seeme to you,
Forgetfull and vnkind for kindnesse showne,
Thinke it not strange their natures I ensue,

---

[1] Over-indulge. G.

[2] = construe. G

[3] Son of John Moyle, of Bake, county Cornwall, by Agnes, daughter of Thomas St. Aubyn, of Clowance, in same county. He had previously married Anne, the only sister of our Worthy, Henry Lok, by whom he had issue, a son John, sheriff of Cornwall, in 1624. See our Memorial-Introduction, *ante*. G.

Where most I liue, whose proofe is dearly
knowne,
The world to me vnkind and carelesse growne,
Conuerts my nature to her temperature ;
My youth—with loue of her puft vp and
blowne—
Is cause that I now iustly this endure :
Yet world's delights, nor cares nere alter'd sure,
So farre my minde, that I ingrate did proue ;
Heauen's faith, Earth's friendship, doth my
soule inure
To take far greater pains where once I loue :
You then—by bloud and friendship's holy
vow—
Right deare take this, and for loue's seale
allow.

T the Gentlemen Courtiers in generall.

Reiect me not—ye peares of gentle spright—
Because I do appeare in plaine array ;
Sometimes for change, the curious do delight
In meane attyres, and homely food we say ;
They are not limbd the best, that go most gay,
Nor soundest meats, that most the tast do please ;
With shepheards russets, shield from cold ye
may,

With hungry meales, preuent oft times disease ;
Such home-wouen robes, such wholesome dyet these,
—Euen these rude lines, of my compilèd frame—
Do offer you, your iudgements to appease,
As may him nourish that doth vse the same :
Not mine—but wisest Salomon's—recait,
So gaine the blessèd state we all await.

To the Right Ho. the Lady Marquesse of Northampton.[1]

The part which I haue taken now in hand,
To represent on stage to common sight,
With my true nature, seemes at strife to stand,
And on an actor farre vnfit to light :
Accustom'd more on vainer theames to write
Then with the taske which now I do pretend,
Which being to be view'd by iudgement's bright,
Makes me to seeke your fauour it defend :

[1] Helena, daughter of Wolfgangus Suachenburg, a Swede, third wife and relict of William Parr, (brother of Catherine Parr, queen to Henry VIII.) who was created Marquis of Northampton 16th February, 1546-7, and died in 1571, without surviving (legitimate) issue. She remarried to Sir Thomas Gorges, and dying 1st April, 1635, ætat 86, was buried in Salisbury Cathedral. G.

Vouchsafe a gracious glose thereto to lend,
I then beseech you—worthy patronesse—
To whose applause, full many more will bend,—
Because they know you vertue do professe,
And vertue is this theame, and that diuine;
With grace consent then, to my sute incline.

To the Right Honourable the Countesse of Darby.[1]

When this my bold attempt to mind I call,
Who Phaeton like would Phebus' chariot guide;
From doubtfull thoughts into dispaire I fall,
How such cleare light, my weake sight may abide:
From one presumption, vnto more I slide,
And give the raigne so much to rash desire
That I make publike what I ought to hide,
And seeke my sanctuary in that heauenly fire,
Whose image of perfection I admire,

[1] Elizabeth, eldest daughter of Edward de Vere, seventeenth Earl of Oxford, and wife of William Stanley, sixth Earl of Derby, to whom she was married 26th June, 1594. Her mother was Anne, daughter of William Cecil, Lord Burleigh. She was buried in Westminster Abbey 11th March, 1626-27. G.

In our rare goddesse, wisdome's clearest light,
Whose grate aspect, my many wants require,
To clense the clouds, which blind my iudgmēt's sight:
And such faire starres, as you—who influence haue
Of her bright beames—to giue some light I craue.

To the Right Honorable the Countesse of Cumberland.[2]

As one whose rashnesse once hath made him bold,
To breake the bands of vsèd modestie,
If of his error he should hap be told,
Will hardly yeeld that he hath gone awrye:
So worthie lady, I confesse that I,
Vnworthie scribe, of such a heauenly stile,
Now that I needs my boldnesse must espie,
Would couer from iust blame myselfe a while;

[2] Lady Margaret Russell, third daughter of Francis, second Earl of Bedford, and wife of George Clifford, third Earl of Cumberland—to whom Lok addressed a previous Sonnet. She was married in 1577. Owing to the misconduct of the Earl she was separated from him for some years before his death: but they were living together at the date of this Sonnet. She died 24th March, 1616. G.

With borrowed grace, therefore I seeke beguile
The cōmon sights, who least would spare my name;
If worthie you therefore but kindly smile,
I know that many more will do the same,
For wisest sort on vertuous do depend,
And vertuous ones will Vertue's cause defend.

To the Right Honorable the Countesse of Warwicke.[1]

In courtly life to keepe a conscience pure,
In youngest yeares to shew a matron's stay;
In honour's type, a lowly mind t'inure,
No doubt a hart regenerate doth bewray:
Such you are held, of such as rightly way
The practise of your life, to your great praise,
Whose vertues all temptations ouersway,
And your rare gifts, vnto the heauens raise:
No common thing it is, in these our dayes,
To see such starres in our darke firmament;

[1] Lady Anne Russell, eldest daughter of Francis, second Earl of Bedford, and third wife and relict of Ambrose Dudley, Earl of Warwick, who died ln 1589. She died 9th February, 1603. G.

Your worth, your soueraigne's influence wel
bewraies ;
Which so transformes, where so her vigor went :
Your birth, your mariage, Natures, gifts most
rare,
With gift of grace herein may not compare.

To the Right Honorable the Countesse of Pembrooke.[1]

Of all the nymphes of fruitfull Britaine's race,
Of all the troopes in our Dianae's traine,
You seeme not least, the Muses trophes grace,
In whom true honour spotlesse doth remaine :
Your name, your match, your vertues, honour
gaine,
But not the least, that pregnancie of spright,
Whereby you equall honour do attaine,
To that extinguisht lampe of heauenly light,
Who now no doubt doth shine midst angels bright ;
While your faire starre, make cleare our darkned sky,

[1] Mary, daughter of Sir Henry Sidney, K.G., and third wife and relict of Henry Herbert, second Earl of Pembroke, who died 19th January, 1600-1. It was to her the Arcadia was dedicated. She died 25th September, 1621. G.

He heauen's; Earth's comfort you are and
delight,
Whose—more then mortall—gifts you do apply,
To serue their Giuer, and your guider's grace,
Whose share in this my worke, hath greatest
place.

To the Right Honorable the Countesse of Essex.[1]

THESE oracles, by Holy Spright distild
Into the hart of wisest happie king,
To you most vertuous ladie here are wild,
As heire to parent worthie in euerie thing:
His carefull trauell countrie's peace did bring,
His solide wisedome vertue did pursue,
His bountie to the poore the world doth sing,
Whose honour him suruiueth, crownd in you:
So nobles—if to God they yeeld His due—
So people ought to nobles render fame,
So shall succeeding ages still renue

---

[1] Frances, daughter and heir of Frances Walsingham, widow of Sir Philip Sidney, and at the date of this Sonnet wife of Robert Devereux, second Earl of Essex, Queen Elizabeth's celebrated favourite—to whom one of the earlier Sonnets is addressed. She remarried to Richard, fourth Earl of Clanricarde. G.

By old records, his euer reuerent name,
Wherein your double blessed spousall bed,
Shall wreath an oliue garland on his head.

To the Right Honourable Ladie, the Ladie Scroope.[1]

The bountie which your vertues do pretend,
The vertues which your wisdome hath imbrast,
The wisdome which both grace and Nature lend,
The gracious nature which so well is plast,
Doth witnesse well the heauens your beauty grast,
With borrowed wisedome not of humane kind,
Which so hath fostred vertues mild and chast,
As benigne Beautie might a dwelling find,
Fit to receiue such presents, as in mind
Are consecrated to that sacred shrine,
Whereon—as vestal virgin—you assignd,
Do worthie waight, whose eye vouchsafe incline,
To take in worth, reade, iudge of, and defend
This worke, weake record of my heart's
intend.[2]

---

1 Probably Ursula, daughter of Sir John Clifton, of Barringtoh, county Somerset, and wife of Sir Adrian Scrope, of Cockerington, county Lincoln, Knight, who died 10th December, 1623. G.

2 = intention. G,

To the Honourable Ladie, the Ladie Rich.[1]

THE perfect beautie, which doth most reclaime,
The purest thoughts from base and vaine desire,
Not seene, nor leuied is by common aime
Of eies, whom coullers vse to set on fire:
The rare seene beautie men on Earth admire,
Doth rather dazell then content the sight,
For grace and wisdome soonest do retire,
A wandring heart to feed on true delight:
Seldome all gifts do in one subiect light,
But all are crownd, with double honour then,
And shine the more, adornd with vertue bright,
But—with Religion grast—adord of men:
These gifts of Nature, since they meet with grace,
In you, haue powre more then faire Venus face.

To the Right Honourable, the Ladie of Hunsdon.[2]

OF soule and bodie both since men consist,

---

[1] Lady Penelope Devereux, daughter of Walter, first Earl of Essex, and sister to Elizabeth's favourite. She was the first wife of Robert, third Baron Rich, from whom she was divorced, and was remarried 26th December, 1605, to Charles Blount, Earl of Devonshire, to whom, as Lord Mountjoy, a former Sonnet is addressed. G.

[2] The dowager Lady Hundson was living at this period,

Of diuers humours since our bodies be ;
Since sundry affects do one selfe thought resist,
Since body, soule, thought, will, are all in me,
Thinke you not strange, these passions new to see,
Which to my wonted humors different seeme,
They both are frute of one and selfe same tree :
The first by younger hold, this elder deeme.
If you of my indeuors will esteeme,
Whom well the world doth know can iudge
the best,
Whose course of life a happie pitch doth cleeme,
In vertuous proues,[1] wherein your fame is blest :
Then shall I haue a part of my desire,
Who for my trauell craue but liking's hire.

To the Honourable gentlewomen, Mistresse Elizabeth and Anne Russels.[2]

THE double giftes of nature and of grace,

---

but the Sonnet was probably addressed to the wife of George, second Lord Hundson, to whom a former Sonnet was addressed. She was Elizabeth, daughter of Sir John Spencer, of Althorpe, county Northampton. After Lord Hundson's death she remarried successively Sir Thomas Chamberlain, Knight, and Ralph, Lord Eure. She survived the latter, and was buried in Westminster Abbey 2nd March, 1617-18. G.

[1] = prowess. G.

[2] Only daughter of John, Lord Russell, (second son of

Redoubled in you both with equall share,
—Whilst beautie shineth in the modest face,
And learning in your mindes with vertue rare—
Do well expresse, of what discent ye are,
Of heauen's immortall seed, of blessed kind,
Of Earth's twise honord stock, which ye declare,
In noble parts composd of either's mind;
Then both in you—rare gems—we blessèd find,
Ye both by them are honord happily:
Then both, vouchsafe what I to both assignd
To read, and to conceiue of graciously:
So ye—like to your kind—the world shall know,
And to your selues—frō hence—some fruit shal grow.

Francis, second Earl of Bedford,) by Elizabeth, daughter of Sir Anthony Coke, of Giddy Hall, Essex, and widow of Sir Thomas Hobby, of Bisham, Berks. Knight. (An accomplished woman: See Ballard's Memoirs of British Ladies p. 136.) Elizabeth, eldest daughter died unmarried, 2nd July, 1600, and was buried with her father in Westminster Abbey. Anne married Henry, Lord Herbert, afterwards fifth Earl and created Marquis of Worcester. She died 8th April, 1639, and was buried at Ragland, county Monmouth. G.

To the Honourable gentlewoman Mistresse Elizabeth Bridges.[1]

Since I haue growne so bold, to take in hand
A theame so farre indeed vnfit for me,
As by the reading you will vnderstand,
Whereto my style in no sort doth agree;
I cannot chuse but feare, lest you should see
Some signe of high presumption in my mind,
Which cause of iust reproch to me might be,
And for my sake the worke lesse fauour find:
Vnto you therfore haue I this assignd,
To craue for me remission at your hand,
Whose vertues show, you cannot be vnkind,
If kindnesse may with modest vertues stand:
And of and for true vertue do I pleade,
Which to desirèd blisse and honour leade.

To the Honourable Lady, the Lady Southwell.[2]

To you the vowèd seruice of my mind,
—Faire Mistresse of the purest thoughts I bred—

---

[1] Eldest daughter and co-heir of Giles Brydges, third Lord Chandos, by Frances, daughter of Edward Clinton, first Earl of Lincoln. She afterwards married Sir John Kennedy, of Scotland, Knight. G.

[2] Probably wife of Sir Robert Southwell, who was knighted in 1585. G.

As youth's conceit could best inuention find,
I dedicated with affection fed.
My elder thoughts with your high honor led,
Haue often stroue to shew continued zeale,
But was discourag'd through mistrust and dred
Of my defects, which did my will conceale:
Yet now compeld my weakenesse to reueale
Vnto a world of worthie witnesses;
I craue to be excus'd, if I appeale
To you for grace, to whom I guilt confesse;
And hope you will for auncient seruice sake,
Excuse my wants, and this in worth will take.

To the Honourable Lady, the Lady Cecill.[1]

In counter-poise of your right high desart,
My dutie made my gratefull mind consent,
To straine my braine to equall with my hart,
In finding forth for you, some fit present:

---

[1] Next to impossible to identify this name, as there were various contemporary who might have been so called. Perhaps the second wife of William Cecil, afterwards second Earl of Exeter. If so, she was Elizabeth, daughter of Sir William Drury, of Suffolk, Knight, and died 26th February, 1658, aged 83. She had the best claim in 1597, to be called "the Lady Cecil." G.

Which to performe, thus will and powre—first
bent—
Was checkt by iust regard of your esteeme:
Which me preuented of my hopes intent,
Since for your worth, vaine things most pleasing
seeme:
Yet—least a meere excuse you that might deeme,
To cloke a thanklesse heart with idle hand—
With more then natiue strength a pitch I cleeme
To treat of blisse, which I not vnderstand:
But God's inspiring grace—to king once
tought—
I here as pawne of dutie, haue you brought.

To the Honorable Ladie, the Ladie Hobbye:[1]

Lest that this change of style at first might breed
A doubt in you, whose worke it were and gift;
I thinke it fit your searching thoughts to feed,
With truth who writ it, and therein his drift:

---

[1] Probably Margaret, daughter and heir of Arthur Dakyns of Linton and Hackness, county York. by Thomasine, daughter of Thomas Guy, Esq. She married Walter Devereux, Esq., brother to the Earl of Essex: second Thomas Sydney, son of the Right Honourable Sir Henry Sidney, K.G., (who died in 1595): thirdly Sir Thomas Posthumous Hoby, Knight. She died in 1635. G.

When scorne of hap, did force my hope to shift,
The place where in felicitie I sought,
As tyr'd on Earth, to heauen my thoughts I lift,
Which in me this strange metamorphos wrought:
But so vnperfect fruit, of what it ought,
Mixt with the dregs of old imprinted phrase,
Require a fauour in the Reader's thought,
With kind construction frailties forth to raze:
To you my wants, to me your vertues tryde,
Giues me good hope, this sute is not denyde.

To the vertuous Lady the Lady Layton.[1]

Since stranger like, to Court, but newly come,
This home-bred child, may hap for to be vsde,
Inquirèd of by most, censured by some
Which cannot iudge, yet will not be refusde:
Where wants are pride into, and soone accused,
If shape, attire, grace, skill, be not the best;
Where curious conceits will seeme abused,
If euery word, phrase, period, bide not test:

[1] Probably wife of Sir Edward Leighton, who was knighted 1521, and was M.P. and one of Her Majesty's Privy Council: ancestor of the present baronet of the name. But perhaps wife of his brother, Sir Thomas Leighton. If so, a daughter of Sir Francis Knollys, and had been maid of honour to Queen Elizabeth. The latter the more probable. G.

Least that this worke too rashly be suppreſt,
Vntried, halfe vnderstood, disgracèd quight,
I needfull thinke it be to some addrest,
Who can and will protect from causelesse spight:
Which that you will vouchsafe, I nothing feare,
Since to the matter, you such zeale do beare.

To the vertuous Lady, the Lady Woollie.[1]

Farre sēt, deare bought, doth fit a lady best;
Such you deserue, such would my will bestow:
Good things are rare, rare things esteem'd you know;
Rare should your's be, as you rare of the rest:
Such hold this gift, fetcht from a forraine land,
Which wisest king, as pretious did prouide,
Who viewing all the Earth, hath nought espide,
Whose worth—herewith cōpar'd—may longer stand:
The price—I dare assure—is very deare,
As puchasd by your merit and my care,
Whose trauell would a better gift prepare,

1 Of the Bridgewater Family. The copy of Lok's volume in the Bridgewater Library, has this sonnet in the Author's autograph prefixed. G.

If any better worthy might appeare:
Then this accept, as I the same intend,
Which dutie to the dead would will me send.

To the vertuous Lady, the Lady Carey.[1]

If anything might in this worke appeare,
Worthy the reading, fit for to content,
I should then hold it best bestowed here,
Where most my time in frame thereof was spent:
By view of your rare vertues I was bent,
To meditate of heauen and heauenly thing:
By comfort of your counsell forward went,
My halting muse, this heauenly note to sing.
And now that time doth forth this haruest bring,
Which must—till need—be layed vp in store,
—As medcine meet to cure care's deadliest sting,
And to restore health's comfort, weake before—
You—Lady—who of right best int'rest haue,
Must here receiue, and keepe, what first ye gaue.

---

[1] Identification almost impossible, as there were so many who might have been called "Lady Carey.". It may even have been a Carew as the names were used indiscriminately. G.

To the vertuous Lady the Lady D.[1]

If kinred be the neernesse of the blood,
Or likenesse of the mind in kind consent;
Or if it be like pronenesse vnto good,
Or mutuall liking by two parties ment:
If kindnesse be in truth of firme intent,
With open heart to testifie good-will;
If true good will, be to contentment bent,
If true contentment cannot be in ill;
I know you will repute this token still,
A pledge of kinsman's loue in ech degree;
Which though it do your treasure little fill,
Yet way to perfect wealth will let you see.
My selfe in kindnesse wish and hope in you,
Profit of mind, and soule's content t'insue.

To the vertuous Gentlewoman Mistresse E. Bowes.[2]

Among the many profits which do rise,
Vnto the faithfull, which the truth do loue,

[1] Even Colonel Chester has failed to identify this lady. G.

[2] The name of the mother of Robert Bowes, to whom a former sonnet was addressed, was Elizabeth: that of his own wife was Anne. Probably then the former is here addressed. G.

A greater comfort can I not deuise,
Then is the sweet societie they proue,
When each doth seeke for others best behoue,
To strengthen that which flesh and bloud doth shake:
Their weakned soules—I meane—which sorows moue,
Through feare of sin, and guiltie thoughts, to quake.
Whereof by you, since I experience make,
Whose mild and kind accord, with neighbours woe,
Doth cause them oft the crosse with patience take,
And forward still in hope and courage goe:
I were vngrate, if I should not indeuer
To nourish that—your grace—I honord euer.

To the Honorable Ladies and Gentlewomen attendants in the Court.

Ye worthy nymphes of chast Dyanae's traine,
Who with our soueraigne's presence blessed bee,
Whereby ye perfect beauty shall attaine,
If ye affect the gifts in her you see:
Scorne not to yeeld your mild aspects to me,
Who with you do attend her high behest;

It can no whit disparage your degree,
To looke on that is likèd of the best:
This worke for style inferiour to the rest,
Which many worthier wits to you present,
Craues welcome yet, as some—no common guest—
Whom best to greet your greatest care is spent.
For king's words these, do guide to blisse you craue,
The fruit of fauour which you striue to haue.

To all other his Honourable and beloued friends in generall.

WHAT shall I do? proceed or stay my pen?
To either side, great reason vrg'd my mind;
Vnto most powrefull would I yeeld, but then
Defect of powre, makes hand to stay behind:
Of well deseruing friends I many find,
Of worthy persons—vnsaluted—more;
Those I neglect may hold my heart vnkind,
And some my iudgement partiall hold therefore:
Yet—as I find—so they must graunt the store,
Of happy England's well deseruing state,
Exceeds the bounds my worke prescribd before
And doth restraine my mind to stricter rate:
But if one word may shew a world of loues,
Vse this and me, to all your best behoues.

From "His Maiestie's poetical exercises at vacant houres. Edinburgh, 4o. 1591":

To the King's Maiestie of Scotland.

If ALEXANDER sighed when he came,
Vnto the tomb where fierce ACHILLES lay:
If he had cause, that blessed age to blame,
Since HOMER lacks his merites to display.
If he with teares his sorrowes did bewray,
To see his father PHILIP conquer all,
And that more Worlds behinde there did not stay,
Which for reward of his deserts might fall:
Then may I moue, our times, our iudgement small,
Vnworthy records of your sacred skill:
Then must our Poets on new Muses call,
To graunt them guiftes to imitate your quill.
I, like the flie, that burneth in the flame,
Should shew my blindnes to attempt the same.

HENRY LOK.[1]

---

[1] On *verso* of 5th leaf: no pagination. G.

Appendix.

Agreeably to promise in Memorial-Introduction there follow here brief specimens of the versification of "Ecclesiastes," neither better nor worse than the rest.

At top of page one, is this verse-summary of the opening of the book:

"1. These sacred words king Dauid's son did preach, who Israel taught
2. All vanitie of vanitie's, he calls: more light then thought."

Well! 'thought' is not the best rhyme conceivable for 'taught' and 'thought' is not necessarily 'light': but so it runs. Again, and rather better, at page 23, is this:

1. All purposes haue proper times, all things fit seasons find:
2. A time of birth and death, to plant and supplant is assigned."

So too at page 59:

"3. A good name sweeter is then oyle: death's day then day of birth.
4. In mourning-house more good is learnd then in the house of mirth."

These must suffice: each couplet is the text of the verse on the several pages.

"Ecclesiastes" thus begins:

"The heauenly words of holy Dauid's sonne,
Who ouer Israel's race sometimes did raigne,
Wherewith to vertue he his subiects wonne,
Whilst in Ierusalem he did remaine;
And to instruct them thus did not disdaine.
Those words, no vaine discourse it is I write,
Pend by a prince, as God did them indite."

One turns expectantly to the vivid and memorable 12th chapter of the original: but here is all that offers even there:

Suppose each ringing knell puts thee in mind,
That thou art in the way vnto thy graue;
Take heed that death thee vnprepar'd not find,
But so in all thy life thy selfe behaue,
As if thou were the man whose turne is next
And wouldst not with a sudden death be vext.
Before—I say—the vital spirits faile,

Or that thy radick humours all be spent,
That cramps do siluer cords of raynes assaile,
  And Nature's intercourse no more be sent,
  From liuer, hart and braine, as earst it went.
Before warme bloud with isey fleame do quailė,
And pulslesse leaue thy ouer emptie vaine,
Before the cesterne—made for liue's auaile—
Thy stomack now no sustenanee retaine;
  But all the wheeles of Nature lacking strength
  To giue them motion, they do faile at length.
For then—be sure—thy dayes are neere an end
And flesh dissoluèd turneth vnto dust:
Then yeeld thereto, before perforce thou bend,
  And in thy strength of youth repose no trust,
  Nor place thy ioy in earth or earthly lust.
Thy nobler part—thy soule—it did descend
From God, first mouer of all life and grace,
Who therefore doth chiefe interest pretend
In thee and it, and will thy soule imbrace,
  Amidst the heauens of the eternall rest,
  If faith and loue haue once thy way adrest.

Thus it closes:

The end of all true wisedome is in this,
To know the will of God, and it obserue:
To know His will, and yet to walke amis,

A double chastisement must needs deserue :
Then feare henceforth therefro so apt to swerue.
No seruile feare which I perswade it is,
But such a gratefull child to parent owes
Who though he feele the smart, the rod will kisse,
Because the fruit of father's loue he knowes ;
And this doth God require of man indeed,
That our obedience should from loue proceed.
The breech whereof will heauie iudgement call,
When God the searcher of the heart and raines,
Shall vnto reckning with vs for them fall,
And pay our passèd ioyes with lasting paines ;
For sinfull worke no other guerdon gaines.
O happie then shall they be most of all,
Whose heedfull liues in holy workes was spent ;
The game of this their trauell is not small :
For blessed they the narrow path that went.
And though this narrow gate few enter in,
Yet who runs in this race, the prize shall win.

Probably the Reader will agree with me that enough of "Ecclesiastes" has been given: and so we will write

Finis.

Epilude.

SINCE our Memorial-Introduction was printed, we haue chanced upon the following interesting *bit* in the Sale-Catalogue of the famous Library of B. H. Bright Esq. (1845) :

"924 Calvin (John) Sermons upon the Songe that Ezechias made after he had been sicke and afflicted by the hand of God, translated by A. L. John Day, 1560.

*** This little Volume is dedicated to Katherine, Duchess of Suffolke. After the Sermons occurs a fresh title, "A Meditation of a Penitent Sinner, written in manner of a Paraphrase of the 51 Psalme of David," the whole of which, including a preface, is in verse.

On the fly-leaf is written, "Liber Henrici Lok ex dono Anne uxoris suæ 1559.". It is most probable therefore, that this lady was the translator."

The initials A. L. of the first title-page, seem to place identification of the translator as Anne Lock beyond dispute. The date '1559-60' shews that she was Anne (Vaughan) mother of our Worthy, rather than his wife, whose Christian name was also Anne.

Besides the sons of our Worthy named in the

Memorial-Introduction there was one daughter at least, viz. Agnes, baptized at Acton, Middlesex, between 25th March and 15th April, 1594, as "dau. of Mr. Henry Lock".

With reference to the Verse of Lok, the Reader will note that very often the rhyme of the second line from the end of the Sonnet has a second rhyme in the middle as well as at close of last line. To mark this as of design, the middle of the line is printed (often very unappropriately) with a capital letter.

By an unlucky oversight an 'f' is dropped out of 'afflatus' in Memorial-Introduction, page 32. G.

MISCELLANIES

OF

The Fuller Worthies' Library.

THE

TEARES OF THE BELOUED:

(1600)

AND

MARIE MAGDALENE'S TEARES:

(1601)

BY

GERVASE MARKHAM:

Edited, with Memorial-Introduction and Notes,

BY THE

REV. ALEXANDER B. GROSART,

ST. GEORGE'S, BLACKBURN, LANCASHIRE.

PRINTED FOR PRIVATE CIRCULATION.

1871.

156 COPIES ONLY.

In our large paper we have the pleasure to present a photo-chromo-lith of the book-plate of Gervase Markham. It must have been among the earliest in England. Cf. that of Cromwell in our Vaughan (Vol. IId. illustrated 4to.) G.

Memorial-Introduction.

IT is vexatious to later Inquirers such as ourselves to discover how perfunctorily the Biography of the Worthies of our Country has been written, and how much has been allowed to perish from sheer neglect. For example, in pursuing our researches for a Memoir of Gervase Markham, we have found in what really is the best of our general biographic authorities, viz. Alexander Chalmers' edition of the General Biographical Dictionary (1815), this summary of a scanty notice: "The time of his birth, death, and all other particulars regarding him are utterly unknown": whereas at the very time in which this was written the MARKHAMS were a prominent family, and one gifted representative at least held family-papers that would (even then) have yielded very considerable information, and doubtless have been willingly communicated on application. But such a thing as making local and personal investigations never seems to have occurred to these compilers, and their successors have too often followed suit. Well-nigh every Life in our Fuller Worthies' Library has called for such a statement and complaint.

It is well that both in our own Country and in the United States of America, increasing attention is being given to utilizing the public and private Manuscript-stores of national and family history. Many of the books that have resulted are printed only, not published: but all, as a rule, are placed in the great Public Libraries, and thus are accessible to the conscientious Worker. The MARKHAMS have a singularly careful and valuable Family-history in the "History of the MARKHAM Family, By the REV. DAVID FREDERICK MARKHAM",

(London, 1854, 8vo: a very limited private impression): and therein is told such a story as few Families have surpassed, carrying within it names and achievements of note in the three spheres of the Law, Literature, and the Church: while at this hour the lustre of the name is unpaled. Our researches have brought us into pleasant correspondence with Lieutenant-Colonel MARKHAM, whose soldierly *esprit* is gratified in counting back to our "Captain" Jervase Markham—to name no more—and CLEMENTS R. MARKHAM Esq, the Historian of the War of ABYSSINIA, the Biographer of FAIRFAX, and in connection with the introduction of Chincona into INDIA, the doer of deeds of daring such as match with the heroes of the Elizabethan days as his chronicle of them does with the grand old folios of Voyage and Travel. There is apparently no liklihood of the name of MARKHAM dying out: and no fear of its whiteness being smirched by its present bearers,—descendents from Dr. William Markham, Archbishop of York, who died in 1807 in his eighty-ninth year and sleeps well in Westminster.

Leaving the Reader to consult the volume named—a copy being in the British Museum—where the most pains-taking and elaborate genealogies are given: and also inviting attention to an interesting supplement to it, called "Entries in an Old Pocket Book, of A. D., 1680, belonging to Sir Robert Markham, Baronet, of Sedgebrook, county Lincoln: from additional MSS., British Museum, 10, 621," (privately printed) by which it seems to us made good that Judge MARKHAM, *not* Judge Gascoigne, was the fearless asserter of the supremacy of Law in ordering the Prince of Wales to prison—we have simply—after a brief retrospect—to present the few facts that survive concerning our Worthy—adding thereto from MSS. unknown to the Family, and hence not used in their Family-History.

Like many of our English families, the MARKHAMS took their name[1] from their lands in WEST and EAST MARKHAM, which are two contiguous parishes

---

[1] A question has long existed in the family, as to what the exact device of our [the Markham] crest is, whether the head of the lion should be surrounded with rays, and what instrument it holds in its paw. This may be set at rest by an entry in one of the Harleian MSS. "Standard of Sir John Markham in temp. Henry VIII. Par fesse, gold and blue. The device (or crest) *a lion rampant gules with wings endorsed or, holding a pair of horse heames of the first*, the lion of St. *Mark* and the *heames* forming a very indifferent pun on the name. (Harleian MSS., fol. 209)" (Family History, as *supra*, pp. 16-17.)

in the county of NOTTINGHAM, and southern division of the hundred of BASSETLAW. They had been seated there from time immemorial or at least un-memorialed, and were says CAMDEN in his Britannia, "very famous heretofore, both for antiquity and valor." The MARKHAMS trace their lineage to a date anterior to the Norman Conquest, and subsequent to Edward the Confessor, the line is unbroken. WEST MARKHAM became the fee of ROGER DE BUSLI, a chieftian of high esteem with WILLIAM THE CONQUEROR, who in addition to this, conferred upon him no less than thirty-nine manors in the county of NOTTINGHAM. Under this Roger, the manor of WEST MARKHAM was held by CLARON or ARON, who is mentioned in Domesday Book, as occupying land there, and Roger—who had a son FULC—held land similarly in East Markham, and so they were styled "de Marcham"—the ancient mode of spelling the name. Fulc's son became SIR ALEXANDER DE MARCHAM, Lord of Marcham. He was born about the year A. D. 1130, and is the first man of mark in the Family, having distinguished himself in the turbulent wars of STEPHEN's reign. I pass as irrelevant here, the numerous marriages and intermarriages and the many remaining lapidary and other family-memorials—resisting the temptation of lingering over the fine love-story and old-fashioned love-verse of SIR JOHN HARINGTON and "sweete Isabella Markham" and their subsequent marriage under the auspices of the PRINCESS ELIZABETH, not long before her committal to the Tower, in 1554,—and come to ROBERT MARKHAM, born at Sireston, (Notts), who succeeded his grandfather SIR JOHN MARKHAM in the family-estates, and like him was a "valiant consumer of his paternal inheritance". He was much trusted by QUEEN ELIZABETH, and was in constant attendance upon her. In the 13th year of the great Queen, he was knight of the Shire for the county of Nottingham, and High Sheriff in the same year. In the twenty-fifth year of the same reign, he again served the office of High Sheriff, and was elected once more, in the thirty-first of Elizabeth, as Knight of the shire for the same county. His name is introduced in the famous distich of the Queen, in which she celebrated her four Nottinghamshire knights.

> "Gervase the gentle, Stanhope the stout,
> MARKHAM THE LION, and Sutton the lout."

SIR ROBERT MARKHAM'S main family-residence latterly, was COTHAM: and hence he is known as MARKHAM OF COTHAM. He was twice married, first, to MARY, daughter of SIR FRANCIS LEEKE, and secondly, to JANE, daughter of William Burnell,—by the latter having only one son ROGER, who died without issue. He himself died in 1606. By his first wife he had five sons, first, ROBERT, who succeeded him, second, FRANCIS, third, GERVASE, fourth, JOHN, fifth, GODFREY: and three daughters. Of the 'fair ladyes" GERTRUDE alone need be noticed, as having become the wife of SIR THOMAS SADLEIR, of STANDEN COURT in Hertfordshire. Their son Ralph is thus mentioned by ISAAC WALTON, through VENATOR: "To-morrow morning we shall meete a pack of other dogs of noble Mr. Sadleir, upon Amwell Hill, who will be there so early that they mean to prevent [= anticipate] the sun rising."

Of the other sons, full details are given in the Family-History. The third, GERVASE, is our present Worthy. It is apparent then, that he was well-born. His cradle was rocked in a lordly mansion. Time's "effacing fingers" have more than defaced it: but evidence remains of its splendor. By the kindness of the Family I am able to present in our (large paper) as vignette at head of this Memorial, the "Site of the House at COTHAM"—great trees enriched by the ancient dust, growing thereon, and where as GOLDSMITH sings, are

> ...."seats beneath the shade
> For talking age, and whispering lovers made"[1]

Gervase—sometimes written *Jervais*, *Jervis*, and simply I and J—was born 'about the year 1566':[2] and in the quaint account given by his elder brother Francis, we get insight into the manner of education of the cadets of good families in England at the time. Here is a short portion: "Francis Markham, second son of Robert Markham of Cotham, borne 7 Eliz. [1564-5] on Wednesday at afternoon between ten and eleven, July 25. First brought up at my lord of Pembroke's, whose wife was Catherine, daughter of yᵉ earl of Shrewsbury, whose mother and his were cousin germans. Brought up after 10 years with BILSON, schoolmaster of Winchester and after bishop there. After, I was put to Adrianus de Saraina, at Southampton, a schoolmaster, who going to his country, the Lowe Countries, my lord put me to

---

[1] Deserted Village.

[2] So in the Family-history. As Robert and Francis preceded Gervase, probably 1568 at earliest was his birth-year. Robert as *supra* seems to have been born in 1654-5.

one Malin, a lowe fellowe, schoolmaster at Paules. Then, 1582, my lord put me to Trinity College in Cambridge, to my tutor Dr. Hammond, and allowed me forty marks per annum. My tutor departing, left me at Dr. Gray's. I contemned him, and went to ye warrs. Whereat my lord was angry and cut off my pension. So lived I in disgrace, till I submitted myself to my father in 1586 :" then follows a strangely chequered career. We cannot go far astray in assuming that the younger brother followed very much the same course. Indeed it is found that foreign tongues were at his tongue's end and that he became a soldier of Fortune in the European battle-ground of the Low Countries, and later followed Essex into Ireland, serving under his command, in company with his brothers Francis and Godfrey, and later still, he took a prominent and heroic part as a Captain under Charles I. But however mixed up with the military services and troubles of a troublous period—earlier and later—he must have lived much in the Country and observed closely the entire range of Agriculture and Arboriculture or Husbandry; while his numerous and strangely varying and rapidly-issued books, attest large literary leisure. The Bibliographical authorities—as Hazlitt—furnish ample information on these technical treatises. This is not the place for recording or dwelling on them. We content ourselves with shortened titles. "The English Husbandman" "The Country Farm", "Cheap and Good Husbandry", "A Farewell to Husbandry", "The Way to get Wealth", "The Whole Art of Husbandry", "The Enrichment of the Weald of Kent", "The English Housewife", "The Pleasure of Princes, containing a Discourse on the Arte of fishing with the Angle, and of breeding the Fightinge Cock", "A Health to the gentlemanly profession of Serving-men or the servingman's comfort", "Country Contentments", "Hunger's Prevention, or the Whole Art of Fowling, by Water and Land", "The Art of Archerie", "The Perfect Horseman", "The Soldier's Accidence or an Introduction to Military Discipline", "The Soldier's Exercise" and "Honour in his Perfection or a Treatise in Commendation of the Virtues of several Noblemen", "The Gentleman's Academy; or the Book of St. Alban's by Juliana Berners, now reduced unto a a better methode". Some of these books passed through an extraordinary number of editions, and each was usually in advance of the former. Some of the earlier indeed are first-forms of the fuller treatises later : others are portions of what were subsequently made complete treatises. Such was his reputation that the Booksellers to guard their interest in his writings obtained the following singular agreement from him: "Mem. That I, Gervase Markham of London, Gent, do promise hereafter never to write any more book or books to be printed of the diseases or cures of any cattle, horse, ox, or cow, sheepe, swine, or goates. In witnesse whereof I have hereunto set my hand the 24th daie of July, 1617. Gervase Markham." Throughout we have been struck with the quaintly-introduced piety of many of the counsels. The 'Gardener' in the planting of his trees and flowers, the 'Horseman' and 'Farrier' in their 'care' of the 'horse', the 'House-wife' in home-arrangements, the 'Archer' in his choice of bow and arrows, the Labourer in the lowliest field-work, is charged to 'go about' all with prayer and composedness of spirit. In his rural books too, there are incidental word-paintings of scenery, utterances of the joys and enjoyments of the country, that breathe of the woodland and which so-to-say alternately flutter and scent the pages with out-of-door freshnesses and fragrances.

Without tarrying longer on these old treatises, with their graphic, vigorous wood-cuts—now rarely to be met with and eagerly snatched up whensoever they occur—we have to do here mainly with his poetical productions. These were very much '*asides*,' and hence are semi-anonymous: our two reprints for example of "The Teares of the Beloved or Lamentation of St. John concerning the Death and Passion of Christ Jesus our Saviour" (1600) and "Marie Magdalene's Lamentations for the Loss of her Master Iesus" (1601) having in the former his initials I. M. only, and in the latter not even his initials.

A hitherto unpublished letter which we have unearthed with others from the Lambeth Shrewsbury papers (709, p. 65) puts somewhat strongly and roughly his 'intermeddling' with Verse and his verdict upon himself as a Poet, albeit the circumstances out of which the letter came must modify our interpretation of the vehement words:

"S^r^,

Y^e^ reuerence I beare to age, & my loue to Modestye shall euer houlde me wth in those gentyle limitts wch beinge brake by any passion of Furye, doth in my conceyt disgrace both age and modestye.

Yow haue chargd me in a letter to my father y^t^ I haue bene an Instigator of those vnkyndnesses wch haue past betwene yow; to wch I doe aunswere, it is altogeyther vntrue, for I did euer and doe styll see yt these ciuille dissentions, and vnhappie disvnions in our owne bloods will if yow will contynewe theyme be the vtter ruine of both your estimations, whylst those yt are ye publique enemyes of our name (and who of my soule haue bene ye first stirrers of this indignation) doe as in a Theater sytt and laughe at our ech others deuowringe. To this instigation yow ade me ye tytle of a poetycall lyinge knave, to wch I thus aunswere.

For my loue to poesye if it be an error, I confes my selfe faultye, and haue wth as greate hartynes as ever I greived for any sinne com̄ytted gaynst the hyest, mourned for myne howers mispent in yt feather-light studye, yet can I name many noble personages who wth greater desyer, and more feruencie have contynued and boasted in ye humor, wch thoughe in others it be excellent, in my selfe I loathe and vtterlye abhorr it; but for 'lyinge knaue', wth him dwell it wch vniustlye gaue it me, and doe but name hym that will in equal place so name me, and I will eyther giue my soule to god or thrust ye lyinge knaue into hys bossome. Sr imagin me as yow wryte me to be trulye my father's sonne, so haue I trulye a feelinge of my father's indignities wch agaynst my mother's sonne I will mayntayne to be false and contrarye, taske me when you will, for in yt I respect no creature ; And so I comytt yow to god, assuringe yow hereafter I will proue no knaue but your nephew.

GERUIS MARKHAM."

The dedication of his book on "Horses" to 'the right worshipful and his singular good father Robert Markham of Cotham in the county of Nottingham, esquire," harmonizes with this vindication as "his father's sonne" in the letter.

We have given this passionate Letter *in extenso* for two reasons, (1) Because it seems to be the only specimen of his that has come down to us: (2) Because of its curious disavowal of Poetry. It may be as well before passing to explain that the quarrel and consequent challenge were between SIR JOHN MARKHAM of Ollerton and SIR ROBERT MARKHAM of Cotham. We are enabled to supply the lack of the Family-History by printing (again for the first time) the extraordinary Letter, to part of which our Gervase wrote as above. It also is preserved at Lambeth (708, p. 45): the close-binding of the volume obliterating here and elsewhere a few words. We adhere literally to the original: and *certes* it is a suggestive glimpse that it gives us into the manners of England's gentry at the period. Nor will the Shakespearean reader fail to mark the mention of the "*Mermaid in Bred Street*".

Y^{or} Worships lre[1] y^{u} sent mee ye 12 of June, dated fro^{m} Winkborne hath not hitherto been aunswered by me, and for that I would be glad better to informe yo^{u} of yor self then yet ye know yor self, I doe take this paines for yor worships sake. Now to the matter. Ffirst yor great conceipted Worship compareth me to Tosse, a man better knowne to mee then to yor self, for when ye Lord Marques carried the order of ye garter to Henry ye ffrench kinge, then I did waite of Henry, Earle of Rutland, al wch tyme ye forsaid Tosse waited of Edward Horsex and ffrancis, both of them my good friends, and diverse tymes pleasured mee wth his service, and from that day to his deathe vsed me ever kindlie when he was himself, but sometimes when he was drunke, then he would waile as your worship will doe when y^{e} are in such like case, as for example at the Fun'all at Sheffield one night

[1] lre (= letter).

at supper in the great chamber, Mr. Carter and yor self maintained great and lowde argument, one of y^u against t'other: now said my Lord, marke Robert Markham for he is drunke, and that maketh him so lowde, therfore I am to advise you to drinke smaller drinke and then I hope I shall not be soe much troubled wth yor Worships drunken lyinge railinge. A better person then yourself shall iustyfy this whensoever you list to bringe it in question.

Also touchinge Charles Chester, a man better knowne to me than yor Worship, for he and I this Michoemas tearme last, mett twice or thrice a weeke at the Mermaid, in Bred St., wheare my Lo^r Compton, Mr. Pope, Mr. Catesby, my brother Sheldon his sonne, with divers others of good account; and then I founde kindness at his hands, whearby I judge him of better and more gratefull nature then yor Worship, so as I thanke God you are not able to compare me to soe arrand an vngrateful knave as y^r self. If you call yt to remembrance I sent my servant Stuffin to yor twice or thrice when you weare in the kinges Bench to see you and to tell you that I would be glad to come to visitt yow, to shew you such poore pleasure as I could, the wch Message by yor aunswere to him you seemed to take kindlie but you did not desire my companie theare, but when you should come into yr countrey you would be glad see me, both in yor oune house and mine: now what befell in this meantyme that made this great alteracon, is better knowne to you than to me. But as I gesse it proceeded from yor vngratefull lyinge sonne Robert, and also the instigation of yor poeticall and lyinge knave Gervas. Thus I find these two shew themselves rightly yor sonnes, presuminge of yr accustomed boastinge of yor bastardlie descent, the wch descent for feare you should forgett it I have sent you hearewth vnder ye Harrolds hand, even of charitie to entreat you to know yor self.

Thoughe yor worship is most vngratfull yet I would haue you remember that by my meanes before yor acquaintance wth that honorable knight Sr Ralph Sadler, I procured the particon of yor ffences at Cotham, which my good father could never doe. Also that favor yow founde in the Starr Chamber against Mr. Jhon Molyneux was likewise by my meanes. To conclude, a ream of paper cannot contain the ffriendships of my parte and the ingratitude of yrs. You and I have been Justices of peace, thereby we know the manner of the Warrants that are to be graunted in that behalf, and in trew faith notwithstandinge yo$_r$ great threates, I will not feare that I am affraid of yo$_r$ person, for all the lands you have, notwithstandinge yo$_r$ priveledge and my delaye, for I thinke my self verie well able to beate you, if you will attempt anie violence against me in yor owne person. Robbin hath not deserued at yor hand the touch you give him in yor letter: he diverse tymes ventured his liffe for you both in feilde and towne.

You had best lett that lyinge bragge cease to say you are the best of my howse, for Griffin may iustly reprove you in that, and soe it is like he will. The lye you made in yor first letter to the younge Countess touchinge ye Stanhops as . . . . that letter you termed them: alas the hearinge of you and by common report knowinge you as they doe, they make a mockerie at yo reports and writings. If it please you to aske Mr. Laurence Wright of it, I thinke he will confidentlie and iustlie reprove you, whose words creditt and state is better then yo^{sr} (whose sonne the more you shame, he beginninge wth little, and you possessing in effect the substance of my father's livinge) is like to overtop yo^{rs} in creditt, estimacon and revenew, ys more my greiffe for his wives sake, whose vertews doe trewlie witnes her desir to be as yt is from an honest worshipfull line. And so I cease to trouble my self to advise you whose graltsnesse[1] will give place to no good Counsell.

ffrom Ollerton the 4 of February 1600.

by me more your frend then you hever deserved.

THO MARKHHAM."[2]

---

[1] *Sic*: or graltsneshe—an unintelligable word, unless it be a clumsy play on *grallatores* = the long-legged or wading class of birds, by which to symbolize his correspondent's stilted and boastful character (alleged).

[2] For full details on the Markhams of Ollerton, see Family History , as before, c. iv. The printed Catalogue of Lambeth thus describes this Letter: "MS. 708-45. Letter of remonstrance, relating many curious circumstances from Thomas Markham to the Earl of Shrewsbury: Ollerton, 4 February, 1600." This cannot possibly be correct, as Robert and Gervase are distinctly designated in it, his correspondent's 'sonnes'. The *Tho.* (not John) is plain enough; but it is a copy (probably a hasty one). This can scarcely have been "Black Markham, of Kirkby Bellers" : for *he* was eldest son of Sir John Markham. of Cotham. One would regret to make out that the writer was the chivalrous Colonel Thomas Markham, who died sword in hand for his king and what he believed to be the cause of his country.

With reference to these Lambeth MSS. the only one that appears to be autograph is Gervase's (709. f. 65): the rest transcripts.

There were other family-quarrels of the same outrageous sort. The Markham Family-History already mentioned repeatedly, gives details of the parties and a somewhat imperfect and inaccurate 'copy' (from the Lansdowne MSS.) of Sir John Markham's "*railing* letter", as it is headed. We present only (also for the first time) the old verse-libels, in all their rage and oddity of phrase:

Lambeth MSS. 701, p. 67.

These are the verses wch weere written the day after Sr Thomas Stanhop's Cooche Lethers was cutt at Newark and dispersed abroade in the streetes, being twentie of them lapped upp like letters wth this direction,

To m^r^ John Markham one of the yonger sonnes of m^r^ Robert Markham of Cotham.

thou crooke backte scabted scurvie Squyer,
thou plaiest the knave for flatterie and hyer:
thou shalte haue to portion, by this birth right,
the Gallowes most fitt for so scurvie a wight.

And for the Cooche cutting and libells sett upp
Thou arte a Calf and a sheepes face, no wiser
than a tupp,

A scurvie knaue thou arte and so thou wilte dye
Farewell scabbed crooke back, not worthie a
flye.

These following mr John Markham wrott in aunswere to these above :

Yf slaunderous woordes may stande for trew
reportes
and whooremongers the honestest defame,
Yf incest be accompted but a sporte
and offered rape to sonnes wief but a game;
Yf these be thus conceited by the knyght
of stanhops race who libellèd on me,
I hope the world will weigh my case aright
And saye that lyes his vsuall Customes be.

The "railing" letter follows: but as it is given in the Family-History need not be reprinted. Only it may be well to note that by mis-reading 'Markham's' for 'Machivael's' the meaning is there confused, and so with other mis-readings, albeit the Lambeth copy is far from an accurate one.

These MSS. have swept us away from our more immediate subject: and yet their fierce satiric, not to say libellous Verse, gives a link of connection. The Markhams earlier and onward seem all to have had something of the Poet or Verse-Thinker and Writer about them. Perhaps the very strong (professed) 'abhorring' of Poetry in Gervase's letter explains his anonymity, seeing the letter and "Teares of the Beloved" both belong to 1600, while the tacit announcement of "Marie Magdelene's Lamentations" in the short Epistle of the first, might cause him to deem even initials supererogatory. His words are definite enough : "I offer thee my harsh and untuned Muse, which being as my talent is, slender and simple, so accompt of the *first part that I may not be discomforted in the second'*.

We must return upon our Worthy's poetical publications. In 1595 he published "The most honorable Tragedie of Sir Richarde Grinville, Knight". Its Italian motto—found elsewhere also—"Bramo assai, poco spero, nulla chieggio" gives point to Bishop HALL's sarcastic hits in his Satires on the practice. "England's Parnassus" (1600) quotes with disproportionate abundance from this small tome, a tomb rather than a Memory-preserving monument to the gallant knight, it somewhat stammeringly celebrates. In 1596 appeared "The Poem of Poems or Sion's Muse. Contayning the diuine Song of King Salomon, deuided into eight Eclogues". It was reprinted the following year, and dedicated to "The sacred virgin, divine Mistress Elizabeth Sidney, sole daughter of the ever-admired Sir Philip Sidney." A copy of the former is preserved among the Grenville books of the British Museum: the latter is in the Bodleian. We have not been rewarded for blowing the dust from them. In 1597 he issued another work paraphrastically translated from the French of Madame Petau Maulette, called "Devoreux: or Vertue's Tears for the Losse of the most Christian King Henry, third of that name, King of Fraunce: and the vntimely death of the most noble and heroicall gentleman Walter Devoreux, who was slain before Roan in France." In 1600 came the "Teares of the Beloved"—copies of which occur with slightly differing title-pages—and in 1601 its sequel "Marie Magdalene's Teares." Until we read in the Markham Family-History that our Worthy was the author of the second poem—the statement resting upon the authority of HASLEWOOD—we had deemed its authorship unknown, and had intended reprinting it as of the too many anonymous productions of the period. But for reasons already given, we have now no hesitation in assigning it to GERVASE MARKHAM: and hence it will follow the other, and by its continuous pagination complete our small revival of his Verse. To 1607 belongs the following: "Rodomonth's Infernall, or the Diuell conquered. Ariastos Conclusions. Of the Marriage of Rogero with Bradamonth his loue, and the fell fought Battell betweene Rogero and Rodomonth the neuer-conquered Pagan. Written in French by Philip de Portes, and Paraphrastically translated by G[ervase] M[arkham]." RITSON in his "Bibliographia Poetica" has this Note on the quaint volume: "In the title of the [British] Museum copy, the name of Gervase Markham is obliterated and that of "Robert Tofte, gentleman" inserted in its stead. R. T. [Robert Tofte] in his translation of Varchi, 1615, says, "read *my* Ariostos Satyres in English; and, in a postscript to the courteous reader, "he speaks of having intended to insert the disastrous fall of three notable Roman gentlemen, ouerthrown through jealousy; but the same was (with Ariosto's Satyrs, translated by him out of Italian into English verse, and notes upon the same) printed without his consent or knowledge, in another man's name": probably Markham's. (The latter part of this note is by the ingenious Mr. Park." It is preposterous to accept a claim of this sort in the face of Markham's own title-page *eight years before*, and when he was still living to be named if TOFTE had any worth or warrant in his statement. The book is an empty one: but we can't withdraw the authorship from him with counter-proof so poor and indefinite.

In 1609 came forth "The famovs Whore, or Noble Curtizan: conteining the lamentable complaint of Pavlina, the famovs Roman Curtizan, sometimes Mrs. unto the great Cardinall Hypolito, of Est. By Garuis Markham". The Author putting on the mask of the Printer thus speaks to the Reader: "Gentlemen, I haue aduentured to bring a whore into your company, but with no bad intent; but to giue you honest recreation: not to hurt you in purse or body. Therefore you must thinke this is a famous, strange whore: for shee seekes the hurt of no man. Wrong her not then, but giue her kind welcome out of Italy." Besides these, wholly his own, our Worthy according to the custom of the period and onward, joined with LEWIS MACHIN in "The dumbe Knight, a pleasant Comedy, acted sundry times by the children of his Maiestie's Revels" (1608) and with WILLIAM SAMPSON in "The true Tragedy of Herod and Antipater: with the death of faire Marriam.' (1622). An address "To the understanding Reader" of "The dumbe Knight" signed by MACHIN, speaks of the part-authorship but does not name MARKHAM. It is only a fair reprisal that in certain copies MARKHAM inserted his own name. Mr. Hazlitt's hasty remark (*s.n.*) that "he was rather an adept at this" has no real basis. "Herod and Antipater" seems to have escaped even his omniverous reading, as it appears under neither MARKHAM nor SAMPSON. The "Dumbe Knight" was reprinted by DODSLEY.

Such were the literary, and more particularly, the Verse productions of GERVASE MARKHAM,—in quantity alone noticeable. He must have held the pen of "a ready writer" and that as the instrument of a very rapid, sharp, vigilant, fecund, receptive intellect and capacious and resolute memory. His culture too must have been considerable. Besides the ancient languages, he was familiar with French, Italian, Spanish and probably Dutch. I fear that in his prose books he acted as what came to be known in later years as the Bookseller's 'hack' or 'drudge', rejecting no topic that offered and assured from his unexampled popularity that his name would 'sell' anything.

Of the Facts of his Life, beyond its literary activities, scarcely anything more remains to be told. Only certain family outrages—one touched on by HUME in his "History of England"—and another which fills a goodly space in the old "Biographia Britannica" under HOLLES. The Family-History gives them in full, and thither and to the B. B. we refer the Reader who cares.

The Family-Biographer remarks that "in reading the account of this extraordinary outrage, (the Holles one) it should be remembered that it came chiefly from partizans of the house of Holles, and that if Markham's version of the story were given, it might assume for him a more favourable aspect." We suspect, to use a vulgar proverb, there were six of the one and half-a-dozen o' the other. The most stolid Conservatism can scarcely regret that such strifes as theirs are now an impossibility.

The HOLLES Narrative informs us that Gervase Markham lived to be "an old man". True, but not so old as the accounts have made him. The usual Notices give 1655 as his death-date, with 1570 as his birth-date *i. e.* at death in his 85th year. Even the Family-History with 'about 1566' for his birth records him to have "died subsequently to the year 1646 at a very advanced age" viz., in his 80th year. All are mistaken. For the first time we are able to give his death-date. In the Register of St. Giles, Cripplegate, is this burial-entry: "1636/7 Feb. 3. Jarvis Markham, Gent".

As there was only one Jarvis or (Gervase) Markham, there can be no doubt this was our Worthy—and it is a gratification to add this *bit* of fact to our literary-biography—one of the many *finds* by my excellent friend Colonel Chester, in his searches and researches among our English muniments.[1] Gervase Markham was married to a daughter of one GELSTHORP, of whom nothing is known. There was no issue. LANGBAINE thus summarizes his brief Notice. "He may be accounted, if not *unus in omnibus* at least a benefactor to the public, by those works which he left behind him, which without doubt will eternise his name. To have lived a military life, which too often engages its professors in a life of dissipation and pleasure, and at the same time to have furnished himself with such various knowledge, and to be skilled in so many languages, entitles him to hold no small rank among those who have been distinguished for ingenuity."

The Poetry of our Worthy now reprinted, including the 'Teares of the Beloved' and 'Marie

---

[1] It was by a lucky accident we got it; for Colonel Chester had merely jotted it down and erased it in sending something else, unaware of its importance and interest to us.

Magdalene Teares' is not at all of the spasmodic sort. It is quiet, tranquil, simple, with only now and again a touch of pathos or quaint symbolism. Occasionally too there are things that lay hold of and stick to the memory. Altogether our early English sacred verse is not so large or opulent as to warrant the keeping out of sight of even GERVASE MARKHAM's russet-clad Muse. If the swallow have no song, we none the less welcome its bright swift wing under our eaves, ay of the House of God—as the "sweet Singer" puts it long long ago.

ALEXANDER B. GROSART.

I.

The Teares of the Beloved.

Note.

The following is the original title-page of the "Teares of the Beloued":

THE TEARES
Of the Beloued:
OR,
The LAMENTATION of
Saint Iohn,
Concerning the death and passion of
Christ Iesus our Sauiour.

By I. M.

Imprinted at London by *Simon Stafford*
And are to be sold by *Iohn* B*rowne*
at the signe of the Bible
in Fleete-streete
1600. [4o.]

Collation: Title-page—To the Christian Reader 2 pp—and 18 leaves. On the title-page is a small wood-cut of Time on a wheel, with the legend "Aut nunc aut nunquam." G.

To the Christian Reader.

MESEEMETH, the same, who had so resolute a purpose to enlarge our Sauiour's suffring, tooke on him a wearisome and needlesse iourney—for that he left the most Sacred Scriptures—and made inquirie after CODRUS, that was sometime King of ATHENS : which CODRUS, begirt with a strong siege of the Peloponesians, hazarded his best health for his citie's good.[1] For though the example appeareth to hold in our head CHRIST, and their ruler, because both beare the titles of kings ; else in this, for that both died for

[1] Codrus, the son of Melanthus, king of Athens, where he reigned, according to tradition, some time after the conquest of Peloponnesus by the Dorians, about B. C. 1068. His patriotic sacrifice of his own life for the deliverance of his invaded country, is a common-place in classic History. (See Herodotus v. 76 ; Lycurg, *c. Leocr.* 20 : Pausanias, iv. 5 §4 vii. 2 : Strabo xiv.) MARKHAM hits doubtless Thomas Nash's " Christ's Teares over Jerusalem" (1593)—full of classical allusions and illustrations, as Codrus &c. &c. G.

the good of their people : yet questionlesse, the oddes betwixt both are wonderfull: for what is the shaddow to the substance? A king for a small time, to a King beyond all time ? the one a creature, the other a Creator? The one for a few, but our King from before all beginning, to the end of the world, is that Lambe of God, &c. Leauing the one which was finite, I commend thee—courteous reader—to the same Who is as He euer hath beene, and will be infinite in His fauors to those that are His : and I offer thee my harsh and untuned Muse, which being as my talent is, slender and simple, so accompt of the first part, that I may not be discomforted in the second.[1] The Highest continue His fauors and graces vnto His Church, and shield vs in these dangerous dayes, from His and our enemies. Amen.

Thine vndoubtedly,

I. M.

---

[1] As shown in the Memorial-Introduction this seems to point to "Marie Magdalen's Teares" published in the next year. It follows this in the present Volume. G.

The Teares of the Beloued.

THOU first and last, Author and Cause of all!
That wast with God, before these worlds were
made!
Thou perfect Good, Whom I God's Word will call;
Most soueraigne grace! do with Thy grace me
trade,
That from Thy fauors, as from fountaine rare
In flowing sort, I may Thy selfe declare.

Euen in Thy might, Thou art beyond esteeme:
For this wide world, Thou art the chiefest King:
For heauen's high Head, the angels all Thee deeme,
Within Thy Church, Thy saints Thy prayses sing.
Vnto my soule, Thou art the chiefe of choyce;
Life of my life, I must in Thee reioyce.

Now that I leane vpon Thy sacred brest,
In Thee I ioy, sweete Sauiour of mankind:
Hauen of health, succour to soules opprest,
Oceans of ease, in Thee the poore shall finde:

For broken heart, pyning away with griefe,
Sorrowing for sinne, findeth in Thee reliefe.

Fly foorth, my soule, for sure this Word diuine,
Hath power on thee, to call thee backe againe ;
Vnseene thou art, my body doth thee shrine,
Bodilesse, and immortall, subiect to ioy or paine.
To none more like, then to that hidden grace
The Godhead hath, which Satan would deface.

O that I might command the moone to stay !
O that the houre of darknes, hence might poast !
But God's decree must stand, though flesh gainsay ;
There's no resist,[1] to that He purposeth most.
His bitter death, from death shall saue mankinde ;
Wonder of angels, to foes that art so kinde.

Come Peter, come Iames, my brother deare ;
Our Lord doth haste, and hasting calles vs hence ;
You knowe the place, although it darke appeare ;
This light so true, and truth is our defence.
More might He hath, then any fencèd tower
More strength He hath, then any earthly power.

Now in our walke, recompt His power diuine,

[1] = resistance. G.

Which like sunne-rayes, shall spread in euery place.
Such strange effects from the chiefe good do shine,
That foggie mists of foes farre hence shall chace.
  Stoope, furious fiends, ye malice Him in vaine,
  He hath great power, your frenzies to restraine.

See how this Lambe, of sinne that hath no spot,
Seemes dombe, and mute, He answereth not at all;
What He foretold, must not be now forgot:
Let vs with teares, record what must befall.
  Exceeding griefe we had, when Thou didst say,
  One of vs twelue, should Thee our Lord betray.

That griefe being past, another is in place:
But may it be that thus Thou shouldest faint?
Ah! show Thy might, those hellish hags to chace,
Who Thee and vs do force to sad complaint.
  I say no more, that must my moane restraine:
  This garden wils, I should a while refraine.

Refraine, said I? no, now began my moane,
Seeing sluggish sloth, my eyes with sleepe opprest:
I carelesse slept, but Lord of Life did groane,
With griefe of griefs, that brought Him such vnrest.
  Woe worth my sinne, the cause of His complaint,
  Forcing my Lord indure such hard constraint.

He wil'd vs stay, and watch with Him a space,
And proofe hereof, he had from sad aspect.
Full fraighted He with griefe for man's disgrace,
Strangely perplext, did yeeld cause of suspect.
  My soule, He said, is heauie to the death,
  Oh stay and watch, sorrow now stops My breath!

Away He went, and fell vpon His face,
Where groanes, and sighes, shewèd a troubled
  minde.
O Father Mine, He said, afford this grace,
If it may be, Thou wilt approue Thy kind:
  Let this fierce cup, I pray Thee, passe from Me:
  Not as I will, but as Thou wilt, let be.

After He came, and found vs three to sleepe,
Simon, said He, can ye not watch one houre?
Watch ye with Me, 'tis prayer must ye keepe
From Sathan's spight; to tempt he hath the power:
  See, see, the spirit is prest, the gole to gaine:
  But flesh is fraile, esteeming labour paine.

Away from vs the second time He went,
Begging againe, oh Father Mine I pray,
If Thou as yet, to fauour so art bent,
Permit this cup, no longer with Me stay:
  If needs I must indeede drinke of the same,
  Thy will be done, vpon Me rest the blame.

And then He came, but found vs fast to sleepe,
Our heauie heads were glad in warre to rest:
He saw our want, and kept vs as His sheepe:
Cause had He none, being Himselfe opprest.
For friends are knowne, when dangers most assaile:
Deeme him thy selfe, that for thee shall preuaile.

Stay here and pawse, before He come againe,
Why what should moue vs three be so vnkinde,
To worke our woe, to seeke our selues such paine,
That what He would, we should so little minde?
Surely the best, in their decline should say,
There is iust cause, Sathan should on vs pray.[1]

Admit before, His preaching did vs stay,
Or such like let,[2] cannot our crime excuse:
He is our Lord, how might we Him gainesay?
For fond resist, proues, we did Him abuse.
Ours was the lot, our Lord thus to offend:
His was the grace, to guide vs to the end.

And though we slept, from heauen an angell sent,
Did comfort Him, Whom we in griefe did leaue:
Great was His griefe; for Hell did Him preuent,
With endlesse pangs, of Heauen Him to bereaue:

---

[1] Prey. G. [2] Hindrance. G.

And gastly sweate, vpon His face was found,
Like drops of blood, that trickling fell to ground.

Ye siluer drops, that from my eyes thus streame,
Crossing that colour, brinish as ye be!
My Lord's were red; for forc't with paines extreame,
He ventured life, from death to set vs free.
His bitter pangs, what pen or wit can tell?
My Lord indured th' extreame paines of Hell.

Cast we our sight on one that parteth hence,
Striuing for life, when soule away must poast;
In such we see cleane gone to be their sence,
They yeld to that, which cleareth euery coast.
So when that Death, His message pale hath done,
He sweeps all hence: and thus the fort is wonne.

Or thinke Thou standst this present at the barre,
Before the iudge, that pries into thy blame,
Thou knowst thy guilt, thy discord makes the iarre:
Thy sinnes preuaile, facing thy vtter shame.
The irefull iudge begins with angry frowne:
And e're He speake, thy conscience casts thee downe.

O Sauiour sweete ! Thou hadst Thy proper sence :
With perfect health, Thou didst approch this
place,
All furious fiends of Hell, Thou driuedst hence,
Death hath no power Thy godhead to deface :
The angry iudge, Thou needest not to feare,
Thou hadst no sinne, and yet our sinne didst
beare.

Our sinnes did force, that far from Nature's reach,
These blooddy drops should still[1] from our sweet
Head :
In these, euen yet, presumers He doth teach,
They be not bold the tract of Hell to tread.
Lest all too soone they fall into the snare,
The angry iudge doth for His foes prepare.

These drops declare His inward sad lament :
For greater griefe no earthly tongue can tell :
They shew His loue to vs, what good He ment
He would we knew, His griefe did farre excell.
Oh, why do men delight with sinnes to dwell,
When sinnes do weigh the sinner downe to
Hell ?

---

[1] = distill. G.

He gaue the checke to vs for former sleepe,
Graunting vs leaue, of ease to take our fill,
That had no care, in anguish Him to keepe,
With good regard Who suffred for our ill.
Behold, quoth He, of darknesse now the hower:
Of Sonne of man, fowle sinners haue the power.

Iudas, that treason harboured in his brest,
Knew well that here our Lord did oft resort
Vnto this place: knowledge had wrought thy rest,
If all in time, thou wouldst haue found comfort:
But murtherous wretch, this onely did thee good:
Thou thirstie went after th' innocent blood.

O monstrous change, that for a friend of trust,
Thou art a fox, and wilt thy friend betray!
Companion once, and now 'mongst thieues to thrust,
As chiefest guide, the spotlesse Lamb to fray.
Cannot great fauours cause thee to returne,
Thou wofull wretch, at goodnes that dost spurne!

How many speeches, tending to our health:
What feruent vowes He sent beyond the sky:
All wayes were sought still to procure our wealth;

His grace to none that would, He did deny.
Might not His grace from treason thee reclaime,
But at His life, thou traitour now wilt aime.

Ye couetuous carles, that for a little gaine
Set soule to sale, as though there were no Hell,
Looke on this Iudas, thinke vpon his paine;
His endlesse pangs all torments far excell.
The very fire, the forgèd far doth passe :[1]
And like hell fire, no torment euer was.

Consider yet, while here we haue a space,
What griefe it is, to be exilde from God;
What ioy it is, to view His pleasant face,
What paine it is, to feele His heauie rod.
Thrise happie they, that cleaue vnto Thy grace :
Thrice cursed they, that will not life imbrace.

O wretched man, bereft of inward peace,
Commest thou arm'd with weapons and with lights?
A cutthroate crew serue for thy shame's increase;
Are these thy mates? belike feare thee affrights.
A guiltie conscience brings a restlesse griefe :
Easless in ease, finding no sound reliefe.

---

[1] = doth surpass that of a furnace. G.

Thou statelie citie of the highest King,
Fitting Thy name, that hadst the prince of peace:
Whilom whose praise, the virgins faire did sing,
What time thy glory, the chiefest did increace:
Thy famous temple deuotion that relieues,
Is now become a den for lothsome thieues.

And must thy rulers now their forces bend,
To send their seruants forth in all the haste,
To binde this lambe, and then His blood to spend?
What doe ye long to see your land lye waste?
All this was done the Scripture to fulfill:
Who can dissolue what God alone doth will?

In these we see, that bring such weapons stoare,
How foes with might God's children do oppresse,
They haue no truth, and as for iustice loare,[1]
They likewise want, which causes should redresse:
Trusting to flesh, this stay as it is wurst,
So for this fault they are of God accurst.

Forward they march, bringing along their light,
Their lanterns, that a little light containe,
With other helpes to guide them in the night,
Vsing the lesse, and from the great refraine:

---

[1] Lore = knowledge. G.

To dim that light each one doth now prepare :
For light of world, no whit at all they care.

Christ knowing well the secrets of mankind,
This instant sawe, what should to Him betyde:
Forward He goeth against the crue vnkind,
From whom He could haue parted cleane vnspyde.
Whom do ye seeke, said He, to Me now tell :
Iesus of Nazareth, said they, and downe they fell.

This hath the taste of His most soueraigne might,
Who with a word could shake them to the ground.
Weake is man's power, if God begin to fight,
His onely breath can all His foes confound.
If slender touch, huge mountains maketh smoke,
How dares then man His Maiestie prouoke ?

The harmlesse Lambe, deuoide of sinfull spot,
Askes the offenders, and doth them preuent.[1]
Wanted they lawes ? was pietie cleane forgot ?
Should they not loue and keepe the innocent ?
Yes, yes, they knew, th' innocent's blood would cry.
For sharpe reuenge against this carelesse fry.

---

[1] =anticipate. G.

Whom do ye seeke? He verely did scorne
Their fond[1] attempt, deriding all their force:
Yet offereth grace to men that were forlorne:
And sure He had, euen of His foes remorce.
For from themselues, He would they should confesse,
That weaponlesse, He could their wrong represse.

Oh, when we heare, that of His francke accord
Our God is good to His professèd foes;
How kinde a good, is this our soueraigne Lord,
Vnto His friends, on whom He grace bestowes?
Oh, loue this well and fountaine of all grace,
Tender His truth, and all His heasts[2] imbrace.

No whit dismaid, Christ said, Euen I am He:
Which ready speech prooueth He fear'd not death.
This holy Sauiour would His owne flocke free,

---

[1] Foolish. G.

[2] Hests: So Bishop Hall, in his "Defiance to Envy" has

"Now ye muses, sith your sacred *hests*
Profanèd are ...."

= behests, commands: from *haitan*, Gothic, to command. Henry Vaughan also uses it. See Index of words in our edition of his works, *s. v.* G.

By suffring shame, and stopping of His breath.
  Learne courage hence: God's cause if we defend,
  He fights for vs, that life for vs did spend.

Now Iudas stood with all this armèd traine,
Like Bayard bold, forecasting no mishap
Vnto himselfe, whereby he might refraine
The further ill, by falling in the trap.
  Thus one vile sinne, another sinne doth chaine,
  Vntill it bring th' offender to his paine.

Whom do ye seeke? the second time He said.
Iesus of Nazareth, they say to Him againe.
That I am He, before I not dennyd:
If Me ye seeke, from these I pray refraine.
  This, that the word fulfill'd might be, He spake:
  Of them Thou gauest, I will not one forsake.

Now louing Lord, I thinke vpon this care
Thou hadst for vs, and I remember well,
Seeing Thou alone, to suffer didst prepare:
For so of old, sweete Esay did foretell.
  And when Thy pangs appeard, fresh to approch
  Thou hadst a care, foes should not vs reproch.

Attend ye pastors, that your flocke should feede:

How that our Lord did say He none had lost.
Your charge is great, ye dayly prayer neede,
To cheere those soules, bought with so royall cost.
They are Christ's flocke, His blood them bought indeed:
My lambs, good Peter, O my sheepe still feed.

Before that Peter heard these words thrise tolde;
He was couragous ere he saw the fight:
His sword he drew, like to a champion bolde,
And Malchus eare, he cutteth off outright.
Into thy sheath, thy sword put vp, let be
Shall I not drinke the cup preparde for Me?

Thus said our Lord, Who by this checke so kinde,
Would take from Peter, his no small offence;
From priuate men, the vse of sword to binde:
Except that kings arme subiects for defence.
And for Religion gladly should we fight:
That cause is good, and God will aide the right.

But Peter's fault appeareth now the more:
For sharpe reuenge belongeth vnto God:
Too saucie he God's taske to take therefore:
Him to resist, is to procure His rod:
For spirituall warre are weapons of that kinde:
Search we the Word, and there we shall them finde.

And now the band, the captaine, with the rest,
Our Sauiour tooke, and fast They do Him binde,
His inward griefe I moand, now is exprest
The outward anguish, that my Lord did finde.
They had no might His person to assaile,
He suffred them, and then they did preuaile.

Not one, but many—then began their spight—
Inflam'd with wrath, incensèd with great yre,
Their masters would them now in blood delight,
And they deuise, how to increase that fire.
If high estates against Religion frowne,
They shall haue mates to cast it headlong
downe.

Ah wicked Ivdas! this was thy consent,
Vsing all meanes that might our Lord betray.
Lay holde on Him, were words with fury bent:
No maruayle then if these from reason stray.
Thy words and workes so treasonfull descry,
Vnder greene grasse a serpent foule may lie.

The father in law of Caiphas was the first
Annas I meane, to whome my Lord was led.
He, and the other, yea all, for blood did thirst:
Not one I saw, as yet with pittie sped.

[1] St. Matthew, xxvi, 51-52. G.

Their violent wrongs prouèd so huge a streame,
Suppressing right, their dealing was extreame.

These I espied, but cruelty with deceight,
And this pretence to stop the common fame :
Matters of state, and those of no small weight,
Were laid to Christ, for which they do Him blame
Their high account, which all in them esteeme,
Must beare them out, whatso'ere men should deeme.

Besides, let Christ with wisdome Him defend,
And them confute, this they did all agree,
The Romanes should His life soon bring to end:
Thus were they bent, no more to set Him free.
Here may ye see the force of Enuye's spight,
Glutted with gall, and doth in death delight.

Caiphas was he, to Iewes that counsell gaue,
How it was meete, that one for them should dye:[1]
A visage fowle, a vizor faire doth craue.
Sathan would not that all his craft should spy.
Oh, such preuaile oft times, who faire pretend:
But giue me him that faithfull proues in end.

I do not muse so much how Nature's kinde
Appeareth changèd, in so corrupt a man:

[1] St. John, xi. 50. G.

For God I know, euen from His foes will finde
Matter of worth, fit for His will to scan.
  So Balaam's asse, against his proper kinde,
  Once checkt his lord when he remainèd blinde.

There was no cause, O Caiphas, thou shouldst feare,
How that our Lord would take from thee thy state.
The Lambe of God, which all our sinne did beare,
Did much abhor His extreame foes to hate:
  Malicious man, whom Enuy so did blinde,
  To vrge His guilt, in Whom no guilt ye finde.

Peter did follow, so did I like case:
But I was knowne, and went into the hall
Without stoode Peter: then I left my place,
And with great care, my fellow in to call.
  I spake to her who there the dore then kept,
  To shew her fauour: who in boldly stept.

The selfe same woman, vnto Peter said,
Of this man's schollers art thou not now one?
The fearefull man to lye was not afraid,
Boldly to say, of them, that he was none.
  Art thou the man, which with our Lord wilt dye?
  And all in haste, doth flatly Him deny?

The officers, and seruants of that place,
Stoode there also, for they had made a fire :
The extreume cold, with heate away they chace :
Peter, and they to warme themselues desire.
It's not amisse, God's graces should be vsed,
So in the vse, His grace be not abused.

Then the high-priest doth these two things propound.
Vnto sweete Iesus, of His disciples first :
Next of His doctrine ; two demaunds profound :
The wolfe was dry, and after blood did thirst.
The hypocrite one thing in shew doth minde,
But is another in his proper kinde.

Our Sauiour said nothing of vs at all :
One Him betraid, another Him denide :
The rest did flee from Christ, being in thrall :
Small was the solace, in so sad a tide.
And for His doctrine, the world might testifie,
What truth He taught, was spoken openlie.

The Synagogue, and Temple for resort,
To all the Iewes, ye euery one can tell :
Who did Me heare, let such of Me report :
Aske these I pray, and then Thou shalt do well.
Herein Christ mouèd him who did faire pretend,

Vnmasking his malice and His doctrine did
defend.

Note the proceeding in a cause vniust,
An officer there smote Iesus with his rod :
Our high priest thus to answere now Thou must?
O great oppression, hatefull indeed to God!
Such blind presumption, mortall man to please.
So great outrage, the highest to disease.[1]

If I, quoth Iesus, haue spoken that is ill,
Then witnes beare vnto the ill thy selfe:
But for good speech thy fury to fulfill,
Why smitest thou Me? what is it hope of pelfe?
For earthly gaine, men ofttimes runne astray:
For stoare of gold, men will whole lands betray.

Annas had now Christ bound to Caiphas sent,
And Simon Peter stoode himselfe to warme.
Thus to and fro, they lead the innocent:
Who still did good, must suffer extreame harme.
But Peter once, being tangled in the snare,
The second time, to deny our Lord doth dare.

What, not content, our Life twise to deny?
For high priest's seruant and a kinseman neere

---

[1] = dis-ease, to distress. So Phineas Fletcher: iii. 194. G.

To Malchus, said, Did I thee not espie
With Christ in garden? 'tis a case most cleere.
  Peter euen then denied our Lord againe :
  Fraile is our flesh, if faintness we retaine.

The crowing cocke must Peter put in minde
Of his offence; for thus our Sauiour said :
And he remembring—Sathan did him blinde—
Poasteth away : his guilt made him afraid.
  He that euen now a firme faith could not keepe,
  Pines for a place with bitternes to weepe.

And now they lead Christ to the common hall:
For day appear'd, high priests not thither went,
For being defil'd were yet to sinne a thrall:
And for to eate the Passouer they ment.
  See how great sinners not so great would seeme:
  Making moats mountaines, and mountains moats esteeme.

For Pilate's place, he being vncircumcizde,
Would them defile, but not the innocent's blood:
Their soules their tongues, with murther were surpriz'd,
They vs'd all meanes, to haue the truth withstood.
  Great sepulchers without are painted fayre,
  But hold within all stench and lothsome ayre.

Pilate perceiued himselfe must take some paine,
To goe to them who frighted[1] were with spight :
Tell me, he said, of Christ sith[2] ye complaine,
So shew the wrong, that I the same may right.
They thus reply, Were not His doings ill,
We would not vrge that thou His blood should spill.

Pilate then said, The man vnto ye take :
Doome him to death as your law shall permit.
The Iewes short time then vnto Pilate spake,
This thy resist doth not our humors fit.
It is not lawfull for any of our traine,
To kill a man ; we must from blood refraine.

This speech of theirs had also this effect :
For He who knew the secrets of mankinde,
Knew long before we did the Iewes suspect ;
His bitter death, and thereof eke the kinde.
He would not faile, our ransome now to pay :
Vs to redeeme, though Hell would Him gainsay.

Let those that list[3] into their dealings pry.
Those wicked men, the rulers and the rest,
False counsell sought, with which they meant to try

[1] = Freighted. G. [2] S nce. G. [3] Choose. G.

Their great vntruth, that Iesus thus opprest,
So foule offenders might be clear'd from blame:
Themselues thus clear'd, were they not neerer shame?

As if a wretch incensèd from deep hell,
Should kill a friend that sauèd once his life:
And seeing on sleepe, the wretch with fury fell,
In sleeper's hand should fast the blooddy knive;
And then abroad, with outcries should maintaine,
His slaughtered friend was by the other slaine.[1]

False witnes sought, but none then found at all:
Though many came laden with vntruthe's stoare;
At last came two into the high priest's hall:
These were the last—like bulles prepard to goare—
Who said that Christ the temple would deface,
And reare it vp againe in three dayes space.

The lovely Sweet, hereat did hold His peace.
Then the high priest incensèd all with yre,
By the liuing God did charge Christ should not cease,

---

[1] This is a scene of Macbeth, in brief, before Macbeth appeared. G.

But answere make to that He would require.
Art Thou the Christ? of God art Thou the
Sonne?
Herewith he hoapt Iesus would be vndonne.

Iesus to this replies, Thou it hast said:
But neuer the lesse, hereafter ye shall see
The Sonne of Man, when ye shall stand dismaid,
All glorious seated on God's right hand to be:
I then will come with glory and great might,
Guarded with millions, compast with clouds most
bright.

Now think ye see vpon this answere prest,
The high priest doth his cloathes in sunder rent:
Christ hath blasphem'd; on witnesses to rest
I see 'tis vaine, that longer time be spent.
What thinke ye now? ye heare His blasphemy:
They answere all, He worthy is to dye.

The fowle-mouth'd monsters spit vpon His face:
Which face, the angels to behold are glad:
They buffet Him, and yeld Him all disgrace,
Smote Him with rods; hereat I waxt most sad.
This to inlarge, as Peter much did moane,
So what insues, must force th'offender groane.

The extreame spight, shewed to God's deare Sonne,

Was for our sinnes, our sinnes causèd this spight.
Vexe Him not fresh, now that the Iewes haue
done:
Such vexe Him still who in their sinnes delight.
All armèd foes cannot such paines procure,
That wilfull sinners for euer shall endure.

This will I proue in one example plaine:
When Iudas sawe our Lord condemn'd to dye,
When he beheld Him led with cursed traine,
When in each place he did all violence spye,
The sense of sinne assailes, and fresh doth fray,
He yeldes, and said, I did my Lord betray.

Let presse in sight, the kindnes of this Lord,
In choosing me vnto so high estate,
In trusting me euen of His owne accord,
In louing me that did deserue all hate.
Ah, brutish beasts are thankfull in their kinde:
I much more brutish, His fauours did not minde.

I others taught, myselfe I did not teach:
I wonders wrought, and now haue wrought a
wonder,
Accursed houre, I after gaine did reach!
Woe to my selfe, God doth with vengeance thun-
der.

Who lookes on me, with this will me vpbraid:
There goes the wretch, his Master that betraid.

I,[1] there's the sting that frets me to the gall:
For ranckerous Iewes excuse them from my spight:
I Christ betraid, on me all vengeance fall:
I am condemn'd, that did in sinne delight.
This monstrous sinne, for which I thus am shent:[2]
With graue forecast, why did I not preuent?

Now mnst I looke vpon my present losse:
And what is that? but an Apostle's place.
That '*but*', brings more, I gaind a little drosse:
And thus lose heauen, the looking on God's face.
Ye greedy gripes, that feede on liuing men,
Hasten to Hell, my lothsome dark'ned den.

Ye monstrous sinners, to my talke attend:
Seducing Sathan snarde me with his baite:
Faire word I had, but these, and deedes, did bend
My couteous minde, on treason now to waite.
If euery sinne should in their kinde appeare,
Ye would detest, siluer to buy so deare.

I feele my sinne a cause my selfe to hate:
I haue no sence, I should for mercy cry:

[1] = Ay. G. [2] Punished. G.

My sinne exclaimes, accursèd is my state:
Iustice is iust, this course I minde to try:
  These thirty pieces of siluer now at last,
  I will againe, to priests and elders, cast.

Good worke this is, but wanteth loue, and faith:
What helpeth it to say I did offend?
The diuell prest, vnto my soule then saith,
'Tis true thou speakst, despaire and life now end.
  Thus he that first did me to mischief traine,
  Doth much reioyce at my perpetuall paine.

I sinn'd a sinne, betraying the innocent blood:
O innocent blood, with cryes that dost affright,
Affright me not: why am I thus withstood?
Withstood with wrath, and with my tainted spright,
  One mischiefe doth vpon another heape:
  Tis good ye looke before the ditch ye leape:

What's that to vs? see Thou to these things looke:
So said the guides, making of me a scorne;
No one I found, that pitty on me tooke:
For I became, indeede, a wretch forlorne.
  A strangling coard[1] made end of all my doubt:
  I hangd my selfe, my bowels gushèd out.

---

[1] Cord. G.

Suffer my speech, who suffer now with griefe :
Death void of death; for death here liueth still :
Barr'd from all hope, shut out from all reliefe,
Most sad complaints, my hearing now doth fill :
  I haue no rest, but in vnrest remaine :
  No tongue, or penne, can well declare my paine.

Now to returne to Pilate, who like case,
To the common hall had entred now with speede :
Who tendring much Cæsar's and his disgrace,
Did aske of Christ, if He were king in deede.[1]
  For rebels wrought the Romanes much vnrest :
  Which caus'd great care, to haue such wrongs
    redrest.

He questioned much if Christ then were a king,
But no aduantage of His words could take ;
Our Sauiour so about His state did bring,
That of His kingdome, thus in briefe He spake :
  My kingly state it is no earthly might :
  For then my seruants would be prest to fight.

Belike the saying of the wise men, much
Moued mens minds, who callèd Christ a king,
But this is true, 'gainst Romanes all did gruch,[2]

---

[1] St. John xviii. 37. G.

[2] Grudge. So HEYWOOD (" Spider and Flie " 1556)
" By taking peace under concluscion such
As maie extinkt (in both partes) all cause of *gruch* ". G.

The hope of freedome, flowing state would bring.
Vaine was their hope, whom God ment not to free:
Who fights 'gainst God, should he with such agree.

Our heauenly King in His especiall grace,
Doth spirituall gifts vpon His friends bestow:
He loueth them that loue Him to imbrace.
Who such sheepe are, this Shepherd true doth know.
Shaddowes haue shewes, wanting their proper weight:
Who wants the ground, are fed with fond deceight.

In this my moane, although I do digresse,
Iust cause I haue, Christ's kingdome me constraines:
This name is it, which Sathan would oppresse,
Herein the wicked most do tire their braines.
The singer sweete of Israel saw this age:
Which causd him muse, why vainely they do rage.[1]

Ye mortall men, who haue on Earth your time,

[1] Psalm ii. 1. G.

Like pilgrims poore, to plod in vncoath wayes,
What are ye here but drosse, earth, clay, and
slime,
Can ye prolong your life, with yeares or dayes?
Your glasse doth run, though sand in glasse do
stay:
But being run, you hence must poast away.

Vpon the charge, Pilate to Christ did lay,
Our Wisedome would he should declare againe:
If of Himselfe He then the words did say?
Or that some other, to speake so did Him traine?
But as Iewes name, the deputy did deny:
So he declarde on whom the blame did lye.

Then he demaunds what our sweete Lord had
done,
Since earthly pompe of kings, He did not claime?
For that with spight, the Iewes this threed had
spone,
'Gainst proper life of Sauiour, so to aime.
The heathen yet, he doth assay to teach,
Though he did here matter aboue his reach.

Hearken to Him who is a glorious king,
Whose gouernment, Whose lawes and other rights,
Are fram'd from heauen, of Him the angels sing:
Of Him to take, each godly one delights.

For ods are great, 'twixt that which shall decay,
And this dread king, which shall indure for aye.

Stoope, stately kings, vnto this King indeede :
Your greatest glory to His is not a sparke :
He you defends, His taske is you to feede :
He is your light, and guides you in the darke :
All possible good, from this great good doth flowe :
His are your crownes, to Him your crownes ye owe.

And Pilate said, a king now art Thou then !
Iesus replyes, Thou saiest I am a king.
This title much doth trouble carnall men
Who causlesse heare, but conscience hath a sting.
Yet of that sting they haue no sence at all,
Which forceth them to greater dangers fall.

Euen for this cause, saith Iesus, I am borne,
Into this world ; for this cause I did come,
Witnes to beare to truth, which most men scorne :
Yet friends to truth that heare My voyce are some.
What is the truth ? thus Pilate then did say,
But turn'd his backe, and would no longer stay.

A question sweete, Pilate, thou didst propound :
Why wouldst not stay, to heare our Lord's reply ?

Thou shouldst haue heard Him error soone confound:
This gracefull Good would not to teach deny:
But Thou foreshewest, how some of chiefest place,
To talke of truth, accompt it their disgrace.

But glorious truth shall in the end preuaile
Against all foes, who seeke to presse it downe;
Sathan doth know, in vaine he doth assaile
This onely good: his ministers yet must frowne,
Banding their might, against this highest grace,
Working their spight, that do this truth imbrace.

Most splendent Truth. Thy glorious golden rayes
Many degrees surmounts the shining sunne:
Thy maruellous might, and Thy most worthy prayse
Who can declare? for when we all haue donne,
We come too short, Thy greatnesse to declare:
Thee to disgrace, yet flesh and blood doth dare.

But sunne to darke, we know a practise vaine,
To warre with heauen, will proue a fearefull fight:
God such doth hate as do His truth disdaine:
Against such foes He girded is with might.
Who for the truth would not his life thus spend,
Seeing God is prest, His owne right to defend?

To Iewes now Pilate goeth yet once againe,
And to them said, in Christ no cause I finde:
Your custome is, I one should loose from paine,
At this your feast: then Iesus he doth minde:
  Ye Iewes, your King if now ye meane to choose,
  Your minds vnfold, will ye I Iesus loose?

Me thought this was like to a sudden stay,
Forc'd to retrait[1] where egre battaile meetes:
Where man, doth man, with mutuall might assay,
And bloodlesse bodies, earth then gladly greetes:
  But then againe, both armies forces tryes,
  Till one of them must yeeld with fainting cryes.

So then this comfort, corsiue[2] I may call,
For what refreshing found my sad lament?
My chiefe of choyce, my soule I saw in thrall,
So I perceiued the Iewes to murther bent.
  Faces of men are tables of their minde:
  By outward signes mens malice ye may finde.

For wicked Iewes their clamours now began:
We will not Iesus, Barrabas we will:

---

[1] Retreat. G.

[2] Contraction of 'corrosive' = anything that corrodes or gnawes the heart. Spenser (F. Q. iv. ix. 15), Drayton (Legend of P. Gav.), Chapman, &c., &c. use it. G.

Like craues their like, let loose a murtherous
man.
Haue ye no care, the spotlesse blood to spill?
Drop blooddy tears, my moysture waxeth dry,
Like Sommer's drouth that for more raine doth
cry.

Poore Iotham[1], now me thinkes, I doe thee see,
Who didst rebuke thy vnkinde countrymen,
In offer made to trees, who king should be:
They rule refus'd: but hooking bramble then
Would needes be king, and then had his desire:
The tyrant's rule is like a consuming fire.

Ah, my Redeemer, this oft Thou didst foretell
In parables, and in Thy preaching plaine,
That of the Vineyard,[2] wherein is vttered well,
How for great good, they Thee requite with paine.
God's heire Thou art, to kill Thee these now
ment,
Thou being slaine, they to possesse are bent.

Possesse ye shall, and cruelly be destroyd:
Oh wicked men, your glory shall decay,
Your pleasant Land shall lye both waste and voyd,
To all the world ye shall become a pray,

---

[1] Judges ix. 5, *et seqq*. G. [2] St. Mark xii. 1-7 G.

Such, who will not that Christ should rule alone,
Must finde His might where they must waile
and mone.

Ye will not Him that would your proper good;
Ye Him reiect that came you to redeeme.
Oh people blinde, that thus God's grace withstood !
So light to set of Him beyond esteeme :
Virtue in place we haue no care to minde :
But being gone, we gladly would it finde.

The first Adiunct.[1]

My sweetest Sweete, my Lord, my loue, my life,
The World's bright lampe, farre clearer then the
sunne,
What may this meane : cannot I end this strife,
This ranckorous spight, by wicked Iewes begunne ?
O man most pure, for wretches most forlorne,
Must my great God to men be made a scorne ?

He made His soule an offring for our sinne ;
His will was such His death doth life prolong ;
He dying for vs, then did our life beginne :
His is the gaine, to Him all ioyes belong.

---

1 '*First*' with relation to the sequel in "Mary Magdalene's Teares". G.

Although our guilt did force our Lord to faint,
Yet all His foes could not with sinne Him taint.

Thou Light of God, in Whom no darknes dwels,
Sole reconciler and worker of our wealth,
Thy bitter pangs all passions farre excels,
Our soules sweete Shepheard carèd for our health.
Thus as my Loue constrainèd was to groane,
So me permit againe refresh my moane.

I grieue that sleepe so sore did me oppresse:
Sinne in my selfe moues me to sad complaint:
For wicked men to watch themselves addresse
To pamper pleasure; where's one that seemes to faint?
What lawes forbid, to that in haste we poast:
The best offends, though hypocrits yet will boast.

Iudas slept not, nor any of his traine:
Night after night men watch, if pleasure call.
Our Head did watch, I could not sleep refraine:
Thus to my will I was become a thrall.
Ah crooked will, that wouldst me so misleade,
That vnder foote my Lord's will I should treade.

I will recount what harmes haue come by sleepe:

While Sampson slept, he then did lose his might :[1]
Sleeping Saule's sonne,[2] his kingdome could not
keepe :
While Sisera slept, Iael him slew outright.[3]
In towne of warre if all should seeke for rest,
Quickly they should with enemies be opprest.

How glad is Satan when we yeld to sleepe :
How sad sweete Iesus when we slouth imbrace :
Sleepe not securely ye that are Christ's sheepe,
With sighes and groanes pray vnto God for grace :
For in our sinne if God with iudgement ceaze,
Late will it be His iustice to appeaze.

Now in my moane to Him I will returne,
Who trayterously had made a cursèd change :
The Vine most true this withered branch did
spurne :
Such wander wide who in by-paths do range.
O treasonfull wretch, my Lord as thou hast sold,
Shall those fowle lips to kisse my Lord make
bold.

The subtill serpent seeking to seduce,
Shroudeth himselfe vnder a faire pretence ;

---

[1] Judges xvi., 19. G. [2] 1 Samuel xxvi. 12. G.
[3] Judges iv. 21. G.

In heart hath hate, with tongue he taketh truce,
His spightfull spirit he shields with sweete defence.
His chearefull looke who gaue the glad 'all haile'.
Fed fowle conceite his treason should preuaile.

Our tainted nature quickly will vs teach,
To follow that we can in others blame.
What needes the serpent th' apple faire to reach?
We hazard all as though we were past shame.
The way to Hell appeareth wondrous faire,
The end whereof doth leade to fowle despaire.

Regard in Iudas, when foule flesh begins
To nibble a little vpon the serpent's baite,
How such will make a sport of all their sinnes:
Doubtlesse such sinners neere to Sathan waite.
For so at first the diuell Iudas tooke,
And held him fast vpon his siluer hooke.

Christ is betrayed of many in this life,
For art thou where religion is abused,
And hast no care then to confute that strife?
There is great feare thy selfe shall be refused.
Thou stragling sheepe, herein thou goest astray;
Thy silence proues, thou Iesus doest betray.

Else doest thou take on thee a Christian's name,
Following not that thou seemest to professe:

Thy owne vilde[1] life Religion much doth shame,
Thou Christ betraiest that doest His truth represse.
Repent thee soone for former life mispent,
And turne to God, while God to grace is bent.

Iesus to Iudas vseth words most kinde:
For, Friend, He saith, a reason to Me render,
Why thou art come? as if He would him binde
From former good his owne estate to tender.
But none more blinde then wilfull blinded bee,
That to renownce which offereth cause of glee.

Traytor, thou camest, another to annoy,
To annoy Him, who euer sought thy good;
Thy good He sought, and thou wilt Him destroy.
But be thou sure thus thirsting after blood,
That thou thy selfe of blood shalt haue thy fill,
Though thou delight the guiltlesse blood to spill.

This to conclude, our Prince of might did foyle
Not onely Sathan, but all his darkesome traine.
Betray not Christ, by giuing backe the spoyle
Vnto His foes; from so vile sinne refraine.
As God in Christ hath shewed His bountie large,
So haue great care still to regard His charge.

---

[1] Vile. G.

On Peter now if we shall cast our sight,
Else on vs all the Apostles to our Lord.
Cause great we haue, not to boast of our might,
That weaknes are, and fall of franke accord.
Yet in our fall as we feele want of strength:
So God relieu es, and succor sends at length.

God suffred vs to see our weak'ned state,
That seeing it, we should detest our sinne :
He did vouchsafe to open wide His gate,
His gate of grace, that we should enter in.
But that His grace to vs did much abound,
He had iust cause for aye vs to confound.

The wounded soule from vs may comfort finde:
For though we fell, yet God did vs uphold,
He tendred vs, and we againe Him minde,
Yelding Him thanks and praises manifold.
How so ere, Lord, of frailty we offend,
Succour Thou vs, and vs with grace defend.

What now remaines vnto the hard'ned Iewes,
Iewes that would not our Lord as King should raigne ?
Raigne yet He must, although they doe refuse:
Refuse that list, He will His right maintaine.
I know, when time of darknes shall expire,
Our glorious King will haue His full desire.

For of this nation our Sauiour did foretell,
That as they sought from Him His state to cleare,
So God in wrath would them from thence expell,
Who did reiect His louing Sonne so deare.
Learne hence therefore if ye desire God's grace,
Haue good regard God's Christ ye doe imbrace.

If Christ alone ye would in you should raigne,
—For He delights within our soules to dwell—
Haue good regard affections to restraine,—
That are not good, but of our flesh do smell,
If Christ us guide, our gaine exceeds esteeme,
We haue more store, then all the world can deeme.

The last of all, yet first in next complaint,
Is the selfe same, who was chiefe actor made.
Who seeth not he did true Iustice taint?
Doubtlesse the wicked make of sinne a trade.
These yet—forsooth—must equitie pretend,
Though to the world oppression they defend.

Why, Pilate, why? thou art a man of might,
Thy country lawes vilde[1] violence doth detest:
As thou art Iudge thou oughtst regard the right,

[1] Vile, as before. G.

And haue great care the poore be not opprest:
Desire to please should not thy minde peruert,
That rightfull cause thou shouldest so subuert.

Finis.

II.

Marie Magdalen's Lamentations

FOR

The Losse of her Master.

1601.

Note.

As explained in our Memorial-Introduction, I accept the ascription of "Marie Magdalen's Lamentations" to GERVASE MARKHAM on the authority of HASLEWOOD, as stated in the Family-History of the MARKHAMS: and also as being confirmed by the Author's own words in his Epistle to his immediately preceding sacred Poem, reprinted by us. The circumstances stated in our Introduction account for the anonymity, and perhaps the giving of it to NICOLAS BRETON rests on an inaccurate reminiscence of a somewhat resembling title-page in one of his numerous publications. The following is the original title-page of the poem:

MARIE MAG-
DALENS LAMEN-
Tations For The
Losse of Her
Master Iesus.
Disce mori mundo vivere disce Deo.
London,
Printed by Adam Islip for Edward White, and are to be
sold at his shop, dwelling at the little North dore
of Paules, at the signe of the Gun.
1601.

Collation: Title and 29 leaves. As before we give a faithful reproduction of the Author's own text of this exceedingly rare poem. For our exemplar, we are indebted to the MARSH Library, Dublin. G.

The Preface to Mary Magdalen's Lamentations.

THE happiest soule that ever was invested
In sinne-staind skin, awakes my woe-
fed Muse,
To sing her loue—whose loue is now celested—
Sith grauer pens so good a worke refuse ;
To wet the world with her sinne-washing teares,
Which well destil'd, each cloudie conscience
cleares.

She shed them once in most abundant wise,
Thinking no future aire should drie them up,
While any drop remain'd in tender eyes,
Or any heart could heartie sorrow sup,
Or any soule could sigh for sinne forepast,
Or feare that God's iust iudgements aye should
last.

But world worse waxing, hath forgot her lore:
Relenting hearts are adamanted so,
They cannot greeue, drie eyes can drop no more,
And sin-clog'd soule[s] doe now so heedlesse go:

They cannot sigh—ah! 'tis too great a paine—
With contrite minds such soure-sweete throbs to stain.

Yea soule-confounding sinne so far hath crept,
Repentant sighes are reckonèd for toies,
And Marie's teares contemnèd long hath slept,
As jems unpriz'd, which corrupt age destroies,
Saue that her Lord because they still should last,
In surest caske hath them invested fast.

For wretched soules let loose to libertie,
So wanton like are weanèd to each wrong,
So licensèd to worke impietie,
And free to fleshly wils haue liv'd so long:
That those fresh springs, whence penitent tears should flow,
Presumption hath so stopt, that none will know

And sencelesse hearts, obdurat to all good,
Haue so perverted their perfixèd end,
That now—O greefe!—their sighs and dearest bloud,
To feed fond fancie they doe vanely spend:
But for their sins one teare for to let fall,
They have—alas!—nor eye nor heart at all.

Ah could they see what sinne from sence hath
shut,
How sweet it were to summon deeds misdone,
To haue their lives in equall ballance put,
To waigh each worke ere that the iudge doe come :
Ah then their teares would trickle like the raine,
And their eye-flouds would helpe to fill the
maine.

They would with Marie send forth bitter cries,
To get the ioies of their soule-saving love,
They would gush forth fresh fountaines from their
eies,
To win His fauour, and His mercie proue :
Eyes, heart, and tongue, should poure, breath
out and send,
Teares, sighs and plaints, untill their loue they
find.

No idle houres ill spent in fond delight,
No teares distil'd for momentarie losses,
No sighs for missing absent lover's sight,
No care contriv'd of common worldly crosses,
Should then be us'd : but all consum'd on this,
To beg amendment and bewaile their misse.

Yea all too little to an humble soule :
—That only sees her ill misgovern'd life—

Would it appeare, to spend whole yeares in dole ;
Yea many ages to declare her strife
Would passe as minuts, wishing Time would stand,
While she with feare her endlesse life had scand.

But farre from this lives sinners—too secure—
Who giving bridle to their selfe-desires,
Cannot alas ! one scanted houre indure
In sacred service, but their mind aspires
In following Pleasure's height, whose froward will
In doing good doth make them carelesse still.

Which seene with pitie on our gracelesse minds,
This blessed sinner, whose so precious teares
Once bath'd His feet, that heaven and earth inbinds,
And made a towell of her trayling haires,
To wipe the drops which for her sins were shed,
Now deignes to tell how our soules should be fed.

And Marie shewes to maids and matrons both,
How they should weepe and decke their rose-like cheekes,

With showers of greefe, whereto hard hearts are
loth,
And who it is her matchlesse mourning seekes :
And when we ought to send our reeking sighs,
To thicke the passage of the purest lights.

And Marie showes us when we ought to beat
Our brazen breasts, and let our robes be rent,
How prostrating, to creepe unto the seat
Of that sweet Lambe Whose bloud for us was
spent:
And that we should giue way unto our woes,
When the excesse no fault or errour showes.

If you will deigne with fauour to peruse
Marie's memoriall of her sad lament,
Exciting Collin[1] in his grauer Muse,
To tell the manner of her heart's repent :
My gaine is great, my guerdon granted is,
Let Marie's plaints plead pardon for amisse.

---

[1] The well-known (self-given) poetic name of SPENSER. Before our Poem (probably) saw the light he had died sorrowfully, viz. on January 16th, 1599. This may be taken as another confirmation that the present Poem was composed contemporaneously with "The Teares of the Beloued :" and hence of the authorship. G.

Marie Magdalen's first Lamentation.

AT THE TOMBE OF IESUS.

WHAT climat will affourd a mournfull mate,
All wo-begon, that vollies out hir grones,
Whose griefs do equalize my sad grown state,
Whose heart poures forth a sea of helpelesse mones!
If to my case, comparison such there be,
Ile help her mourne, if she will mourne with me.

But since, no such associat there is,
My Muse may tell a greefe without compare,—
A blacke rehearse of metamorphos'd blis,
And sad memoriall of untimely care,
Lugubre carmen fitteth best my use;
In waining state best fits a wailing Muse.

The deepest passion of true burning loue,
That euer any loue-sicke heart possesst,
—Drown'd in distresse—I silly woman prove,
Whose ardent zeale is nurse of mine vnrest,
But euen to death—O haplesse death!—alone
I ru'd His death when other friends were gone.

I did behold my Love's too cruell death
With these sad eyes, made red with brinish teares:
My soule did sorrow for His losse of breath,
By whose sweet life, my life was free from feares.
  Oh had I dy'd, when He dy'd on the crosse,
  I needed no complaint to waile my losse.

But that—too sweet a favour—was deny'de,
I, might not I consort[1] my louer dying;
My course of life doth sorrow still betyde,
Which moves my soule to such a ceaselesse crying:
  Oh haplesse soule, so clog'd with care and greefe,
  For losse of Him that was thy comfort cheefe.

My Lord is dead, to Whom my soule did live;
He dy'd for me, I wretch am left alive;
Now to the dead I lasting praise must give,
Sith light is lost, which did my life revive,
  And all in darkenesse I desire to dwell,
  In death's dread shade my saddest griefes to tell.

My Jesu's tombe my mansion is become,
My wearie soule hath there made choise to inn;[2]
Vpon His crosse my comfort shall consume,

---

[1] Querq—comfort? G.

[2] = to dwell. See our Ph. Fletcher, II. 294, 302: IV. 35. G.

And ioies shall end where ioies did first begin.
Oh eies gush forth your fast distilling force
Of ocean tears upon His tombe and corse.

Oh life-containing tombe of my dead Lord,
From thee no chaunce shall hale me hence away;
Ile linger here while death doth life affourd,
And being dead, my twining armes shall stay,
And cleave unto Thee: nor alive or dead
Will I be drawne from whence my Lord is laid.

Thou art the altar of all mercies meeke,
The temple of all truth, the grave of death,
The sanctuarie which lost soules doe seeke,
The cradle of eternall living breath.
Oh sweetest heaven of my eclipsèd Sonne,
Receive this silly star, whose light is done.

Oh whale, that my deare Ionas swallowed hast,[1]
Come swallow me—more sweet to be thy prey—
'Twas I, not He, that should in right have past
This bloodie tempest: I was cause I say:
Vnequall doomer, what hast Thou misdone,
To rob the Earth of her celestiall Sonne.

Oh cesterne of my Joseph innocent,
Let thy drie bottome take me prisoner,[2]

---

[1] Jonah I. 17. G. [2] Genesis xxxvii. 20. G.

Sith I, not He—oh wretch most impudent—
Gave cause that so enrag'd my brethren were.
What pitch clouds darken our translucent[1] way,
And on what shore doth Truth's sweet preacher
stay?

Aye me accurst, why did I not before
Thinke upon this, which now I aske too late?
Why did I leave Him when I had Him sure?
To rue His losse, and more my ruthlesse state.
Oh had I watchèd, as I waile Him now,
None could have taken Him without me too.

But being too precise to keepe the Law,
The Lawe's sweet Maker I have thereby lost;
And bearing to His ceremonies too much awe,
I misse His sweetest selfe, of far more cost;
Sith rather with the Truth I should have beene,
Than working that which but a tipe was seen.

The Sabbath day so strickt solemnizèd
The standing by his coarse had not prophan'd;
By which, prophanest things are sanctified,
And that made pure which earst was foulely
stain'd;

---

[1] A Miltonic word *e.g.* Sampson Agonistes, 511: Comus 861. G.

Whose touch doth not not defile the thing that's
clean,
But most defilèd maketh faire againe.

But when I should haue staid, I went away,
And when it was too late, I came againe;
In time of helpe—ah then!—my helpe did stay,
Now I repent my follie—but in vain—
My carelesse heed hath brought a heape of care,
And carefull I, must ceaselesse teares prepare.

Ah! let my heart into sad sighs dissolve,
Let eies consume their flouds in brinish teares,
Let soule—Care's captiue—in dislikes resolue,
To languish still—sunke with despaire and feares—
Let all I have endure deseruèd paine,
That pennance due, sin's losses may regaine.

But ah! my sweetest Iesu—my deare heart—
Thou art not now, where Thou went but of late;
And yet, alas! I know not where Thou art:
—O wretched care! O lamentable state!—
Such haplesse state, unhappie I live in,
To better it, I cannot yet begin.

Alas! my ioy, my hope, my cheefe desire,
How hast Thou left me wavering thus in doubt?
In mazèd moodinesse my thoughts to tire,

Wandering in woe, and cannot find way out.
  If I stay here I cannot find Thee so,
  To seek elsewhere I know not where to goe.

To leave the tombe, is for to gaine vnrest,
To stand still helpelesse, is a curelesse paine ;
So all my comfort in this plot doth rest,
Helpelesse to stay, or going, hope in vaine.
  And to this choise poore soule I am left free,
  Which is to say, with what death I will die.

And yet—euen this—too happie a choice would be,
For me, so vile, so base, unhappie wretch :
For if to chuse my death it lay in me,
How soone should I that execution catch ?
  How willing would I be to stop live's breath,
  If I might 'point the manner of my death ?

I would be nailèd to the selfe-same crosse,
With those same nailes, and in the selfe-same place,
Where bloudie Iewes did butcher up my losse ;
His speare should wound my hart, His thorns my face,
  His whip my bodie : I would tast all smart
  To tread His steps with an embrued hart.

But oh ambitious thoughts, gaze not so hie,
Vpon so sweet divine felicitie,

Thinke not with such a glorious death to die,
Whose life is privie to such infamie :
  Death I deserv'd, not one, but many a death,
  But not so sweet a meane to stop my breath.

So sweet a death seasoned with such deepe ioy,
The instruments whereof, dead corpes would
    raise,
And most impurest soules from sinne destroy,
And make it pure, to yeeld Thee pure due praise :
  A scourge too much—ah ! where alas !—too
    small
  For my offences to be beat withall.

And therefore am I left, more deaths to tast
Than I live houres, and far more woes to shun,
Than I haue thoughts for my lost ioy to wast,
Which are in number more then motes in sun.
  Vnhappie me whose weake estate must beare
  The violence of such confusèd care.

But sith I cannot as He died, die,
Nor yet can live where He now liveth dead,
To end my dying life I here will lie,
Fast by His grave, and leane my wearie head
  Vpon His tombe, on whose most sweete repose
  Ile leaue to live, and death my eies shall close.

Better it is after His bodie's losse,
—His sacred bodie which all creatures ioy'de—
To keepe His sepulchre from farther crosse,
Than losing one to let both be destroy'de;
Though I haue lost the Saint of clearest shine,
I wil at least have care to keep the shrine.

And to this shrine I'le sacrifice my heart,
Though it be spoilèd of the soveraigne host;
It shall the altar be and sacred part,
Where I my teares will offer with the most;
My teares distillèd from my heart's deepe paine,
Which going out, my sighs shall blow againe.

Here in this place—oh happie place!—I'le lead
Yea lead and end my wofull loathèd life,
That at the least my cold grave may be made
Neare to this tombe, where I haue told my griefe:
Neare this stone-couch, my eies their light shall lose,
Which my Lord made the place of sweet repose.

It may be so this sindon[1] lying here,
Thus emptie left and sezing to no use,

---

[1] From σινδών (Latin *sindon*) originally = a fine Indian cloth or muslin (and hence the derivation from Ἰνδός): later, as in text = fine linen, and so the Lord's 'grave-clothes.' G.

This tombe being open without any there.
May pierce some piteous heart for to peruse,
My naked bones, whose rights for to preferre,
This shroud may wrap and this sweet tomb interre.

But oh too fortunat a lot to craue,
For her that is a wretch so unfortunate;
No, no, I seeke not such a blisse to haue,
Alas! I dare not beg so good estate:
But yet if such a sinne may proue unblam'd,
I would forgiue by whom it first was fram'd.

And if to wish no presumption were
In me alive then to permit it dead,
If I knew him that that should prise me here,
My teares should woo to haue my corpes so laid,
And with my praiers I that man would hire,
To blesse me with this blisse which I desire.

And though I dare not wish that anie do it,
Yet this without offence to all I say,
This sindon hath my love so tyde unto it,
Above all clothes I love to it will pay.
And this same tombe my heart more deare doth deeme,
Than anie prince's hearse of most esteeme.

Yea and I thinke that coarse is favoured much,
That shall my Lord in this same tombe succeed :
And for my part—as my resolue is such—
Vpon this plot to meet Death's fatal deed ;
  So doe I wish, that in the readiest graue,
  My breathlesse bones the right of buriall haue.

But this is all, and I dare say no more,
My bodie I will leave to what befals ;
And in this paradise all ioy will store
For my poore soule, which flesh and bloud inthrals,
  Which from this brittle case shall passe even
    then,
  Into the glorions tombe of God and Man.

Marie Magdalen's second Lamentation.

FOR THE LOSSE OF THE BODIE, WHICH SHE CAME TO ANNOINT.

UT stay my Muse, I feare my Maister's love
—The only portion that my fortune left
  me—
Would languish in my breast, and chillish prove,
Sith warmth to cherish it, was quite bereft me.

His words, His presence gone, which fed my
flame,
And not the ashes left to rake the same.

My spice and ointment shall be then prepar'd,
To pay last tribute of eternall dutie;
Though others have thereto devoutly car'd,
And brought the best in worth, in worke, in
beautie;
Yet such desire my dutie doth inherit,
That I must yeeld my loue my latest merit.

My love each quantitie too little deem'd,
Vnlesse that mine were added thereunto;
Best quantitie too meane and not esteem'd,
Except with mine it somewhat have to doe:
No diligence ynough for to apply,
Vnlesse my service be employed by.

Nor doe I thus sharpe censure others' deeds,
But 'cause love makes me covetous of doing;
Though Joseph's worke no reprehension needs,
Though to my wish his baulme he was bestowing:
Yet all he did cannot my love suffise,
But I must actor be to please mine eies.

Such is the force of true affecting love,
To be as eagre in effects t' appeare,

As it is zealous, fervently to move
Affections firme, to what it holdeth deare.
  This loue devout sets my poore heart on fire,
  To show some deed of my most deepe desire.

And to embaulme His breathlesse corps I came,
As once afore I did annoint His feet,
And to preserue the reliques of the same,
The only remnant that my blisse did meet:
  To weepe afresh for Him in deapth of dole,
  That lately wept to Him for mine owne soule.

But loe alas! I find the graue wide ope,
The bodie gone, the emptie sindon[1] left:
The hollow tombe I every where doe grope,
To be assur'd of what I am bereft,
  The labour of embaulming is prevented,[2]
  But cause of endlesse weeping is augmented.

He wanting is unto my obsequies,
That was not wanting to my ceaselesse teares;
I find a cause to moue my miseries,
To ease my woe, no wisht for ioy appeares.
  Thus though I misse, whom to annoint I meant,
  Yet have I found a matter to lament.

---

[1] = fine linen wrapper, as before. G.
[2] = anticipated. G.

I having settled all my sole desires
On Christ my love, Who all my love possesst,
In whose rare goodnesse, my affection fires,
Whom to enioy I other ioies suppresst,
  Whose peerlesse worth unmatcht of all that liue,
  Being had—all ioy—and lost—all sorrowes—give.

The life of lives thus murthering in His death,
Doth leaue behind Him lasting to endure,
A generall death of each thing having breath,
And His decease our nature hath made pure :
  Yet am poore I of ornament bereft,
  And all the world without perfection left.

What maruell then if my heart's hot desire,
And vehement loue to such a lovely Lord,
To see life's wracke, with scalding sighs aspire,
And for His bodie's losse such woe afford,
  And feele like tast of sorrow in His misse,
  As in His presence I enioed blisse.

And though my teares, destil'd from moistned eies,
Are rather oile than water to my flame,
More apt to nourish sorrow in such wise,
Then to deminish or abate the same.

Yet silly soule I plung'd in deapth of paine,
Do yeeld my selfe a captiue to complaine.

Most true it is that Peter came and John,
With me unto the tombe to trie report,
They came in hast, and hastily were gone,
They—hauing searcht—dare make no more resort ;
And what gain'd I, two witnesse of my losse,
Dismaiers of my hope, cause of more crosse.

Love made them come, but love was quickly
quail'd,
With such a feare as cal'd them soone away;
I—poore I—hoping, in despaire assail'd,
Without all feare, persevering[1] still to stay,
Because I thought, no cause of feare was left,
Sith Whom I feard was from my sight bereft.

For I—poore soule—haue lost my Maister deare,
To whom my thoughts devoutly were combin'd ;
The totall of my love my cheefest cheare,
The height of hope in Whom my glorie shin'd ;
My finall feare, and therefore Him excepted,
Nor other hope, nor love, nor losse respected.

---

[1] See our Ph. Fletcher for like pronunciation of 'persever': I. 37: III. 166, 223, 357. G.

Worse feare behind, was death, which I desired
And fearèd not—my soule's life being gone—
Without which I no other life required,
And in which death had been delight alone:
  And thus—ah thus!—I live a dying life,
  Yet neither death nor life can end my strife.

Yet now me thinkes 'tis better die than liue,
For haply dying, I my loue may find,
Who while I liue no hope at all can giue,
And He not had, to liue I haue no mind:
  For nothing in my selfe, but Christ I lov'd,
  And nothing ioies, my Iesus so remov'd.

If any thing alive to keepe me, striv'd,
It is His image, cause it should not die
With me, whose likenesse love in me contriv'd,
And treasured up in sweetest memorie:
  From which my love by no way can depart,
  Vnlesse I rip the centre of my heart.

Which had been done, but that I feard to burst
The worthlesse trunck which my dear Lord inclosed,
In which the reliques of lost ioy was trust,[1]
And all the remnant of my life imposed:

---

[1] = trussed: cf. our Ph. Fletcher III. 11. G.

Else greefe had charg'd my hart to bleeding
tears,
And fatall end had past from pittious ears.

Yet pittious I, in so unperfect sort
Doe seeme to draw my undesirèd breath,
That true I prove this often-heard report,
Love is more strong than life-destroying death:
For what more could pale Death in me have done,
Than in my life performèd plaine is showne.

My wits destraught, and all my sence amaz'd,
My thoughts let loose, and fled I know not where;
Of understanding rob'd, I stand agaz'd,
Not able to conceit what I doe heare:
That in the end, finding I did not know,
And seeing, could not well discerne the show.

I am not where I am, but with my Love,
And where He is, poore soule I cannot tell;
Yet from His sight no thing my heart can move,
I more in Him than in my selfe doe dwell:
And missing Whom I looke for with sad seeking,
Poor wo-worn woman, at the tomb stay weeping.

Marie Magdalen's third Lamentation.

IN FINDING THE ANGELS AND MISSING WHOM SHE SOUGHT.

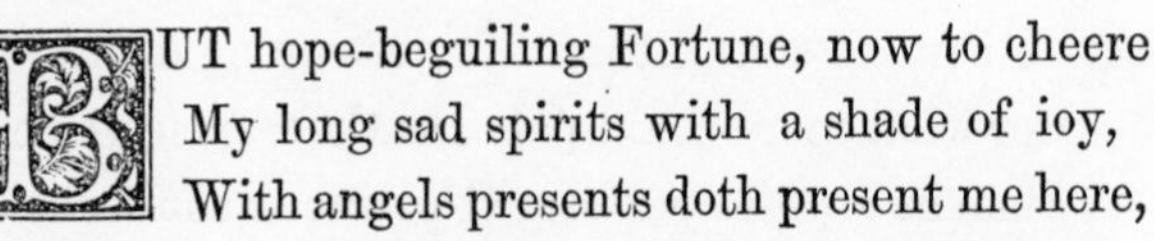

BUT hope-beguiling Fortune, now to cheere
My long sad spirits with a shade of ioy,
With angels presents doth present me here,
Granting a moment's mirth to increase annoy.
For lacking[1] Him, though for Him I find twaine,
To thinke on Him, redoubleth still my pane.

Yet for a time I will revive my soule,
With this good hope, which may my hopes exceed:
Comfort, sweet comfort shall my cares controule,
Releefe may hatch, where greefe did lately breed;
I seeke for One, and now have found out twaine,
A bodie dead, yet two alive againe.

My woofull weeping, all was for a Man,
And now my teares have angel bright obtained:
I will suppresse my sigh-swolne sadnesse than,
And glad my heart with this good fortune gained:
These Heaven attendants to a parle envite me,
Il'e heare what they will say; it may delight me.

[1] Misprinted 'looking' G.

For I assure my selfe, if that the corse
By fraud or mallice had removèd bin,
The linnen had not found so much remorse,
But had been caried too away with Him:
  Nor could the angels looke so chearfully,
  But of some happier chance to warrant me.

And for to free me from all feares—even now—
They thus encounter, these their speeches were,
And thus they spake, Woman why weepest thou?
As if they bad me weeping to forbeare:
  For ill it fits a mortall eye should weepe,
  Where heauenly angels such reioicing keepe.

Erewhile they said, thou camst with manly
    courage,
Arming thy feet, through greatest thornes to run,
Thy bodie to endure all tyrants rage,
Thy soule no violent tortures for to shun:
  And art thou now so much a woman made,
  Thou canst not bid thine eies from teares be
    staide.

If that thou hadst a true disciple's name,
So many certaine proofes would thee persuade,
But incredulitie so blots the same,
Thou of that title art unworthie made:

And therefore woman—too much woman now—
Tell us—O woman—wherefore weepest thou?

If there were any coarse here lying by,
We then would thinke for it thou shedst thy teares,
That sorrow for the dead inforst thee cry:
But now this place, a place of ioy appeares,
Thou findst no dead, but living, to be here,
Oh! then why weepst thou with mournfull
cheere?

What is our presence so discomfortable,
That seeing us, thou art inforst to weepe,
Thinkst thou if teares were so availeable,
That we ourselues from flowing streams could
keep:
Or is thy kindnesse in this cause extended,
That we with teares should thus be entertainèd.

If they be teares of loue to shew goodwill,
As love is knowne, so let them be suppressèd;
If teares of wrath, denouncing anger still,
To shed them here, thou shouldst not haue
addressèd:
Here where all anger lately buried was,
But none deserv'd, ah! none deserv'd alas!

If they be teares of sorrow, dead men's duties,
—The dead revivèd—they are spent in vaine;

If teares of ioy destillèd from the booties
Of happie fortune—flowers of ioyfull gaine—
  It better were that feuer had been spent,
  And fitter tokens might expresse content.

And angel's semblance visible, presents
The will invisible of His dread Lord,
Whose shapes are shaddowed after the intents
And drift of Him, that rules him by His word:
  They brandish swords when God begins to frown,
  They sheath in scabbards when His wrath is
    downe.

When He would fight, they armèd come to field,
When He would terrifie, their forme afright,
When he would comfort, they their countenance
  yeeld
To smiling lookes, and signes of sweet delight:
  Mirth in their eies, and mildnesse in their words,
  All favour, grace, and comeliness affourds.

Why weepest Thou Marie then when we reioice?
Thinke not our nature can degenerat,
Or faile in dutie—which we hold so choice—
Ours is no changing or sin-working state:
  Doest thou more love or more His secrets know,
  Than we that at His Throne our service show?

Oh! deeme not Marie, deeme not then amisse.
Against so plaine apparent evidence;
At our request forbeare, and leave of this,
Leave weeping Marie, and with teares dispence:
  Exchange thy sorrow for our offered ioy
  Accept sweet comfort, and forsake annoy.

No, no, you saints of glorie, ever shining,
Persuade not me to harbor ioyfull glee,
But thinke to whom my sorrow is enclining,
And beare with my poore love-bound miserie:
  Alas! I weepe for this one only losse,
  For whom all ioy doth but inferre new crosse.

For while He liv'd, I made my Paradise
In euery place where I His presence found;
A speciall blisse was euery exercise;
Wherein I shewed my service to Him bound:
  Each season wherein I inioy'd my King,
  Did seeme to me a neuer dying Spring.

Mary Magdalen's fourth Lamentation.

MARIE BEWAILES THE LOSSE OF THAT PART WHICH CHRIST PROMISED HER: WHEN HE SAID, MARIE HATH CHOSEN THE BETTER PART, WHICH SHALL NOT BE TAKEN AWAY FROM HER.[1]

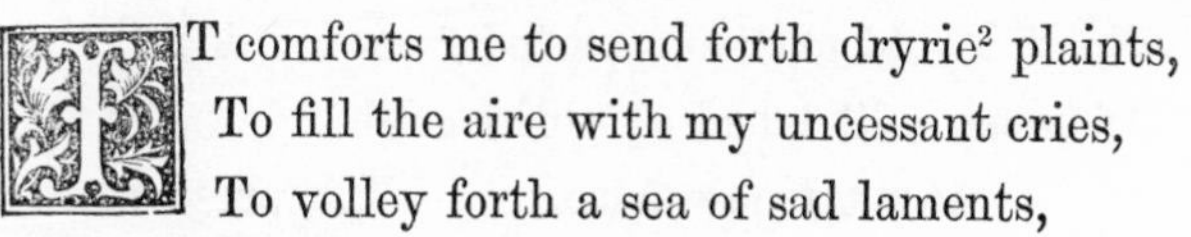

IT comforts me to send forth dryrie[2] plaints,
To fill the aire with my uncessant cries,
To volley forth a sea of sad laments,
With liquid teares to moisten still mine eies:
Yet neither plaints, nor cries, laments, nor teares,
Can serue, can ease, can salue, can shew my feares.

For all inioin'd to doe their best availe,
To helpe the mourne[3] of my greefe-burthened soule,
Persuade me still it is my best to waile,
And spend the day in pittie-pleading dole:

---

[1] St. Luke x. 42. G. [2] = dreary. G.
[3] Query—moane? G.

Sith whom I chose, the comfort of my heart,
Is now bereft—oh care-increasing smart!

That I did chuse the best and precious part,
It is no doubt, sith Christ I only chose;
My Lord, the soveraigne of my zealous heart,
Whom to possesse, I wish my life to lose:
But how I haue it now I cannot say,
Sith He that was that part, is tane away.

Ah! could I still haue kept Him with me here,
I would not thus haue lost him from my sight;
No, I would not haue parted from my deare,
If to my will I had obtainèd might:
And might I now with teares His presence buy,
Rather than lose it, I all chance would trie.

Sith then I nothing seeke, but what I chose,
And losse of choice is all my combat's cause,
Either vouchsafe this part I doe not lose
Or I see not how to averre this clause:
Or how—poore wretch!—I now may truly say,
I chose best part, which is not tane away?

But happily, His heavenly meaning was,
That it should not be taken from my heart;
Though from mine eies Thou suffered it to passe,
Thy inward presence should supplie this part:

And yet I thinke if Thou within me were,
I should Thee feele—and felt—not seeke Thee here.

Thou art too hotte a fire to heat my breast,
And not to burne me with Thy scorching flame;
Thy glorious light would not leave me to rest
In this blind darknesse, if I had the same;
For if Thy glorie in me duly shin'd,
It would reioice and cheere my dying mind.

No, no, if that I had the virgin's Boy,
My innocent heart—which never yet hath knowne
To counterfeit an outside of hid ioy—
Could not complain and make such greevous mone:
Nor should my thoughts feed on a dead man's grave,
If they at home so sweet a feast might have.

My love would not retaine a thought to spare,
Nor have an idle minute for to spend,
In any other action for to care,
But in the sweet amplecting[1] of my friend:
Ah nothing could withdraw my mind from this,
To abridge least part in me from such a blisse.

---

[1] = lamenting. G.

My starving thirst for His lost sight is such
The sea of my still flowing ioies againe,
So able is to let me drinke as much,
As may suffice to fill my longing paine :
That though each part whole tides of ioy should drinke,
Yet all too few my greedie drought would thinke.

In true loue's hearts each part is made an eie,
And every thought prefixèd for a looke ;
Then I so sweet an obiect soone would spie,
That 'mongst so many eyes should darkenesse brooke :
So cleare a shine, so bright, so cleare a light,
Could not be hidden from a lover's sight.

Yea doubtlesse had the Lord in me a seat,
I would not envie at the fortunes sweet
Of mightiest prince—or empresse ne're so great—
Yea I could more—if so He thought me meet—
Reioice in Earth to be His tombe or shrine,
Than be in Heaven, a throne, or saint faire shine.

But peradventure now 'tis with my mind,
As earst it was with His apostles eyes,
Who on the sea thought they a ghost did find,

When there He walkèd in miraculous wise:
  And I knowing more His bodie's shape than
    might,
  Take Him but for a fancie in heart's sight.

But oh! sad soule—it seemes too strange that He,
He whom I seeke, and Hee for whom I weepe,
Should to my plainings thus estrangèd be,
And leave me to these fits which sorrow keepe:
  If that in me a cause He did not see,
  For which He will not yet be seene of mee.

For hence it comes that water-wasted eies,
Commaund a fresh incessant shower of teares,
And drive my breast, which under burthen cries,
Vnto a new made storme of sighs and feares:
  And last my soule—oh soule with woe opprest—
  Is made a prisoner to my owne unrest.

My heart shall never cease to tire my toung,
My toung shall never rest to tell my smart,
My smart shall cause me still to waile my wrong,
My wrong—bereaving me of my best part—
  So heart, so toung, so smart, shall all accord,
  To sigh, tell, shew, my greefes for my dead
    Lord.

I silly soule, sith I my mirth have lost,
For my part will make much of heartie sorrow;

And sith my ioy with such deepe woe is crost,
In bitter teares all comfort I will borrow:
  Which I presume I lawfully may sheed,
  Fetching my warrant from His latest deed.

Alas! what need had my sweet Lord to weepe
Vpon the crosse, but for my learning's sake?
Which cannot sure be ill for me to keepe,
That He thought good to give, 'tis good to take.
  My weeping cannot preiudice my blisse,
  A world of teares cannot bewaile my misse.

I still will draw to my distressèd mind,
All sad conceits, all heavie pensive musing;
My heart to daily languour I will bind,
Where it may pine in withered care perusing:
  Taking no comfort for my woe's redresse,
  But in consenting to be comfortlesse.

Oh would to God I were as privie made
Vnto His blessed bodie's sweet remoue,
To know where that pure vessell now is laid,
As He is witting of my faithfull love:
  Oh Thou my Lord and owner of my soule,
  That knowes my heart and can conceiue my dole.

If skies bright sunne to shew his beames did shame,
When light of lights was darkenèd with disgrace;

If heavens their beautie did with louring staine,
Suting their colours to their Maker's case.
  If Nature's frame did—melting—shake to see
  Nature's faire Author us'd unnaturally.

Why should not I, whose ouer-burthening smart
Hath equall cause to waile His heavie case,
Helpe in this bad consort to beare a part?
Especially sith in this little space,

His bodie's losse hath mourners number lessened,
And yet the cause of weeping is increased:
The Apostles all are fled, His friends afraid,
And I alone to weep for all am staid.

Marie Magdalen's fift Lamentation.

MARIE'S PERSEVERANCE AT THE TOMBE, AND THE AP'RING OF CHRIST IN THE LIKENESSE OF A GARDINER.

OH my deare Lord, Thy griefe the greatest was
That euer was in man or manly heart,
And my greefe is as great a greefe alas!

As euer came to woman for her part:
  For out of Thine my loue hath carvèd mee,
  A part not small, and yet too small for Thee.

Thy losse my torment hath redoublèd,
And all sad soules pay me what they did borrow;
I beare the griefe, which them too much hath
    troubled,
Yet I am made vice-gerent of all sorrow.
  Sorrow, ah sorrow thou O tombe with me,
  And thaw to teares you stones that hardest be.

The time is come—now is the very time—
That leave it had and license for to cry,
To tell the Pharises their sinfull crime,
Now for the Lord, the breach of silence try:
  Who said, if His disciples held their peace,
  The very stones would crie for sin's increase.

Sith then their lips be lockèd up with feare,
And sadnesse makes them mute, and not a word
Oh crie you stones, and no exclaimes forbeare,
Crie out against the murtherers of my Lord:
  The robbers of His sacred coarse bewray,
  Bring them to light that stole my Lord away.

For sure it was some Pharise's fell spight
Or bloodie Scribe—not suted with the paine

His bodie felt—but bloud their hearts envite
To practise some worse crueltie againe :
  And now to glut their brutish mind withall,
  Have stolne His coarse to use unnaturall.

Oh rockes and stones, if euer you must crie,
Now is high time to poure your loud exclaimes;
Now let your clamours to the welkin[1] flie,
Sith light is darkened, dead the flame of flames,
  The world's great Monarch foulely massacrèd,
  The life of lives outrageously misusèd.

Doth not His tongue—whose truth infallible is—
Whose word omnipotent rules sea and wind,
Whom creatures—most insensible—doe kisse,
With aw'd obedience, which His power doth bind :
  Promise the whole world shall defend the iust,
  Against those sencelesse soules, which selfe-
    power trust.

And who more iust than He, of Iustice king?
Who then His barbarous murtherers, sencelesse
    more?
Whose innocent bloud could not a staunching bring
Vnto their greedie thirst, slaughterèd before;
  Vnlesse they to this impious act proceed
  To worke—His bodie dead—some hellish deed.

---

[1] A noticeable early use of this word. G.

Why doe not then all creatures them applie
To be revengèd in a cause so iust,
Vpon the Iewes incivile tyrannie,
Bereft of sence and blinded in mistrust,
  Their hearts made inhumane, of reason barrain,
  Void of good feeling both to God and Man?

But sure it cannot be in humane might
To steale the bodie of the Lord away,
No bloudie theefe, nor any mortall wight
Had sufferance to beare so wicked sway:
  It cannot be that any sinfull soule
  Would undertake a deed of such deepe dole.

No, no, He was no bootie for a theefe,
Nor for a cruell Pharisee a pray,[1]
Nor were the angels slacke to attend Him cheefe,
As my suspition doth presume to say:
  If this thing cannot change my mind from feare,
  Yet looking on the clothes, my doubts may cleare.

Would any theefe have so religious beene,
To steale the bodie and the clothes not take?
Would any theefe so venterous have been
    seene,
To stay, so many feare-delaies to make,

---

[1] Prey. G.

As to unshroud the coarse, order the sheets,
And fold the napkins with such seemly pleets ?

I know that mirrhe makes linnen cleave as fast
As pitch or glue well temperèd or made ;
And could a theefe's stolne leasure so long last,
As to dissolue the mirrhe, and bare the dead,
Breake up the seales, open the tombe and all ?
Where was the watch when these things did befall ?

If all this yet cannot persuade my mind,
Yet might my own experience make me see :
When at the crosse they strippèd Him, unkind,
I saw His garment would not parted bee
From goarie backe, but tare His tender skin,
Much more if it with mirrhe had 'nointed bin.

I'le looke into the sheet, if there remaine
Any one parcell of His mangled flesh,
Or any haire pluckt from His head's soft vaine,
If none that shall my wearie woe refresh :
I'le think a better chaunce betides my loue,
Than my misdeeming feare will let me prove.

A guiltie conscience doubteth want of time,
And leand[1] attempts are still dispatcht in hast,

[1] = lean or destitute of good qualities. G.

Offenders doubt least light make known their
crime,
And in Night's sable weed commit their wast:
With dread and horror acting fearefully,
And cannot marke when things well ordered be.

But to unwrap a bodie mangled so,
Out of mirrhe, cloathes, and not the flesh to teare,
Leaving them thus so cleanely wip'd in show,
It is a thing most marvellous to heare,
And most impossible for man to do,
Vnlesse they had light, helpe, and time thereto.

But oh! the great effects of rarest loue!
If loue a langour be, how then liue I?
If life, how do I then such dead fits proue?
If it bereaveth sence, how did I see
The angels then? if it revive the same,
Why did I not know Iesus when He came?

And doe I in such zeale thus seeke for One,
Whom when I have found out, I do not know,
Or if I know Him that of late was gone,
Now having Him, why doe I seeke Him so?
Behold my Christ is come, He whom I sought,
Doth talke with me, and I my selfe know
nought.

Why doe I not then wipe my dazled eies?
Ah hath my Lord in this world liv'd so long,
Di'de with such paine, shed shours of tears with
cries,
Laboured so much, and suffered so much wrong,
And hath thereby no more preferment cought,
But for to be a silly gardiner thought?

And hath my kindnesse so much cost bestowed
Vpon this ointment which I did prepare?
Have I in anguish pin'd and so long sorrowed,
Shead all these teares, and had such heedlesse
care:
And was all done for One, and one no better
Than is a silly simple gardiner?

Alas! and is a silly garden plot
The best free-hold that my loue can afford,
Is this the highest office He hath got,
To be a gardiner now that was my Lord?
He better might have liv'd and ownèd me,
Than with His death to have bought so small a
fee.

Marie Magdalen's sixt Lamentation.

JESUS SAID UNTO HER (MARIE): SHE TURNED, AND SAID UNTO HIM, RABBONI.[1]

OH loving Lord, Thou only didst deferre
My consolation, to encrease it more,
That Thy delightfull presence might preferre
The better welcome, being wisht so sore;
In that Thy absence little hope had left.
Vnto my heart, so long of blisse bereft.

It may be that I knew not former blisse,
Till I a time was from the sweetnesse wean'd,
Nor what it was such treasures rich to misse,
Which in Thy presence I of late attain'd;
Vntill my povertie had made it cleere,
Of what inestimable rate they were.

But now Thou shewst me by a proofe most sweet,
That though I paid Thee with my dearest love,
With water of my teares to wash Thy feet,
With my best breath, which all desire could move:

[1] St. John xx. 16. G.

Yet small the price was that I did bestowe,
Waying the worth, which now Thou letst me
know.

I sought Thee dead, pind in a stonie gaile,[1]
But find Thee living, and at libertie :
Shrin'd in a shroud, Thy visage sad and pale,
Left as the modell of all miserie :
But now invest in glorious robes I find Thee,
And as the president of blisse I mind Thee.

As all this while I sought but could not find,
Wept without comfort, cal'd unanswered to :
So now Thy comming satisfies my mind,
Thy triumphs please my teares, which long did
wo ;
And all my cries are husht with this one word,
—Marie—'cause sweetly spoken from my Lord.

For when I heard Thee call in wonted sort,
And with Thy usuall voice, my only name,
Issuing from that Thy heavenly mouth's report :
So strange an alteration it did frame,
As if I had been wholly made anew,
Being only nam'd by Thee—Whose voice I
knew—

---

[1] = gaol. G.

Whereas before my griefe benum'd me so,
My bodie seem'd the hearse of my dead hart:
My heart— soule's coffin—kil'd with care and wo,
And my whole selfe did seeme in euery part
  A double funerall presented plain,
  Of Thee and of my selfe together slaine.

But now this one word, hath my sence restored,
Lightned my mind and quicknèd my heart,
And in my soule a living spirit poured,
Yea, with sweet comfort strengthened every part:
  For well this word a spirit dead may raise,
  Which only word made Heaven, world and seas.

Marie I was when sin possest me whole,
Marie I am, being now in state of grace;
Marie did worke the ill that damn'd her soule,
Marie did good in giving ill a place,
  And now I shew but what I was and am,
  This word alone displaies my ioy and shame.

For by His vertues that did speak the same,
An epitome of all His mercies sweet,
A repetition of my miseries came,
And all good haps I did together meet:
  Which so my sences ravishèd with ioy,
  I soone forgot my sorrowes and annoy.

And thus my heart a troupe of ioyes did lead ;
Mustered in rankes, to mutinie they fell,
Conspiring which might worthiest be made ;
With them my owne unworthies doe rebell,
  And long in doubtfull issue they contend,
  Till view of highest blisse the strife did end.

He was my Sunne, whose going downe did leave,
A dumpish night with fearefull fancies fild,
And did each starre of glistering shines bereave,
And all the world with mystie horror kill'd :
  And every planet reigning erst so bright,
  Were chang'd to dismall signes in this darke
    night.

Yet now the cleareness of His lovely face,
His words, authoritie which all obay,
This foggie darknesse cleane away doth chace,
And brings a calme and bright well-tempered day :
  And doth disperse clouds of melancholie,
  Awakes my sence and cures my lethargie.

Rapt with His voice, impatient of delay,
Out of His mouth His talke I greedily take,
And to His first and only word I say,
And with one other word this answere make,
Rabboni : then my ioy, my speech did choke,
  I could no more proceed, nor more hear spoke.

Some would have spoke, but Fear conceal'd the
clause,
Hope framèd words, but Doubt their passage staies :
When I should speake, I then stood in a pause,
My suddaine ioy my inward thoughts quite slaies :
My voice doth tremble, and my toung doth falter,
My breath doth faile, and all my sences alter.

Lastly, in lieu of words, issue my teares,
Deepe sighs in stead of sentences are spent ;
Their mother's want they fill with sighs and feares,
And from the heart halfe-uttered breath they sent :
Which so in passion's conflict disagree,
To sounds perceiv'd they cannot sorted be.

So fares the heart that's sicke for suddain ioy,
Attaining that for which it long did fire :
For even as Feare is Loue's still servile boy,
And Hope an usher unto lost desire,
So Love is hard, a firme beleefe in gaining,
And credulous coniectures entertaining.

And though desire be apt for to admit
Of wisht for comfort any smallest shade,
The hotter yet it burnes in having it,
The more it cares to have it perfect made :
And while least hope is wanting which is sought,
The best assurances avantage nought.

And even as hope doth still the best presume,
Inviting ioy to welcome good successe,
So Fame suspects true blisse can hardly come,
And cals up Sorrow, making it seème lesse:
With greefe bewailing the uncertainetie.
Of that which should be sole felicitie.

And while as these doe mutually contend,
Feare sometime falleth into deepe despaire,
Hope rising up, his fierie darts doth send
Of wrath, repining to the emptie aire:
Making a doubtfull skirmish, dead they stand,
Till evidence of proofe the strife have skand.

For though—poore I—so suddainly repli'de
Vpon the notice of His voice well knowne,
Yet for because so rare a chaunce I spi'de,
His person chaung'd, Himselfe unlookt for showne:
The sight my thoughts into sedition drew,
Then were they purg'd from doubts by stricter view.

And then though speeches would have issued faine,
And my poore heart to His haue dutie sent,
Yet euery thought for utterance taking paine,
Which first might be receav'd, so hastily went,
That I was forc'd—indifferent iudge to all—
To act by signes, and let my speeches fall.

And running to the haunt of my delight,
My cheefest blisse, I straight fell at His feet,
And kindly offer in my Saviour's sight,
To bath them now with teares of ioy most sweet :
  To sanctifie my lips with kissing His,
  Once greevous, but now glorious wounds of blis.

To hear more words I listed not to stay,
Being with the Word it selfe now happie made,
But deeme a greater blisse for to assay,
To have at once my wishes full apaide,
  In honoring and kissing of His feet,
  Than in the hearing of His speech, lesse sweet.

For euen as loue, in nature coueteth,
To be united, yea transformèd whole,
Out of it selfe into the thing it loueth;
So what unites, loue most affecteth sole,
  And still preferreth least coniunction euer,
  Before best ioies, which distance seemes to seuer.

To see Him, therefore, doth not me suffice,
To heare Him doth not quiet whole my mind,
To speake with Him in so familiar wise,
Is not ynough my loose-let soule to bind :
  No, nothing can my vehement loue appease,
  Least by His touch my wo-worne heart I please.

Marie Magdalen's seventh Lamentation.

HER FALLING AT CHRIST'S FEET TO KISSE THEM, HIS FORBIDDING HER: SAYING, DO NOT TOUCH ME, FOR I AM NOT YET ASCENDED TO MY FATHER.[1]

H loving Lord, what mysterie is this?
Being dead in sinne, I toucht Thy mortall feet
That were to die for me, now may not kisse
Thy glorious feet; yet Thou hast thought it meet
They should as well for my good now revive,
As for my good they dy'de, being late aliue?

Thou didst admit me once to annoint Thy head,
And am I now unmeet Thy feet to touch?
Thou wonted was for to commend the deed,
Which now Thou doest command me from as much:
O Lord, sith I and others shall them feele,
Why doest Thou now forbid me so to kneele?

What meanest Thou, good Lord, that Thou restrainst

---

[1] St. John xx., 17. G.

My heart of such a dutie so desirèd,
Sith Thou 'mongst all Thy friends, to me hast
deign'd
The first of Thy selfe—of all requirèd :
With Thy first words my eares sole happie be,
And may I not be blest with touching Thee ?

If teares haue woon such favour, from mine eies,
If longing earnes a recompence so sweet,
Why doest Thou Lord my feeling hands despise,
And barre my mouth from kissing Thy sweet feet :
Sith lips—with plaints—and hands—with will
to serve—
Doe seeme as great reward for to deserve.

But notwithstanding, thus Thou doest prevent,
My tender offer, which I would effect,
Forbidding me to touch—as if Thou meant—
I should the difference of Thy state respect :
Being now a glorious, not a mortall bodie,
A life eternall and not momentarie.

For sith the bodie's immortalitie,
The glorie of the soule together knit,
Are both of them indowments heavenly,
For such as in sweet paradice doe sit :
Rights of another world well maist Thou deeme
This favour, than nothing of small esteeme.

Though to my Father I have not ascended,
I shortly shall; let thy demeanure then
Not by the place where I am, be intended,
But by that place which is my due: and when
With reverence thou farre off wouldst fall,
I will consent that thou Me handle shall.

If thou My former promises beleeve
My present words may be a constant proofe;
Doe not thy eies and eares true witnesse give,
Must hands and face most feele for heart's be-
hoofe?
If eies and eares deceivèd be by Me,
As well may hands and face deluded be.

Yet if thou feare lest I so suddaine part,
That if thou take not leave now of My feet,
With humble kisse, with teares fetched from thy
heart,
Thou never shalt so fit a season meet:
License that doubt, for all those loves of thine,
There will be found a more convenient time.

But goe about what now more hast requires,
Run to My brethren, tell them what I say,
That I to satisfie their soules desires,
For them in Gallilee will goe stay:

And there before them shortly will I bee,
Where they My sacred heavenly face shall see.[1]

And I preferring 'fore my wish His will
Even like a hungrie child, departed from Him,
Puld from a teat, which store of milke doth fill,
Or like a thirstie hart from brookes exil'd :
Sorrie that I by carrying ioyfull newes,
Should leaue my Lord, Whom I did rather chuse.

Alas! then—said I—cannot others be
Made happie, but by my unhappie crosse ?
Cannot their gaine come in by none but me,
And not by me, but by my heavie losse ?
Must dawning of their day my evening be,
And to enrich themselves, must they rob me ?

Alas! goe seeke to better thee—deare hart—
And ease thy woe in some more happie brest,
Sith I unworthie creature for my part,
Am nothing freèd from my late unrest, :
But in the tast of high felicitie,
The want whereof doth worke more miserie.

Thus lead by dutie, and held backe by love,
I pacèd forward, but my thoughts goe backe,
Readie eftsoones a sounding fit to prove,

[1] St. Matthew xxvi. 32. G.

But that firme faith supported me from wracke :
  And towards the tombe in breathing oft I turn'd,
  As if that aire with new refreshing burn'd.

Sometimes poore soule my selfe I do forget :
Love in a sweet distraction leading me,
Makes me imagine I my love have met,
And seems as though His words were feeding me :
  I deeme His feete are folded in my armes,
  And that His comfort my chill spirit warmes.

But when my wits are all againe awake,
And this a meere illusion is found,
My heart halfe dead, its wonted woe doth take,
And greater greefe my sicke soule doth confound,
  That I—alas !—the thing it selfe must misse,
  Whose only thought so much delightfull is.

And as I passèd where my Lord hath beene,
Oh stones—said I—more happie farre than I,
Most wretched caitife ! I alas ! have seene.
When unto you my Lord did not denie,
  The touch of His for euer blessed feet,
  Whereof my ill deserts make me unmeet,

Alas ! what crime have I of late commit,
That cancels me out of His good conceit ?
Or doth my Lord His wonted love forget ?

May I no more His wonted love a wait?
  Had I for tearme of life His love in lease,
  And did my right expire in His decease?

Oh in His feet with teares at first I writ
My supplication for His mercie sweet,
With sobs and sighes—poore soule—I pointed it,
My haire did choisely fold it, being wet;
  My lips impression humbly seal'd the same,
  With reuerent stamp, which from my sicke soule
    came.

They were the dores that entrance first did giue,
Into His favour, and by them I came
By kind acceptance in His heart to liue;
By them I did my humble homage frame,
  Vnto His head, while it did yet containe
  In man, a mirror of God's brightnesse plaine.

But now alas! I must contented be
To beare a lower saile, and stoope to time,
To take downe my desires that sores so high,
To meaner hopes, and leaue aloft to clime:
  Sith former favours now are markes too high,
  Either to levell at, or to come nigh.

But oh! ambitious eies! for so weake sight,
He is too bright a sunne; your lookes are ty'de,

And now are limited to meaner light,
And rather like a batt, than eagle ey'de:
You must your selves t'inferiour lookes submit,
For Him to see, such substance is unfit.

No, no, sith I am from His feet reiected,
How can I thinke, but that my want of faith
Is cause I am so slenderly respected,
And that His heart to yeeld me love gainesaith:
Yea, that I am from all possession throwne,
Of His kind favour, which were earst mine owne.

Yet why should I stoope to a feare so base,
When want of faith with sinne was worse agreeved:
He did vouchsafe to graunt me of His grace,
And shall I now, cause faintly I beleeued,
Thinke that my Lord so rigorously will deale,
As to abridge me of this wishèd weale?

Is the sinceritie of my pure loue,
—Wherein He hath no partener at all—
In no respect availeable to moue?
Or in account is it so slight and small,
As that it may not hope some sparke to find
Of wonted mercie, and His grace so kind?

I will not wrong Him with so vniust a thought,
Sith His appearing doth approve the same,

His words o'rethrow that such suspition wrought,
His countenance doth tell I am to blame :
  Why then should I from such a vaine surmise,
  Sucke so much sorrow in such foolish wise.

Thus as I travailed in this iourney short,
My fantasies long voiages did make,
And heal'd[1] my mind in such a wavering sort,
Hope could not win nor Feare would not forsake :
  But twixt them both my vision made me glad,
  And greefe of my deniall made me sad.

But as I was in this perplexèd wise,
Rising and falling in uncertainetie,
The other holy women I espie,
That first with me came to the grave to see :
  To whom the angels had made demonstration
  Of Christ my Lord and Maister's resurrection.

---

[1] = held G.

The Conclusion.

JESUS MET THEM, SAYING, ALL HAILE.

H how profound are all Thy iudgements
Lord!
How doest Thou take my sorrow to Thy,
heart!
How doth Thy eies such bleeding drops afford,
To see my wounded love and greevous smart:
That Thy refusall late, requited is
With such a grant so free and full of blis.

Full of content, the baulme of troubled mind,
That tooke no pleasure where Thy presence wanted:
But oh! that grace hath gracèd me to find
The love wherewith my soule is cheefe acquainted:
His love's my life, by His love my life liveth,
For to my soule His love the life breath giveth.

Now are the dolefull, darke, and pitcht-fac'd
clouds
Dispearst and driven from my comfort's face;
Those melancholy, moist, and wat'rie shrouds,
That did the brightnesse of my ioies displace,

Wrapping me up, as in eternall night,
Vanisht they are, seeing my heart's delight.

Delight in Him, to Whom all love is debt,
Seald with the heart, the soule, and all the might:
A paiment that admits no worldly let,
To linger or defraud, a heauenly right:
Which if I cannot pay as due requires,
Accept—O Lord !—Thy debtor's true desires.

Let me Thy everlasting prisoner be,
Chain'd in the linkes of an eternall love;
My want and will is only knowne to Thee,
A willing debtour I will ever prove:
And what I have, I freely doe bestowe,
Take all my worth, for past of that I owe.

Oh Christian soule take Marie to thy mirrour,
And if Thou wilt the like effects obtaine,
Then follow her in like affections fervour,
And so with her, like mercie shalt thou gaine:
Learn sinfull man of this once sinfull woman,
That sinners may find Christ, which sin abandon.

That love recovereth Him that sinne did lose,
That firme beliefe recalleth that againe.
What fainting faith did quite forsake to chose,
That what nor force nor favour can obtaine,

Nor pollicie by mortall meanes bring in,
Continued teares of constant loue, can win.

Learne then of her for Christ no force to feare,
And out of Christ no comfort to desire.
With Christ His loue, all loue—though ne're so
deare—
To ouer-rule, to quench fond fancie's fire:
Rise earely soule, in thy good motion's morne,
Sleepe not in sloth, when diligence may per-
forme.

Run with repentance to thy sinfull hart,
Which should the temple undefil'd have bin,
But through thy fault, deserves no better part
Than be the tombe for Christ to burie in:
For wanting life to tast this heavenly bread,
He seem'd to thee as if He had been dead.

Remoue the loads that presse thee downe in sin,
The stone of former hardnesse roule away,
Looke to thy soule, if Christ be lodg'd therein,
And if thou find that there He doe not stay,
Then weepe without; in other creatures mind
Him,
Sith had in all, in any thou maiest find Him.

Make Faith thine eie, Hope guide, and Love thy
light,

Seeke Him, not His; for Himselfe, not His meeds:
If Faith have found him in a cloudie night,
Let Hope seeke for Him when the Day spring
breeds:
If Hope to see Him have thee luckly led,
Let Love seeke further, in Him to be fed.

If Sorrow knocke, Remorse is Mercie's porter,
And euer opens to let Dolour in;
Vnto that dore be thou a quicke resorter,
'Tis much to save the losse that comes by sin:
He that of sorrow is true mournefull taster,
Doth feel Sin's smart, and also Sin's salving-
plaster.

Striue with thy thoughts, being all prepar'd
together,
To rise out of mortalitie's foule mire,
Which hath no standing, nor firme footing neither;
Prevent the danger, and in time retire:
Crave to be cleane of that same filth sinne urged,
For who is pure, that Iesus hath not purged?

He can the ruines of thy soule repaire,
He yet distributeth His mercie's treasure,
The dore stands open yet, thy suite prepare,
Let not repentance stay old age's leasure:

When the meridian of thy sun's once past,
The night of Nature hies upon thee fast.

Awake therefore, watch th' evils hourely nie,
Provide before thou be surpriz'd of breath ;
Vpon the pale horse heedfull cast thine eie,
Note him that sits thereon, whose name is Death :
Be readie for the stroke he is to give,
For feare thou die ere thou begins to liue.

Oh mild Physician, how well didst Thou know !
Thy corosive so sharp did greeve my wound :
Which did by ignorance, not errour grow,
Therefore no sooner felt, but helpe was found :
Thy linative appli'de, did ease my paine,
For though Thou did forbid, 'twas no restraine.

And now to shew that Thy deniall late
Was but a checke to my unsetled faith,
And no reiecting of my fault with hate,
Thou letst me wash Thy feet in my teare bath :
I kisse them too, the seales of our redemption,
My loue renewèd with endlesse consolation.

Thus hast Thou Lord full finishèd my teares,
Assured my hopes, contented my desire,
Repair'd my loves, extirpèd quite my feares,
Perfected ioies with all that heart requires.

And made the period of expiring greefes,
The preamble to euer fresh reliefes.

How mercifull a father art Thou Lord,
To poore forsaken orphans in distresse!
How soft a iudge, that iudgement doth afford
With mildest grace, to sinners comfortlesse!
How sure a friend unto a syncere louer,
Whose pure and faithfull loue doth alter neuer!

Thou then that art with diligence prepar'd,
Going with speed, standing with hopes lift hie,
Humbling thy heart, thy haughtie will impar'd,
If Thou with Marie none but Christ would see,
Himselfe will to thy teares an answere giue,
And His owne words assure thee He doth liue:

That sweetly He, unto thee being showne,
To others thou maiest run, and make Him knowne.